Nick Faldo

THE AUTOBIOGRAPHY

Life
Swings

headline

First published in 2004
by HEADLINE BOOK PUBLISHING

10 9 8 7 6 5 4 3 2 1

Cataloguing in Publication Data is available from the British Library

ISBN 0 7553 1120 5

Typeset in Centaur MT by Palimpsest Book Production Limited,
Polmont, Stirlingshire
Text designed by Ben Cracknell
Printed and bound in Great Britain by
Clays Ltd, St Ives plc

Headline's policy is to use papers that are natural, renewable and recyclable products and
made from wood grown in sustainable forests. The logging and manufacturing processes are
expected to conform to the environmental regulations of the country of origin.

HEADLINE BOOK PUBLISHING
A division of Hodder Headline
338 Euston Road
London NW1 3BH

www.headline.co.uk
www.hodderheadline.com

To Valerie, Natalie, Matthew, Georgia and Emma

CONTENTS

FOREWORD
by Jack Nicklaus

Nick Faldo once said that the inspiration he had for first picking up a golf club came after watching me on television during the 1971 Masters tournament at Augusta National. As someone who has since watched his rise up many a leaderboard, and someone who has competed and captained against him in four Ryder Cup matches – and personally seen him record 11 victories in those four matches – I consider it an honour and a privilege if, as Nick says, I was among the early motivations behind what we have all witnessed to be a truly remarkable career.

The numbers speak volumes by themselves: three Open Championships; three Masters titles; and a member of four victorious Ryder Cup teams, including the distinction of owning more appearances and Ryder Cup points than any player on either side of the Atlantic. Add in another 34 professional tournament victories across the globe and Nick is arguably not only the most successful British golfer of all time, but among the greatest players ever to have walked the world's fairways.

At the peak of his game, Nick was considered among the purest strikers of a golf ball since the peerless Ben Hogan. Like Hogan, Nick had to work to become such a heralded ball-striker, and perhaps what has impressed me most about watching Nick Faldo evolve into a champion was the work ethic that brought him to that point. Nick was a great athlete, who applied his ability to golf, yet he was not content on being just another golfer. I would argue that no one worked harder to achieve greatness than Nick Faldo. As he learned how to win, he taught himself how to win more. Once he tasted success, his appetite for more grew. Along the way, he became not only a decorated champion but a beloved hero in Great Britain.

When it came to Major championships, Nick's swing and game were at their finest. I have always believed that the Majors are the measuring sticks for greatness, and I recognised at an early age that the success of a golfer is usually weighed against his or her performance in those four events each year. Thus, much of my preparation was focused around those dates. Nick shares that passion for Major-championship golf, and it is reflected in his six victories in a nine-year stretch. Ironically, we both won our first Open Championship at fabled Muirfield, and we each count victory at St Andrews among our crowning achievements. So, when future generations flip through the pages of our game's history books, Nick Faldo should be remembered among the greats of this or any era.

Just as there is far more to the greatest game of all than one's victory total, there is much more beneath the surface of Nick Faldo's success. As long as I have known him, Nick has played the game of golf in the wonderful spirit in which it was originally intended – with sportsmanship, with humility in victory, and, what is an even more noble trait, graciousness in defeat. He has always been the first to offer his hand in congratulation or commiseration.

As someone he has cast in a supporting role in the genesis of his career, I have come to regard this young man with affection. Given the warmth of the receptions he receives when he walks up the 18th fairway, be it at St Andrews or Augusta National, it suggests that affection is shared by legions of fans. Those who understand and appreciate this game certainly recognise and respect a true champion.

Britain has produced many a sporting hero – from Roger Bannister, the first man to break the 4-minute-mile barrier, to three times world Formula One champion Sir Jackie Stewart; to gold medal Olympian and world record holder Sebastian Coe, and on to Lennox Lewis, the heavyweight boxing champion of the world – but without question, Nick Faldo has earned his rightful spot among his country's most revered athletes and champions.

Good golfing.

ACKNOWLEDGEMENTS

There are so many people to thank for the life I have enjoyed:

Jack Nicklaus, for the inspiration to make me pick up and swing a golf club. Thank you for that Jack. And for the contests we have enjoyed and the standards we try to emulate on and off the golf course.

My parents, George and Joyce, for the trust they have had in me. Trust which I hope I have never abused. Their wonderful support and belief throughout my life allowed me to mature into the golfer I became. I would like to hope they are as proud of me as their son, as I am of them as my mum and dad.

The late Ian Connelly, for his help and guidance in the early years.

David Leadbetter, for the time and groundbreaking work we enjoyed together in search of the perfect golf swing.

To all my friends, past and present, for the support they have given me. In particular, thank you Danny Desmond, a great mate for more than 25 years, for always looking out for me. And also Kjell Enhager, for your laughter and your wisdom.

In my business enterprises I have been lucky to meet and work with some wonderful colleagues. Thank you all for sharing your energies, experience and passion to succeed with me.

Robert Philip, for working with me on the writing of this book. Thank you for your skill in helping bring all these memories alive on the page.

To Gill, for giving me Natalie, Matthew and Georgia, three

wonderful characters who bring me so much pleasure and make me so proud.

To Fanny Sunesson, my buddy, confidante and caddie supreme.

And finally to my wife Valerie. Thank you for granting me your love, for bringing to life the person I really am, and for giving me Emma, who brings so much joy to my life every day.

CHAPTER ONE

DESIRE FOR GREATNESS

It is difficult to reach for the stars when you cannot even see them twinkling through the impenetrable glare of the streetlights. But I knew that somewhere up there they shone brightly and so each night I would perch upon my bedroom windowsill gazing out into the night sky above Welwyn Garden City, painting pictures of the future in my mind's eye. However, as a young teenager, even in my wildest imaginings I could never quite conjure up visions of Open Championships or US Masters victories – some things are just too fantastical to contemplate. Deep in my heart, though, I believed destiny had determined that I should become a professional golfer. I studied faded photographs of Tony Jacklin, who had won the 1969 Open at Royal Lytham and the US Open the following summer, standing in front of his mansion or Rolls-Royce, and fantasised, 'Yeah, one day I'll have those sorts of things. One day I'm going to be famous . . .' After all, the Faldo family lodger, a scientist based at the Malaysian Rubber Company in town, had analysed my handwriting and discovered 'a desire for greatness'.

My first opportunity to fulfil this desire came to pass not on the green fairways of St Andrews or Augusta but in the somewhat less glamorous surroundings of Stevenage public swimming baths, venue of the 1966 Hertfordshire County under-10 breaststroke final. I had come through the various qualifying heats and there I stood, on the starting block, all bony knees and elbows, a-shivering and a-shaking with nerves, and watched by Mum, Dad and hundreds of strangers. I was so determined to win, so frightened of losing in front of all those appraising eyes, so overcome by the intensity of this monumental occasion in my life, that I promptly peed myself. Can you imagine what an abjectly humiliating experience it was for a nine-year-old to stand there, fondly imagining himself as an early-day Mark Spitz, with pee leaking out of his trunks and trickling down his spindly legs? Fortunately, so burning was my childish passion to succeed, I also covered myself in something approaching glory one minute 42 seconds or whatever later by splashing my way to victory, thereby collecting my first sports trophy.

I had embarked upon my flirtation with the swimming pool three years earlier during a family holiday in the south of France; Mum, Dad, me, tent, camp-beds, stove, pots, pans, you name it, all squeezed into an Austin A40 with the approximate dimensions of a tele-phone box. Our tent alone took up half the space, for this was not one of your little canvas kennels. Oh no, this was a real posh affair right out of *Lawrence of Arabia*, with two separate sleeping areas, plastic windows, sun canopy, the lot. It took us three days to arrive at our destination, given that our humble Austin was possessed of a top speed of 45mph and not one single mile per hour more. We meandered down the idyllic west coast of France, through the exotic-sounding – to this unsophisticated and excited six-year-old at least – Le Mont St Michel and St Georges-de-Didonne to our beautiful little camp-site near Narbonne-Plage.

To a mite born and raised on a suburban council estate, here was paradise. Our tent was situated 50 yards from the sandy beach, there were trees to be climbed, coves to be explored, the sun always seemed to shine, and, gourmet that I was, even the food, given my suspicions that it would be no match for fish fingers and baked beans, proved reassuringly edible. A local fisherman ran a stall selling steamed mussels and for the princely sum of two francs he would fill any container of your choosing. Most evenings, I was despatched with Mum's dustbin-sized pressure cooker to collect a shellfish supper, which the three of us would scoff using chunks of baguette for cutlery (it remains one of my favourite gastronomic experiences to this day) while sitting in the sand-dunes looking out to sea.

I had always enjoyed splashing about in the water and this particular summer I pestered Dad to teach me to swim. I took to it like a duck to water (no, I will not apologise; what else did you expect me to say?) and the very night we returned from holiday I persuaded my parents to take me along to enrol at the Welwyn Garden City Swimming Club.

Alas, my big reward for becoming county champion three years later was to be invited to London's Crystal Palace for a three-day, intensive training programme, which I loathed and detested from the moment I arrived. I had never swum in a 50-metre pool before in my short life, so after 33 metres what did I do but pop up my head to see where the blasted wall had gone. Now there were two hundred kids in the water at the time, so instead of the relatively calm surface you might expect to find in an Olympic pool, there were waves, and the breakers generated by eight hundred thrashing limbs were better suited to surfers than breaststrokers. One of these chlorinated rollers hit me smack in the face, all but knocking me out, and I was forced to swallow a mouthful of the vile-tasting water. Thereafter, I hated every single length I was forced to swim; our daily routine consisted of swim, get out, shower, dry off, have something to eat, swim, get out, shower, dry off, and so on and so forth for three interminable days. On the final length of the final afternoon, I nearly drowned, because I was laughing fit to burst at the thought that my sorry ordeal was almost over.

Mum continued taking me to Stevenage for training but I realised I was finding more and more imaginative excuses to remain longer in the changing room rather than peel off and dive into the pool.

My keenness was also dampened somewhat, despite all his enthusiastic efforts, by the presence of my coach, Mot Salmon (with a moniker like that he just had to be a swimmer didn't he?) barking at me from poolside. Blessed with a gravelly voice that made Marlon Brando in *The Godfather* sound like Julian Clary, Mot could have put the fear of death into the US Marine Corps, never mind a group of quivering 10-year-olds. One of his favourite keep-fit exercises was to 'walk' down the terraces of a football stadium on his hands, an exercise we were, fortunately, spared. He ruled over us with a rod of iron, but he loved us nonetheless.

One Easter, Mot thought it would be character-building to take us to the outdoor pool in Welwyn Garden City where it was so cold, if they had left us there any longer than for a few lengths they would have had to chip us out. Mind you, we should have been used to that with the summers we had. I was an alarming shade of blue by the time I re-emerged to be greeted by my parents holding a large fluffy towel and pouring a welcoming mug of tomato soup from a vacuum flask. Having lost all sensation in my body from the scalp down, needless to say I burned my lips on the scalding liquid.

It was time to find a new hobby. Watching 'Grandstand' one Saturday afternoon, I was intrigued by a canoeing competition and badgered Dad into building me a boat. Like a Laurel and Hardy movie, we assembled the kit in the back bedroom – 13 feet of spanking new canoe – and then, despite our best endeavours, could not manoeuvre it around the corners of our narrow hallway. Dad had to remove the bedroom window and lower our prized construction into the back garden on ropes; as we had spent six months locked away building the blasted thing, Mum was less than impressed by our DIY skills.

Eager to launch the precious craft, the following morning we tied it on to the roof of our Austin A40 and headed for the River Lea in Hertford. I was paddling away merrily when I was attacked by an irate swan in a 633 squadron-style raid. Little did I know that this was, famously, the meanest swan in Hertford – so much so that when the brute died it made the papers. I capsized in a panic, which scared the hell out of me. Being upside down in dank, murky river water quickly put pay to my canoeing career.

The fascination with competitive water sports over, and inspired by scenes of the athletics events at the 1968 Mexico Olympics, my desire for greatness aroused hitherto dormant ambitions of becoming the king of track and field. I suppose I could have succeeded as a decathlete because although I preferred the 800 and 1500 metres, I was also pretty nifty with the javelin which, in turn, led me on to the discus. Now this was a smart move because the headmaster at my school, Rex Treganar, just happened to be the discus coach, so although I was not what you would call a distinguished pupil, I suddenly found myself in the beak's good books. I managed to rack up a string of victories in Sir Fredric Osbourn colours at various schools' competitions and, if I say so myself, became something of a legend in the county for my prowess in that most cruelly underrated sport, cricket ball distance-throwing. If this had ever become an Olympic discipline, then, in all modesty, Nicholas Alexander Faldo would most surely have been a gold medallist and world-record holder.

One of my first successes with a cricket ball came a couple of years earlier when I was about 10. I had been out bird's-nesting, as small boys the world over are wont to do despite dire warnings of parental retribution if caught, when one of my teachers drove past.

'Oi, Faldo . . .' he bellowed, through the open window of his car.

Guilt-ridden and with my pockets stuffed with purloined eggs, I was ready to surrender myself into the hands of the adult justice system when he opened the passenger door.

'Get in,' he commanded. 'Where the heck have you been? You're meant to be throwing a cricket ball for the school this afternoon and I've been searching everywhere for you.'

He drove me to one of our rival schools, and I can still hear the sickening sound of the eggs cracking one by one in my trouser pocket. I picked up the cricket ball, threw it – *whoosh* – and won the competition with that single throw. 'Can I go home now, sir?' I asked, wriggling with discomfort as the first gooey yolk began its inexorable slide down my leg.

'Yeah, OK,' he replied, and I waddled off home. It is hard to whistle nonchalantly when you have something decidedly unpleasant hidden in your pants.

Whether that incident left me with a deep-seated psychological scar I cannot say, but I promptly abandoned the pursuit of athletics stardom and cajoled my parents into buying me a racing bike so I could join the Welwyn Wheelers Cycling Club – the desire for greatness had turned my focus firmly upon the Tour de France. I also briefly toyed with the notion of becoming Wimbledon champion but the coach at my local club told me I was too tall at 6 feet 3 inches to conquer the tennis world.

None of this would have been possible, I need hardly add, without the encouragement of my parents who supported each and every new fad not only with their time, but also with their hard-earned cash. My dad, George, worked in the financial planning department of ICI Plastics; Mum, Joyce Smalley as was, earned some extra pin-money as a part-time dressmaker. We were never what you would describe as well-off, so I guess they had to make certain sacrifices to raise the £30 required to purchase my new two-wheeled racing bike.

Not that my pursuit of the Yellow Jersey had got off to a flying start. One of my very first failures in life was the police-organised cycling proficiency test at Blackthorn School. I was gutted when I failed the test and cried my eyes out, but the disappointment may have actually made me more determined to succeed. Fortunately, as with swimming and athletics, I had been blessed with a modicum of natural talent for cycling and managed to win quite a number of age-group events. I discovered it was one tough sport; the club officials used to enter us in 10-mile time-trials after which I would fall off my bike and throw up over my coach's shoes. 'Good ride, son . . .' Brendan McEwan would mutter approvingly. Looking back on my early sporting career, if I was not dripping with pee or broken eggs, then it was vomit.

It was Brendan, a bronze medallist at the Tokyo Olympics in 1964, who gave me one of the most important pieces of advice I have ever received. 'When you get on that bike,' he said, 'you've got to hate the other guy's guts. That's the attitude you must display if you entertain serious hopes of becoming a champion . . .' Perhaps 'hate' was the wrong word to use. Brendan's philosophy returned to haunt me some years later when, as a young rookie on the European tour, I innocently related this anecdote to golf writer Bill Elliott. Thus the first line of his story in the following morning's newspaper began, 'I hate Sandy Lyle's guts . . .' 'No, no, no . . .' I thought as I read it. 'That's *not* what I said, or what I meant.' I got my own back about twenty years later when Bill was caddying for me in a pro-am event with Bruce Forsyth. I slipped a brick into the bottom of the bag and Brucie – who was in on the joke – kept commenting on how amazing Fanny was as a caddie because Bill was making it look like awfully hard work. I gave Bill the brick at the end of the round, wrapped up as a gift; fortunately, he saw the funny side of things.

If my childhood sounds like one long, blissful adventure from dawn until dusk, that is exactly how I recall those golden years; I may have been an only child – Mum, bless her, explained she did not want any more children because she felt it would be impossible to love another as much as she loved me – but I was never, ever lonely. By day I romped and stomped in the woods; at night we would gather round the wireless (we did not own a television until I was about 10) to listen to Max Miller, Frankie Howerd, 'Round the Horne' or, my personal favourite, 'Hancock's Half Hour'. Later, on the nights I had a cub scout meeting, my big treat was being allowed to stay up late to watch 'Till Death Us Do Part', which probably explains why I developed such a colourful vocabulary.

My earliest memory is of a Lego set the size of Windsor Castle, which I was given for Christmas, aged three. My favourite 'toy,' however, was the garden shed and ladder, which graced the back garden of the house where I was born, 285 Knella Road. I would play for hour upon hour on my own, quite contentedly, transforming the shed into a pirates' galleon, a spaceship, a treasure island, a smugglers' cave, anything and everything, depending on whim. I took my wife, Valerie, to see the house shortly after we were engaged and I was delighted – and a bit misty-eyed, I have to confess – to discover nothing had changed. The washing line still ran the length of the garden, fixed at each end to those horrible old square, concrete posts, but, best of all, my shed was standing exactly as I remembered. When I pluck up the courage, some day in the future, I am going to knock on the front door and ask if I can buy the shed to reassemble in the grounds of our present home near Windsor – unless, of course, there is a new child in residence to whom it represents Hogwarts School of Witchcraft and Wizardry.

As a tiny tot, the whole garden spread out before me like a magic kingdom. Apart from the shed, there were two trees and a bank of huge bushes, and across the other side of the road were the woods, which I came to know like the back of my hand, complete with a railway line at the far end. My children have every diversion known to man – computers, PlayStations, you name it – but one of the great thrills of my young life was to run down to the level-crossing with my dad to watch the steam trains hurtle past, especially if *The Flying Scotsman* was due through.

Along with my best pals Gazza (Gary) and the daredevil Susie, who was a real tomboy, I invented a terrific game that we could play only after it had rained. Armed with our mothers' brooms, we used to push the rainwater along the roadside gutters. We would assemble a stream about 30 yards long and then sweep it down a drain in a single, surging tidal wave. All the neighbours loved us because there was never a single puddle in our street. Ah, the simple pleasures of youth!

Little wonder I was always filthy. I took to wearing two sets of clothes and would emerge from the bushes like the wild man of the woods, a grimy vision resplendent in grubby T-shirt and jeans, but with a clean T-shirt and shorts underneath. Thus, whenever I called at a chum's house and his mum or dad enquired, 'Are you wearing your spare clothes, Nicholas?' I could whip off the top layer of mud on the doorstep before being granted admittance.

Family holidays in the summer or at Christmas were another source of unbridled fun and laughter, even though I was the only child in the company of a posse of adults. Usually, these occasions included Uncle Charlie Faldo, who was married to Gladys, Uncle Harry Faldo, who was married to Gwen, plus Auntie Dolly who was married to Percy Slywockji, who had come over to England from Poland during the war. Along with Grandad, Charlie and Harry, who were the archetypal naughty uncles, wore those long, dark 1960s coats in winter, which made them look like the Chigwell Mafia.

My school chums would come back raving about the various charms of Blackpool or Bournemouth, but I was as happy as a sandboy on my family holidays. Uncle Harry was a great character and story-teller – one of his favourite yarns was 'How do they get the hole in the doughnut?'. I was too young to understand many of the tales but I realised from the reactions of the adults that here was an hilarious account to be treasured. 'Oooo, Harry,' my mum would say. 'You are awful . . .' At Christmas we used to go to

Sheringham in Norfolk where family tradition demanded that we run down to the beach and splash our faces in the sea. The water was minus degrees, as you would expect in England in December, black and horrible – it was certainly not the type of beach on which you would choose to go sunbathing – yet no matter how often we enacted this curious ritual, we still fell about laughing every time.

It was Uncle Harry who inadvertently brought about one of the rare disappointments of those halcyon days. Every Christmas Day for as far back as I can remember, Santa Claus would walk into the room at precisely four o'clock carrying a sack of fabulously wrapped presents all bearing my name. I was 10 when I spotted 'Santa' was wearing an identical ring on his left hand to the one Uncle Harry wore.

'Hey,' I blurted, 'you're not Santa Claus, you're Uncle Harry.' He might have succeeded in maintaining the charade by explaining there were many such rings in the world but Auntie Dolly gave the game away by interrupting.

'Oh, Harry, you've gone and bleedin' spoiled it all . . .'

Ah, well, I would not have swapped Uncle Harry for Father Christmas any day.

In summer, we would usually embark *en masse* for village life, also in leafy Norfolk where Uncle Charlie Faldo kept a caravan. Once my parents twigged to load my bike on to the roof rack, I was gone. Imagine being a 10-year-old with mile upon mile of pine forests to explore. They would set up the primus stoves and, unerringly, I would bowl up through the undergrowth just as my mother was serving lunch, grab a sausage sandwich or whatever was on offer on my high-speed way past, and disappear again still covered in leaves, twigs and accumulated foliage.

I always had an enormous appetite except when I was dragged along for Sunday lunch with Gran Faldo, who was a firm believer that vegetables – cabbage, carrots, sprouts, it made no difference in her cookbook – should be boiled until they turned grey and surrendered any semblance of crunch or flavour. On the other hand, she could have won a Michelin Star for her steamed pudding, the secret ingredient of which I will now divulge, should you wish to make note of Gran Faldo's famous recipe. The menfolk were despatched to the pub, Grandad very proper in his polished shoes and braces, where I was placed at a corner table with a glass of Tizer and a bag of crisps. After a few pints we would dutifully troop back to be force-fed our cremated meat and two indistinguishable soggy veg before Gran would disappear into the kitchen, re-emerging proudly bearing her prize-winning steamed sponge high above her head, snugly wrapped up in Grandad's old vest. It may not sound particularly appetising, but those were the ways of the Family Faldo.

Like all children, I could behave like a brat at times when the mood was upon me, especially when I felt thwarted in my desires. Mum and I used to pass a toy shop in Welwyn on our Saturday morning shopping trips and I became entranced by a big, red fire-engine in the window calling my name. 'Mum, Mum, Mum, I want it . . . I want it . . .' I wailed, and Mum patiently explained that she would, indeed, buy me this treasure some day. I was gazing through the window of the toy shop in wonderment one morning when up strolled another mother with her angelic-looking son who immediately spied *my* fire-engine. 'Mum, Mum, Mum,' he bleated, 'I want it . . . I want it . . .' I could have pointed out, quite reasonably, that I had first claim, instead of which I thought 'sod that', turned round and smacked him; I gave him four bells. Imagine my mother's embarrassment. There was this strange child lying on the pavement, rubbing his jaw and screaming in righteous indignation, with me hopping about in a rage yelling, '. . . but he wanted *my* fire-engine'. I was clearly forgiven, however, because I later took possession of my wooden dream-machine in which I careered around the streets like a thing demented.

Like all free-spirited youngsters, I found myself embroiled in a number of scrapes during my childhood but the only time I can recall incurring the genuine wrath of my parents was when I strayed off my own patch into another section of the woods 'owned' by the gang of kids in the next street. They spotted my brand new shiny bike and proceeded to launch a fusillade of gravel – ping, ping, ping – all over my proudest possession.

'Oi, stop that . . . don't do that again,' I shouted indignantly, whereupon another shower of gravel arrived. So I picked up a stone and although I was maybe 30 yards from my tormentors – remember, I was as unerringly accurate with a cricket ball as Robin Hood was with his bow – I got one of them right in the middle of the forehead. David had slain his Goliath, which seemed like the appropriate time to make good my escape. I was just sitting down to supper, knife and fork in hand, when there was a furious knocking on the door and Goliath's irate father was standing there, with the victim at his side sporting an egg-sized lump. When you are in deep trouble, as I was, you are never given the chance to put your side of the story. 'But he scratched my bike, Dad . . .' I pleaded my case in vain.

I was reminded of this incident when I took my son Matthew to a funfair, where he was immediately attracted by the crowd gathered around the coconut-shy. He had to knock over four of the targets with five balls to win a prize. I stood back with an indulgent smile to watch him. One . . . hit . . . two . . . hit . . . three . . . hit . . . four . . . miss. One ball and one target to hit. Knowing all about pressure, I thought, 'This will be interesting.' Matthew took aim . . . I couldn't believe it. He hit the coconut square on and number four was gone. The guy behind the stall looked at me and muttered, 'No one's done that all day.' Matthew won the biggest-fluffy pink pig you have ever seen for his little sister, Georgia. I admit it is a curious talent to pass on; Matthew's prodigious throwing arm has clearly been in his genes from birth. Should some unsuspecting kid ever decide to pepper Matthew's bike with pebbles, I guess he will do so at his peril.

My cycling adventures came to an abrupt end in my early teens when I was chosen to attend an Outward Bound school at Ullswater in the Lake District during the Easter holidays. It was the first time I had ever been away from my parents so I was understandably apprehensive, especially when I discovered I was about to embark on a six-hour train journey to Penrith. Six hours north of Welwyn? By my estimation that placed Penrith somewhere near the Polar icecap. I was not far wrong as things transpired.

Penrith was cold and bleak when I arrived. I threw my rucksack and myself into the back of a ramshackle open-bed truck with about nineteen grudging gears and, as someone who always suffered from car-sickness, had turned a fetching shade of bilious yellow by the time we finally arrived at what turned out to be a fabulous big old house on the shores of Ullswater. Now, having grown up in Welwyn Garden City in the 1960s, I had never had a black friend before, so when I found myself sharing a bunk with a lad from London whose parents had come over from the West Indies, it was a whole new experience. He was a super guy and we became inseparable over the course of the next four weeks. It may sound naive, but to this day I firmly believe that if you bring children of every race and religion together at a young age, they will not acquire the curse of prejudice in adulthood.

On our first night in Ullswater, I pulled on my pyjamas and lay in bed shivering; I drew up another blanket but was still shivering. I got out of bed, put my clothes back on, climbed back in and was still shivering. I got up again, put my coat on – still shivering. About three o'clock in the morning, just when I was finally dropping off, the blasted fire alarm went off, so we all charged outside and assembled in the garden, blue with cold and teeth chattering.

'Right,' announced the group leader, 'the next time will be for real.' Welcome to Outward Bound.

As it turned out, the first two weeks were spent in brilliant sunshine, canoeing on the lake and tackling commando assault courses, which I absolutely loved, but we came down for breakfast on the second Sunday morning to find Ullswater blanketed under two feet of snow. For the next fortnight we camped in the hills and trekked around Coniston Water. I was the supposed cook but trying to light a campfire in heavy snow demanded an ingenuity beyond my powers. We had to use powdered food and I was forever adding too much water to whatever mush I was preparing. It was entirely inedible until I came up with the wheeze of pouring in plenty of porridge as a thickener. 'Mmmm,' I would lick my lips while the happy campers looked on aghast, 'get that down your throats . . .'

If I make it sound like a frozen hell, nothing could be further from the truth; we all had a ball and must have learned something because we even joined in a genuine mountain rescue at four o'clock one morning when a walker was reported missing in the hills. Needless to say, we set off in one direction around the time this lost soul was making his way down by another route. He ended up enjoying a cup of tea and a Kit-Kat by the fire in the local police station while we were still out there freezing our nuts off.

My mum always says, 'Nick went away a boy and came back a man . . .' but man or not, my visit to Ullswater ended my career in the saddle. With all the preparations, I suppose I missed about six weeks of the cycling season and by the time I returned, the other guys were operating at a different level. I would set off and they would be out of sight – gone!

By now, the cupboard under the stairs of our new home at 11 Redwoods had come to resemble Steptoe's yard, crammed as it was with unwanted swimming goggles, home-made dirt-bike, canoe, racing bike, football and rugby boots, tennis racquet, cricket bat and balls, all discarded in my guise as sporting butterfly. There had been sundry other diversions along the way. My parents, both being keen on amateur dramatics, fondly imagined I might become the next Sir Laurence Olivier but, alas for their vision, Hollywood never beckoned. Next came music, so certain was Mum that I had the talent to win the Tchaikovsky music prize. They even took me to the ballet. Not any old ballet mind you, this was one of the Bolshoi's very first visits to London. Covent Garden no less. But the sight of a grown man prancing around in green tights is enough to put a boy off Brussels sprouts for life. Following this came a maternal belief that because I was possessed of such 'smashing legs' fame and fortune could be achieved as a catwalk model. I seem to remember it was during a fashion show at Harrods that I told Mum that although I could envisage myself on the cover of *Sports Illustrated*, *Vogue* was not on my agenda.

Some years ago, I was amused to read a remark by television commentator Peter Alliss that I was the product of a spoiled childhood. You cannot be serious. Indulged, yes; spoiled, never. I was forever being chased out of the back door by my irate mother, round the washing pole and back into the kitchen where I would receive a wallop with some implement or other depending upon the gravity of my misdemeanour. She gave up that tactic when I was about 10 – I had grown into such a big lug, these smacks genuinely hurt her more than they hurt me, and so I was made to stand in the corner with my back to the room like a school dunce by way of discipline.

At the dinner table, 'stomach in, chest out, don't fidget, Nicholas' became her mantra, which obviously had the desired effect because on my first train journey to London I sat there as good as gold like Little Lord Fauntleroy, inspiring a grey-haired old lady across the aisle to present me with a bar of chocolate as a reward for being 'a perfectly adorable child'. Now, in the Faldo home, this represented a mega-treat since sweeties of any variety were considered a banned substance, Mum being a fervent member of the anti-sugar lobby.

Even as a young lad I was on the Gaylord Hauser diet. No sugar. Nothing. And it obviously made an impact on me. Years later when dining with friends our hostess served a homemade pie to which she had forgotten to add any sugar. No problem for me of course, so while my fellow diners were all pulling faces at the sour taste, I was munching away quite happily. It wasn't until I was about halfway through that I realised everyone was looking at me in amazement. I couldn't see what their problem was.

My various sporting whims came and went, and although I still cycle as part of my fitness regime, continue to support Leeds United from afar, and while away the long hours in hotel bedrooms across the world watching everything and anything from lacrosse to tractor-pulling on the local sports channel, the only sport that has truly sustained me throughout the passing years is fishing. What began as a hobby has matured into a passion. Like so many things in my life, it was Dad who introduced me to it, gently guiding me through the intricacies of the sport from the riverbanks and reservoirs of Hertfordshire. From chasing perch, bream and roach with basic rod and line, I am now in the fortunate position of being able to fish the finest trout streams and salmon pools in the land, and there can be no more relaxing way to unwind after the strains and stresses of tournament golf than taking yourself off to the peace and solitude of a lonely stretch of river.

Fly-fishing and golf have much in common; you are constantly striving to improve your technique, and, above all, perfect timing and a slow backswing are essential. Just like moments of high pressure on the golf course, that slow backswing is especially difficult to perfect during the excitement of a rising fish. Although fishing is one of the few pleasures best enjoyed alone, it can also be a highly social pastime. During a golf tournament at Kapalua, Hawaii, some years back, I fell into conversation with American rock singer Huey Lewis, an enthusiastic low-handicap golfer and avid angler, and I have since stayed with him on his ranch in Montana where he owns a few miles of Spring Creek. On fishing trips with him, he keeps me enthralled with his tales of the curious world of rock music.

I recall that it was after Dad and I got home from a fishing expedition that we switched on the television and, at nearly 14 years old, I belatedly discovered the instrument through which I would finally fulfil my 'desire for greatness' — not a fishing rod, but a golf club.

CHAPTER TWO

A PROFESSIONAL
AMATEUR

My first golf club had been delivered into my hands some years earlier when Grandad Faldo gave me an old hickory-shafted iron. Unaware that what lay before me was, in fact, a golf club, I committed what I now know to be sacrilege by using it as an axe, sword, spear or whatever other weapon came to mind during my youthful games in the back garden. As a machete, it was ideal for cutting my way through the jungle on the days the neighbourhood woods and nettles were magically converted into an Amazonian rainforest bristling with snakes and incredible man-eating plants. Needless to say, the head duly snapped off and the club was consigned to the dustbin of history, which is a pity because it would have been nice to display this relic from the past among my mementoes.

Although my dad and uncles would frequently take me for a game of tennis or a two-a-side football match on the beach during our family holidays, strangely, we never once considered a round of golf; not even a light-hearted game of putting. I was aware of

Welwyn Garden City Golf Club only because our local scout hall lay 50 yards across the lane from the green on which, lo and behold, I would later spend two years building my game after leaving school at the age of 16. We made use of the course during our rambles – my parents were both enthusiastic walkers – but golf's mysteries were exactly that; so much so that I have no recollection whatsoever of watching or reading about Tony Jacklin's victory at the 1969 Open. You might think that this would have made some sort of impression on me considering he was the first Briton to win it since Max Faulkner at Portrush in 1951, six years before I was born.

Colour television was still a great novelty and had the 1971 Masters from Augusta been broadcast in black and white, my future might have turned out to be very different indeed. Switching through the channels on the Sunday evening of the last round after an afternoon's fishing with Dad, I was entranced not only by the beauty of the place, the flowers, lakes and lush green fairways, but also by the power and personality of Jack Nicklaus. A lot of people wrongly think I was inspired by the sight of Nicklaus pulling on the green jacket but it was the little-known Charles Coody who actually won that year, although I had eyes for the Golden Bear only. I never fail to marvel that this patch of golfing heaven came to gain such a special place in my heart in later years.

Mesmerised by the scenes I had witnessed, I came downstairs for breakfast the next morning and blithely announced that I would like to take up golf. 'Well, you'll need to have your hair cut,' replied Mum primly, reaching for the scissors and her best pudding bowl, which was not Fortnum & Mason's in our house but good old Pyrex. Suitably turned out as a choirboy, I was then accompanied to Welwyn Garden City Golf Club where I enrolled for six lessons. Having paid the assistant professional, Chris Arnold, the fee, I wanted to get on with it. 'Right, let's get started,' I said, and made ready to exit the pro shop stage left in the direction of the practice tee. Being a man with previous and more important appointments,

Chris politely explained he could not possibly fit me in until the next day, which to a 13-year-old is an eternity when destiny has come calling.

'Aaaooow,' I wailed, like Norman Wisdom, 'I want to start hitting shots now . . .'

My disgruntlement deepened when lesson one comprised learning the correct grip; with lesson two came the stance and alignment; lesson three, the backswing – did Chris not realise Augusta was awaiting my presence? After four lessons, I was finally allowed to hit a ball. It was perfect discipline, however, and Chris's insistence that I should not run before I could walk is something that has had a major influence on me over the years. I am constantly asked at the clinics I run these days for one tip, and I have to say the most important thing is always to be aware of the fundamentals – grip, alignment, posture and balance. I have kept them in mind from day one of playing this game and I still do over thirty years later.

From the moment Chris permitted me to launch my first ball into the sky, I was utterly head-over-heels in love. I instinctively knew that this was no mere infatuation like swimming, cycling or athletics had been; golf was to be my grand passion, my partner for life. At Sir Fredric Osbourn school, where I had never been the most attentive of pupils, I now spent most of the day practising the overlapping grip Chris had so painstakingly taught me. I came to live for Saturday mornings and my now weekly golf lesson. Even then, I thoroughly enjoyed practice, and so when Chris had finished his 30 minutes' tuition, I would take myself off for hours at a time, assiduously perfecting everything I had learned.

My parents must have been mightily impressed by this display of dedication because on my 14th birthday – 18 July 1971 – they presented me with my first half-set of clubs: nothing particularly grand, but to me they represented the ultimate in golfing equipment, especially as the heads were stamped 'St Andrews'. I flew – and I use the word advisedly – round to the golf club where I was disconcerted as I arrived on the first green to find the sprinklers operating at full whirl and water cascading everywhere.

Uncertain about the correct procedure, I skipped putting out and hastened on to the second hole where the green was under similar preparation; and so it was the third hole before I actually set foot on a putting surface where I promptly three-putted. 'Well that's daft,' I said to myself. 'I'm never doing that again!' I also remember thinking that the green was so soft, so luscious underfoot, that I felt I should have been wearing carpet slippers instead of cruel spikes. Ah, but what did you score, I hear you enquire. Well, I struck 82 shots but lost three balls, which, not knowing the rules, meant nothing to me, so I'm afraid there is no official record of my very first outing although I would definitely have broken 90. Alas, my St Andrews specials were not long for this world; through sheer brute strength, one by one the shafts simply snapped and so, not for the first time, my parents indulged me by purchasing a full second-hand set bearing the master's name, Ben Hogan.

By this time, Chris had decided to turn me over to the head professional, Ian Connelly, a Scot of infinite wisdom and patience. A vastly knowledgeable historian of the game, it was from Ian that I first heard about the deeds of legendary figures of bygone days – Sam Snead, Henry Cotton and, most importantly of all perhaps, Ben Hogan. During the winter months when the course was frozen or flooded, I would spend hours by the electric fire in Ian's pro shop, listening to him spin those magical tales in his rich Dundonian tones.

I could not have passed into better care because it is my continuing belief that few, if any, teaching professionals in the world can compare with Ian Connelly in the art of nurturing young talent. He became my biggest fan and my sternest critic, instilling in me not only the need to behave like a gentleman at all times on the course, but also the understanding that without hard work and dedication, all the natural talent in the world will not turn you into a champion. My admiration and appreciation for Ian remains unbounded and it says everything about his skills as a mentor that, by the age of 15, little more than a year after holding a golf club for the very first time, I was playing off a handicap of 5.

Maybe it was because I was something of a loner, perhaps it was my barely disguised burning ambition to succeed, but I was less than popular with certain individuals at the club. And so, when I was practising by myself as usual one Sunday morning and was approached by a member inviting me to play in the monthly medal competition, I naturally jumped at the chance. As the first tee was more crowded than Oxford Street on Christmas Eve, we dashed across to the 10th, whereupon I proceeded to shoot a 72 minus 5 for a medal-winning 67, and duly repaired to the clubhouse for the prize-giving ceremony. I was sitting at the bar with my glass of lemonade when the club captain strode up.

'I'm afraid we've disqualified you,' he barked, sergeant-major style.

'And why's that?' I demanded indignantly.

'Because you teed off at ten-forty-five and juniors are not allowed on the course until eleven o'clock.'

Crushed by this blatant miscarriage of justice, I never played in another monthly medal competition in my life.

Fortunately, Clive Harkett later took over as captain, a true gentleman who fully appreciated that the juniors represented the future of the club. He was tremendously supportive, and has only recently retired after giving 35 years of service, support and encouragement to Hertfordshire golf. We won the Herts County Junior Team Championship in successive years with a team consisting of myself, Trevor Powell and John and Colin Moorhouse, and suddenly the membership was proud of us, but that original atmosphere of superiority is something I detest about golf clubs even now, and part of the reason I launched the Nick Faldo Series to encourage and assist young talent.

Under Clive, the Welwyn members became wonderfully helpful and even created the Commemorative Jug tournament after my first

Open Championship victory at Muirfield in 1987; but in the bad old days I think I was regarded as a young upstart who should have been at home doing his homework instead of cluttering up their precious course. All of that, you will not be surprised to discover, made me even more determined to succeed. 'Sod you,' was my attitude, 'I'll show you . . .' That is when all the famous trademarks were probably ingrained in my psyche. Head down, blinkers on, I cocooned myself in a private world of my own. My parents were both hard workers, and they had instilled in me the ethic that if I worked harder than everyone else, I deserved to win, simple as that.

Although I had briefly entertained childish notions of working as a ranger for the Canadian Forestry Commission (well, you have to admit, it makes a change from wanting to become a fireman or a train driver), by now I was committed to playing golf for a living, which was a surprise to a youth employment officer who interviewed me at school one afternoon. After studying my grades, which were fairly miserable to be truthful, not to mention the size of my navvy's hands, he informed me that he could probably find me a placement on a building site or in a factory. As it happened, my form class had already endured an 'outing' to the nearby Vauxhall car plant, just to scare us into action, I reckon. When you hear the noisy machinery and see guys screwing on door handles all day, it certainly concentrates the mind. When he asked me if I thought I might be interested in manual labour, I replied, 'No, no, no, none of that for me. I'm going to be out in the fresh air; I want to be my own boss. I'm going to be a professional golfer.'

'But only one lad in ten thousand makes it, son,' he explained kindly.

'Yeah, but I'm the one, I'm that one,' I insisted.

I remember round about the same time my headmaster Rex Treganar asking me when I was sitting in my classroom on a rainy afternoon, 'How good are you?'

'Well, I'm a great putter,' I replied. 'I could beat any professional on the greens.' That was probably true at the time, to be honest, because you don't need physical strength to putt; if I did not hole every putt from 15 feet I was outraged.

After that, what little interest I had in school disintegrated completely. I never played truant – George and Joyce Faldo would never have stood for those shenanigans from their son – but I could not see how algebraic equations were going to improve my golf swing, even if I somehow managed to pass my exams in English, mathematics, technical drawing, woodwork and metalwork. Mr Harvey, my PE teacher, accepted the inevitable when he wrote on my report card: 'Nick's future will undoubtedly be in sport. He sets his standards high and his dedication will be the key to his success.' Prophetic words. But the moment the school bell blessedly rang at four o'clock I was out of the blocks like an Olympic 100 metre finalist. I used to cycle home with such haste to collect my clubs that I was actually stopped by the police for speeding on one occasion when they clocked me doing 35mph, which means I would probably have overtaken Dad in our original Austin A40.

Already a full-time golfer in my own mind, I officially ceased being a schoolboy on my 16th birthday with, and again I have to stress this, the encouragement and financial assistance of my parents. I am so grateful to my dad for the opportunity he gave me. Being an accountant he had worked out the maths. If I'd worked in a pro shop I'd have received £4 a week. As it was, child allowance was also £4 a week so we would have ended up losing out if I'd done that. And of course I wouldn't have had the same amount of time to practise. It also meant that I could remain a free agent, and that was, as I'd told that youth employment officer, one of the two goals of my professional life – being my own boss and working outside. Dad's decision to support me sowed those seeds at an early age. They trusted me implicitly in the sense that here was a 16-year-old kid cycling off into the distance every morning saying he was going to the golf club and returning home every night after dark. I doubt they ever spied on me because I have never shirked any responsibility — even school — which is why they were confident I would be out there on the practice ground as promised and not hanging about street corners. Rain, hail or snow (and I frequently had to sweep the practice green after a snowstorm), if they had come out to look for me, they would have found me hard at work on the golf course. Yes, it was a dream come true to be able to play the game I loved every day, but I genuinely thought of myself as an ordinary working man whose office or factory just happened to be the golf course.

Every morning I awoke to the sound of Mum scraping the burnt toast — who needs an alarm clock when you have a culinary arsonist in the kitchen? — and breakfasted on home-made yoghurt, porridge and a boiled egg before leaving the house at eight o'clock on the dot. For my working lunch I ate the same thing for the following two years — cheese and pickle sandwiches, or cheese and salad cream if I fancied a change, a chunky date bar, a chocolate bar and a yoghurt, plus an apple or an orange. This feast was crammed into one of Mum's round tupperware containers, which meant the sarnies always came out a funny shape. I had to carry this and all my clubs every day because I had not yet been granted the privilege of a locker in the clubhouse. So I designed and built a wooden contraption to carry my clubs, which I tied across the handlebars of my bike with wire, and off I would shoot. The outward journey was no problem because it was mostly a gentle uphill climb through the woods but the return trip was hazardous in the extreme, especially if it had been raining, when the path was transformed into a muddy version of the Cresta Run. I lost count of the times I surrendered control and crashed, clubs flying everywhere, and had to painstakingly put my DIY two-wheeled bag-carrier back together again.

That, then, was my life for two years. I would arrive at the course about 8.15 and spend all morning on my little bit of practice ground, which even then was probably no more than a 7-iron, and that was where I learned to improvise. With Ian Connelly's instruction, I learned to hit a slow-motion 2-iron a 7-iron distance, pitching it oh-so-gently on to the green 160 yards or so away. This was an invaluable exercise, which certainly came into its own when I was on the European Tour. In the good old days we used to have to practise in cow fields and I remember being at one event where the practice area was only 180 yards and we were informed by the Tour official that we weren't allowed to hit drivers as a result. That's fine, I thought. No problem, and proceeded to hit a number of nice, slo-mo drives to 180 yards. Little did I know that thousands of miles away, this was Ben Hogan's party piece to demonstrate his swing. Around noon, I would allow myself a half-hour break and sit on a log to have lunch, then pitch and putt for an hour or so. After that, I would play a minimum of 27 holes, but frequently 36. Unless the course was formally closed because of the weather, I never missed a day. I had a pair of proper waterproof trousers and Mum, being a dressmaker, knocked me up some sort of jacket to keep out the rain. There could not have been a happier or more contented worker in the land. My hands were in a terrible state, having hit thousands of shots a day. Dry spots would crack open and I had blisters. I frequently cycled home with my hands dripping in blood. Invariably Mum would have my supper waiting for me on the stove but I always went back out immediately after finishing to clean my clubs. They were the tools of my trade after all. Following dinner I would swing the night away thanks to an outside light on the shed wall that created a mirror image of me in the kitchen window, allowing me to study my swing. Now, thirty years on, sports psychologists will tell you the power of being able to see and feel your swing to mentally endorse your positive image.

Critics who claim I am obsessive should have known me back then. As well as practising under the light of the shed, you would also find me hitting full-blown drives in the back garden. But it wasn't as dangerous as it sounds. I would tee up little mud balls the size of peas and if I hit one sweetly I'd run in and show Mum the patch of mud on the head. She was suitably under-whelmed, I must confess. Another one of my routines, which I copied from Harry Wheetman's book, was to swing a pickaxe over and over again in order to swing slowly and develop my tempo. (Harry actually used an axe but there wasn't one in our shed.)

Occasionally, when the weather was too atrocious even for me to venture out on the course, I would offer my dubious services to Ron Marks, a long-time friend who ran a one-man carpet-fitting business. It was hard work for two quid a day, lugging van-loads of best Axminster up and down innumerable flights of stairs, but eventually, as I picked up the secrets of the craft, I was promoted from human donkey to assistant fitter, laying the underlay, hammering in the gripper rods, then cutting the carpet to fit. Those were hilarious interludes because you came across some real nutty folk. One five-year-old kid was annoying me so much, poking his grubby hands everywhere they were not wanted while I was trying to lay carpet on his parents' blasted stairs, I eventually said, 'Come here, son, I've got a terrific game we can play.' So saying, I tied him to the banisters. The wee fella was delighted with this unexpected game of cowboys and Indians – I thought of it as cannibals and missionaries, I have to confess – and chirruped away quite contentedly, allowing me to finish the job. I did not feel a shred of guilt, especially when his mother offered Ron and I a cup of tea and thoughtfully provided a saucer into which I was expected to drop a few coins to pay for my biscuit.

Another customer went out shopping, leaving me to look after a yappy little dog. The creature thought carpet-fitting was tremendous fun, snapping at my ankles, chewing the underlay, running off with my tools, thereby leaving me no alternative but to drop-kick the damned mutt out of the back door on to the lawn.

'Oh, what a perfectly lovely job you've made of the library,' she trilled toffily on her return. 'And where's my beloved Tiddles?' (or some such drippy name).

'He's frolicking in the garden,' I replied, mimicking her snooty accent.

'Perhaps you would like to join him,' she continued. 'Tiddles does enjoy a game of football ever so much.'

'I know. Tiddles and I have already had a game together,' I muttered, making a beeline for the front door.

We later branched out into carpet cleaning, which is how I came to be at the Hammersmith Palais, cleaning the carpets from top to bottom, from 12 midnight to 12 noon the following day – a back-breaking task that had my stomach muscles screaming in agony for days. But the worst, the very worst, experience was when we were contracted to rip up and dispose of all the carpets in a Welwyn Garden City hotel, which was being refurbished. It started well; I was allowed to kick down the doors like Starsky and Hutch before pulling up the carpet and underlay. Being a smart lad, or so I fondly imagined, instead of rolling up each roomful, carrying it along the corridor, down the stairs and into the car park below, I came up with the wheeze of simply chucking all the old stuff out of the window. We swept through three floors in this manner but, of course, when we finally ventured outside, there was a huge mountain of carpets and underlay staring at us accusingly. Having blithely thought our task was nearly done, we were another two hours rolling everything up and carrying it to the skips 50 yards or so away – and I was the boy who had wanted nothing to do with manual labour (like Lee Trevino, I preferred to think of Manuel Labor as a Mexican freedom fighter).

It was excruciating work but deep in my soul I was convinced that fame and fortune awaited. Driving through Ayot St Lawrence to a job one particularly bleak Monday morning, we passed an idyllic, chocolate-box house called Tudor Cottage whereupon I turned to Ron and blithely told him, 'I'm going to own that place some day.' It was wishful thinking, a spur-of-the-moment daydream, but by a strange quirk of fate, when I started making some money on the Tour in 1978, Tudor Cottage became available and it was the first home I ever owned.

There was much hard graft to come before that event but I have always believed that if you visualise what you want, the logical next question is, 'Well, how do I do it?'. I was fortunate in being blessed with strong mental discipline but in golf, as in any sport, you need every advantage you can gain over your rivals, which is why I first consulted a sports psychologist as far back as 1982, long before it became fashionable to do so. I kept those visits secret at the time because I was worried outsiders might think I had gone 'loopy-loo'. I have always considered inner or mental strength, call it what you will, every bit as important as natural talent, and that is why I admired Bjorn Borg. He was one of my early sporting heroes for the way he conducted himself, never permitting his concentration to waver no matter what was going on all around him, so it is no coincidence that on the golf course I was more of a Bjorn Borg than an Ilie Nastase.

Borg was a past master in the art of appearing aloof and that was the way I liked it during my two-year 'apprenticeship' on the practice ground at Welwyn. There were very few other kids around acting as a distraction, no boss on my back telling me to do this or that. I was out there hour after hour, day after day, week after week, through my own discipline, my own determination, not forgetting the four quid a week child allowance my parents were paying me. Ian Connelly was constantly offering advice and encouragement, I hasten to add, and I became an avid collector of tips, whatever the source. When I heard that Gary Player used to hit bunker shots for half a day, that is precisely what I did, spending all morning playing out of this one little sand-trap at Welwyn. The members came to hate the sight of me because whenever they turned up on the practice hole after my Gary Player sessions, there was little or no sand left in the bunker; I was forever asking the greenkeeper to refill the darned thing.

Having read about Gary Player and all the other great players, imagine my excitement when Dad arranged for us to travel to Royal Troon for the 1973 Open. We had swapped the old Austin A40 for a second-hand white Volkswagen Beetle by then, and up the M6 we trundled through the pouring rain, scared out of our lives every time we were forced to overtake a lorry in the spray. We bowled into Troon on our very last drop of fuel, so headed straight for the nearest petrol station, and there was Tony Jacklin in his Rupert Bear checked trousers and bright pink cashmere sweater, filling up his Rolls-Royce, with Tom Weiskopf sitting in the passenger seat. 'That'll be us in a few years' time, Dad,' I promised. Whereas Jacklin and Weiskopf were probably staying in the five-star Marine Hotel, which overlooks the 18th fairway at Troon, the Faldo duo took up temporary residence on a local camp-site. Not unlike at Ullswater, it was so cold day and night that not only did I sleep with my clothes on over my pyjamas, when I woke up I went out in the self-same rig-out. God knows what I smelled like at the end of the week.

Every morning we headed straight to the practice ground to watch all the legends close up – Gary Player, Arnold Palmer, Lee Trevino and Bruce Crampton, who hit every drive so accurately his caddie would catch the balls on the fly in a baseball glove. We quietly studied their rituals and routines, then made our way to the first tee. One time, Jack Nicklaus – wow, Dad, that's Jack Nicklaus! – jumped over a wall and disappeared into a portaloo. Like any kid of 16 would do, I immediately followed him in and went down the line peeing in every urinal so I could say I had peed in the same place as Jack Nicklaus.

Weiskopf came down to the range late one evening and proceeded to practise in his street shoes; he chatted away to Jack, all the while clipping these marvellous shots, and the noise his club made on the ball and turf was simply mesmerising. Weiskopf possessed one of the most majestic swings of all time, as sweet as chocolate sauce, and I stood there amazed, trying to take in his rhythm and tempo.

'They can give him the trophy now,' I told my father and, sound judge that I am, Weiskopf duly emerged triumphant.

Watching Weiskopf at that Open was truly magical. Because the crowds were so much smaller then I could run the course and watch every single shot – from the practice area, to the first drive, on to the second and so on. At this year's Open I bumped into Tom and his son Eric who informed me that – after his dad of course – I was his hero and had inspired him through his college days in the 1990s. We had a chat and I told Eric that his dad was my hero, recalling how I had followed him in 1973 and had seen him take a divot on the 7th tee that took my breath away. It was as long and thin as a finger and I just had no idea how that was possible. My divots were great big clumps at that time.

Back in Welwyn Garden City, inspired by what I had seen, I would play out imaginary matches – me versus Trevino (who fades) and Player (who hooks), or Nicklaus (the master tactician) and Palmer (the muscle man). I'd play all three balls, trying my hardest to mimic the style and strokes of my playing partners. I guess even then my ability to visualise was developing unwittingly. I was emulating my golfing heroes and playing against them, so that my practice had a competitive edge – even more so when I created, from the relatively ordinary surroundings of the Welwyn Garden City course, imaginary bunkers and lakes to be avoided. The power of this approach is something I teach today. If you don't feel you can make a shot, who can? Imagine Tiger Woods is doing it and jump into his shoes. With that mental attitude it is possible to get lost in the vision and forget about your own swing, turning a negative into a positive.

The following summer, we attended the Open at Royal Lytham where I was deeply impressed by Jerry Heard who came equipped with a big, syrupy swing, which was absolutely gorgeous. Jerry became my instant role model and I spent many a long day replicating his style on my return to Welwyn. Two years later, when I played my one and only round of golf with Mark McCormack, he turned to me and said, 'You look just like Jerry Heard,' and I thought, 'Little do you know, mate.'

I offer no apologies for practising so assiduously. It was my future at stake, and being the stubborn person that I am, I simply used any criticism of my methods that reached my ears to make me strive even harder. It was sweet music therefore when, after winning the Royston Boys' Championship in 1974 by shooting 67 in a blizzard, on a course where you needed a Sherpa as a guide, I entered the clubhouse to hear one of the other fathers complaining, 'It's unfair because Faldo practises such a lot. He's really a full-time golfer, you know.'

My major breakthrough came in 1975 when I started the season by winning the Berkshire Trophy, one of the most prestigious events on the English amateur calendar. I telephoned my parents who, with unfortunate timing, were out shopping, and set off for home more excited than I had ever been in my life. Having recently passed my driving test in an Opel Kadette, I had cajoled my dad into buying a similar model (which turned out to be a 'pup', I regret to admit) and, strapping this most beautiful of trophies in alongside me, I raced down the country roads like Jackie Stewart, eager to impart my news. I was so overwhelmed, so joyous, so ecstatically happy, I wound down the windows and screamed and shouted to release all those pent-up emotions (and there are those who believe I am as cold and dispassionate as Mr Spock).

That summer was truly amazing; after winning the Berkshire Trophy, I then finished well in the Brabazon, won the British Youths' Championship, and qualified for the British Amateur Championship at Royal Liverpool where I achieved national recognition by beating the favourite, John 'Badger' Davies, in the third round. Mind you, he had been warned. While driving to the tournament, Gerald Micklem, one of the great figures of the amateur game, had told him that he was about to play against a young lad who 'shouldn't be taken lightly'. John was wondrously sporting in defeat and was quoted thus by one newspaper: 'I've just been beaten by the best amateur I have ever seen. What a boy . . . what class. There was nothing I could do . . . he has no weaknesses.' With that tribute ringing in my 17-year-old ears, 24 hours later I lost at the first play-off hole to the unheralded Dave Moffatt. How quickly are the mighty humbled in golf.

It was marvellous to bump into 'Badger' again recently. He recounted a story of the 1992 European Open at Sunningdale, which took place following my Open victory that year. Badger told me that he had come out to the practice ground to watch me hit a few balls and was suitably impressed with my form that he decided to walk round for three holes. He ended up staying for 72 which, he said, was something he had never done before. Badger is one of the true gentlemen of golf – and not just because he was a member of the ultra-exclusive Sunningdale and drove a Jensen Interceptor at the time. Such was his reputation he had even employed Willie Aitcheson as his bag carrier. Aitcheson was perhaps the most famous caddie in professional golf during his highly successful partnership with Lee Trevino. Despite the wretchedness of my defeat by Dave Moffatt, Willie, wise old owl that he is, must have spotted something he liked because he promised that should I qualify for the forthcoming Open at Carnoustie, he would arrange for me to play a practice round with Super-Mex.

'How can you arrange that?' I asked, suitably awed.

''Cos I'm the boss,' came Willie's response.

I duly celebrated my 18th birthday by failing to qualify by two agonising strokes at Monifieth but, being in the area and with nothing else to occupy mind or body for the next week, I took myself along to Carnoustie to watch Trevino, Open Champion in 1971 and 1972, up close and personal.

'How did you get on?' whispered Willie when he espied me on the non-business side of the first tee.

'I messed up big-time and I'm gutted,' I confessed.

'Ach, dinnae worry, son, just stick close . . .'

And that was how I came to accompany Willie and the incomparable Lee Trevino throughout three rounds of practice. Oh, yes, I had won the Berkshire Trophy, but Lee had never met this fresh-faced kid in his life before yet he could not have been more helpful or friendly.

Lee related a wonderful story about how he first came to work with Willie at Royal Birkdale in '71, having sacked his original caddie after nine holes of practice.

'So Willie joined me at the tenth and we marched down the fairway to my ball. "How far is it to the pin?" "Five-iron, surrr" announced this Scottish voice at my side. "I didn't ask you that, I asked you how far it is to the pin." "Disnae matter whit ye asked, it's still a five-iron, surrr." "How . . . far . . . is . . . it . . . to . . . the . . . pin?" I repeated a third time before reaching into my bag and pulling out five balls. I then hit a wedge, a seven-iron, a three-wood, a three-iron and a putter straight on to the green. So I looked at Willie and said, "Don't ever tell me what club it is. Just give me the yardage."'

Five days later, Super-Mex's name was writ large in the headlines when he secured his first old Claret Jug.

Being with Trevino during that 1975 Open was an incredible experience for me. Can you imagine what it was like to walk those three practice rounds with him? It took him two and a half days to miss a green. I remember in particular two of his drives on the par-3 16th. There was a howling crosswind but that didn't deter Lee. On the first day he hit it within two feet and on the second within three. Trevino really could make a ball talk.

A lasting impression of our first meeting was when I first shook hands with him. I couldn't believe it, I'd expected them to be hard and calloused but they were like squidgy pads. Just like Sam Snead's hands. They were both powerful men with fantastic touch. And the best thing he did for me over those three days? 'I'll show you how to putt,' he told me. 'Address the ball, push your hands slightly forward and rock your shoulders.' How incredible is that? From Lee Trevino to a young amateur. He also explained to me how he started playing golf. He was allowed to hit balls at a range (although he had to go and pick them all up) – he would hit a thousand a day and in so doing he developed his swing. He had a mega strong grip, and on his backswing he would take the club outside and drive through with his leg action. In that way he became a master fader of the ball. As he said to me, you can talk to a fade to bring it in, but a hook will never listen.

The 1975 English Amateur Championship at Royal Lytham proved to be a highly successful week in more ways than one because I met a girl called Angela in the clubhouse and fell in love for the first time in my life. Up until then, my devotion to golf meant I had missed out on the 'youth experience'; girls, and, indeed, friends in general, could not be permitted to interfere with my daily routine. I regret to say that the day I left school I said goodbye to my best chum, Steve Ellis, at the end of the road, and didn't see him again for years. 'See you then,' I said, as Steve went off to be a plumber and I set off to pursue my desire for sporting greatness. Steve now lives and works in Australia, and we meet up for a beer whenever I am there.

Angela became a constant presence at my side at Lytham; I was faffing around in practice one day, as only I can, when a pearl of wisdom dropped in my ear. 'Oh, just hit it, Nick,' she said in her Lancashire accent, and that became our private code for the week. Following Angela's expert advice, I kept 'hitting it' as I cut a swathe through my half of the draw, assisted by the defeat of defending champion Mark James. There was a mightily satisfying victory over Gordon Edwards, a real English Golf Union toff, in the quarter-finals. As we came off the 14th green, one of his cronies brayed, 'I say, Gordon, let's have a picture of you two chaps.' I was one down at the time and they wanted a happy-snap for the photograph album.

'Doesn't smile much, does he, Gordon?' sneered the cameraman.

'Yeah,' I muttered under my breath, 'but I'll be the one smiling at the eighteenth.'

I did not have to wait that long as it transpired, a run of three holes earning me a 2 and 1 victory on the 17th.

Thus I qualified to meet Philip Morley in the semi-finals. Phil was not only my room-mate for the week, but he, Angela and I had spent many a night in the local pub listening to Elton John singing 'Don't Let The Sun Go Down On Me' on the jukebox. There was no way of knowing it at the time, of course, but in later years Elton would become my nearest neighbour in Old Windsor. Shortly after moving into my current home, I was strolling round the garden one evening when I heard Elton and a few friends enjoying a jam-session the other side of the wall. Pouring myself a glass of white wine, I settled into a lounger and listened to a free concert of his greatest hits. With Elton John living next door, you never have to complain about the noise.

I knew playing Phil Morley would be difficult, given our friendship, and that is when the earlier words of my old cycling coach, Brendan McEwan, came to mind – 'When you get on that bike, you've got to hate the other guy's guts.' Phil was far too likeable to engender any sense of hatred, but I managed to 'dislike' him sufficiently that afternoon to record an improbably straightforward 4 and 2 win to reach my first major 36-hole final. It also helped that by the end of the week I was getting more and more comfortable with the course – especially the 6th and 7th. Every time I went through those two holes I recorded an eagle on one of them. Given my mixed emotions about beating Phil, I was understandably relieved when Chris Allen, another good friend and fellow Welwyn Garden City member, fell to David Ecclestone in the other semi-final.

With Angela still cajoling me to 'just hit it,' I was six up at lunch in the final and, although I struggled to reproduce that form in the afternoon round, nine days after turning 18 I became the youngest winner of the English Amateur Championship by beating Ecclestone 6 and 4.

Perhaps the most important aspect of the week – apart from being handed the trophy – was the discovery that I was not afraid of winning. There is many a richly talented golfer out there who, in a head-to-head battle, stands on the 18th feeling genuine terror. I was still a teenager but I had tamed that particular demon.

I'd been almost invincible on the greens that week, where I had used my new Lee Trevino putting style to devastating effect. When I arrived at Lytham I had been mesmerised by the putting surfaces – these really were like carpet, and about as far removed as is possible from the green I had created at home. Very generously I had offered Dad that I would cut the grass for free, but what I ended up doing was scalping it as close as I could to make the surface as fast as possible, and digging out the holes with a garden trowel. After practising on that, no wonder I couldn't miss.

The snipers were out in force, criticising me for being a 'professional amateur' because I spent so many hours practising and, horror of horrors, actually working out yardages. But happily, not everyone was so grudging and I am proud of the following words offered by Pat Ward-Thomas in the *Guardian*. The cutting adorns my first scrapbook, which is still in the possession of my parents:

> It would be surprising if this success was a sudden flash of glory because there is a distinct quality of the unusual about Faldo. The exceptional strength of his wood and iron play would stand favourably in any company, and is achieved with less effort than I have seen in any young golfer for many years. This plainly is a natural gift. For a boy, his approach to the game is uncommonly mature.

Within a heady six-month spell, I had won the English Amateur, the British Youths', the Berkshire Trophy, the Commonwealth Trophy Invitational in South Africa, the Scrutton Jug, the Champion of Champions' Trophy, the Hertfordshire County Championship, the

Hertfordshire Boys' and the Royston Junior, and been in joint first place in the King George V Coronation Cup. I was costing Mum a small fortune in silver cleaning liquid. In some regards, I was still a naive young thing as I discovered when I competed in the South-East Boys' Championship at Sunningdale. Having been accustomed to staying in cheap and frequently not so cheerful bed-and-breakfast establishments, and even a YMCA at the Brabazon, we were put up in a super-posh hotel complete with chandeliers, velvet drapes and French windows opening out on to manicured lawns. Being unfamiliar with dining in such surroundings, on the first evening I even took a bite out of a delicious-looking Mediterranean prawn – with its shell on. I only did it once mind you.

Disappointingly, my golden six months came too late to earn me a place in the Walker Cup team to play the United States at Hoylake – in a typically British move the squad had been selected during the previous winter – and it gave me no satisfaction whatsoever when we were duly thumped 15½–8½ by an American side containing Jerry Pate, Lanny Wadkins, Craig Stadler, George Burns and Jay Haas. Having been denied a crack at the Yanks by this curious selectorial procedure, and despite my misgivings, it was time to take on the Americans on their own soil in the company of Sandy Lyle and Martin Poxon. Being a great admirer of the US college system, Ian Connelly was firmly of the belief that a two-year stint in the States would prove far more beneficial than remaining in England, even if it meant relinquishing any hope of competing in the 1977 Walker Cup contest at Shinnecock Hills.

Although Tom Weiskopf had sent a personally written letter inviting me to consider Ohio State University (where Jack Nicklaus had honed his skills as a bear cub), we decided to opt for the University of Houston, mainly because the coach there was so persuasive.

'You're a lion, you're a real competitor, aren't you?' he would growl down the transatlantic phone line.

'Oh, yeah,' I agreed, displaying nary a shred of false modesty. 'I'm the best in the country right now, mate . . .'

And so the three of us departed little ol' England for Texas where we were collected at the airport in a car as big as the Faldo family home – Dad's Austin A40 would have fitted in the boot, sorry, trunk. Then, after checking into our dormitory, came the first little stinger when we were informed we would have to sit an entrance exam. Martin and I managed to scramble a pass but Sandy was the luckiest out of the three of us; having failed, he was instructed to attend a junior college to prepare for his re-sit, whereupon he decided America was not to his liking and caught the first plane home.

How I wish I had accompanied Sandy rather than remained cooped up studying mass communications, physical education, hotel and restaurant management, media and public speaking, not all of which were vitally important subjects for a wannabe professional golfer. I was thoroughly miserable, having been transported from the practice ground of Welwyn Garden City to a classroom. The golf courses were 45 minutes away from the campus so there was no time for practice before a match; you simply arrived, changed into your golf gear, teed up and you were away. My game gradually went to pieces although I was still playing well enough to retain my place on the team. Worst of all, when it came to the weekend, which represented my first chance to hit a few practice balls, college tradition demanded that you troop down to the Barbery Coast Diner on a 'honey hunting' expedition. There we would sit, surrounded by pitchers of beer, burgers and fries, abjectly failing to sniff out any suitable 'honey'. I did about six weeks of school but then thought 'sod this' and started skipping classes to mooch about in my room, putting on the carpet, anything to kill time until the next college match.

Eventually, I asked to be left out of the team so I could spend a few days practising; the coach did not respond but at our next team meeting delivered a less-than-coded message when he announced, 'Boys, I've had a complaint about the amount of time devoted to practice. Well, let me tell you all something – the great players out there are just that, players, they're not practicers.' I sat there and thought, 'Player, Hogan, Nicklaus – you're trying to tell me they're not, as if such a word existed, *practicers*? Give me a break.'

Space City, as Houston was called, might be a delightful place if you want to walk on the moon, but, for me, it was hell upon earth as a golfer. For reasons known only to himself, however, the coach granted my wish and I was allowed to go off by myself for three days to practise before a small inter-collegiate event in Houston, which I won.

'Well done, Nick,' he muttered.

'Yes, isn't it amazing what you can do with a spot of practice?' I answered darkly.

Come the next team meeting and up stepped the coach to deliver his latest sermon: 'Boys, if you want to be great players, you've got to practise. If you want to be a great driver of the ball, you've got to practise your driving. If you want to be a great chipper, you've got to practise your chipping . . .' and so on, and so on.

I reported to his office the next morning, looked at him across the desk, and told him, 'I'm out of here, that's enough for me.'

He drummed his fingers for a few moments, clearly planning a campaign and replied, 'You're homesick, son, aren't you? You're missing your parents, you're missing your girlfriend . . .'

I twigged him immediately, but thought, OK, if that is your story, why not? So I went along with his so-called motives for my departure after a mere 10 weeks in Houston, but I arrived home to find myself the subject of a *Sunday Times* article headlined: 'Faldo's So Wet!' According to the writer, Dudley Doust:

Faldo, a prodigy, is suffering a disease common to too many British golfers, both amateur and professional; things have come too easily for him. He was, perhaps still is, a glorious prospect.

He has come out of it poorly and, as the reigning English amateur champion, doubtless has left a bad taste behind him.

I strenuously disagreed with this assessment. It had been a great experience and the only problem for me was that I had lost out on my practice time. The set-up there simply didn't allow for enough golf for me. But I am pleased I gave it a shot and I didn't regard it as a failure. And I certainly did not think I was being 'wet'. In my view, having the guts to try something and then deciding it isn't for you is not a failure. Rather it is a learning experience and it means that I can talk with some authority on the subject now. To be fair to Dudley Doust, a few years later he retracted every word in print.

The next decision was whether to remain amateur, defend my English title and qualify for the 1977 Walker Cup side, or turn professional; the notion of continuing in the unpaid ranks held great appeal but I could not expect my parents to support me financially indefinitely and so I applied to the PGA to become a professional on 14 April 1976, three months before my 19th birthday. Little did I know that 20 years later to the day, I was to win the Masters. My last appearance as an amateur was in the King George IV Trophy at Craigmillar in Scotland where I shot 68, 70, 76, 68 to beat seasoned Walker Cup campaigner George McGregor by four shots, reinforcing the belief that my hasty departure from Houston had been entirely justified.

As a safety-net, I initially wanted to become the touring professional at Dyrham Park where Ian Connelly had recently taken up residence as club pro, but the committee, in their infinite wisdom, decided 'the club neither desires nor needs the publicity that such an attachment would bring.' Cue the entrance of the agents. The first character over the horizon claimed to manage Pink Floyd, complete with 1970s kipper tie and flared trousers. I told him that if I won a tournament I'd expect to make £50,000 from it. He obviously did not agree with my arithmetic because I never saw or heard from him again after that initial meeting.

Next up was James Marshall who was managing a young Australian bloke of whom I had never heard called Greg Norman.

'Nick, you're going to be big in Japan, that's the circuit for you.'

'It doesn't quite work that way,' I pointed out. 'You see, I have to play in Britain if I want to make the top sixty in the money list and qualify for exemption.' That was exemption from the grind of Monday pre-qualifying events. Unfazed, he went on to outline his grand scheme.

'Out of the first quarter of a million, I'll take twenty per cent, then up to half a million it will be thirty per cent and above that forty per cent [those were the kind of numbers he was bandying about] and I'll give you three thousand pounds pocket-money . . .'

Now I was an 18-year-old with about 50 pence in his pocket, so it was impossible not to be impressed. Dad and I arranged to talk to Marshall again at his house, which turned out to be a moated castle with the prerequisite Mercedes sports car in the drive. My dad being a smart cookie – remember he worked in the accounts department at ICI – took himself off to the local village where he grilled, in the politest possible way, the High Street florist, discovering that our Mr Marshall was not only renting the east wing of the castle but the Mercedes was also on hire. After making a few more discreet enquiries, Dad said, 'Son, I may be burning you a million but I don't think you should do this.'

If you are as confident in your own ability as I was, striking out on your own is not as big a gamble as it might seem; sure it must be comforting to know someone is paying all your expenses, but a lot of players never fully appreciate exactly what they are signing until their attention is drawn to paragraph 17, sub-section XXXIV, line 397 of a contract, which might have been written in invisible ink the print is so tiny. Colin Montgomerie received some financial help from a group of guys in his early days and, when approached by IMG, revealed he was on an 80/20 cut. 'That's OK,' said the man from IMG, 'that's what we charge our clients.' 'You don't understand,' replied Monty. 'They take eighty per cent and I get twenty.'

Dad's attitude seemed to be that if I was as good as I thought I was, I would soon be earning sufficient money to make it unnecessary for me to employ a manager to find me sponsors. He also insisted that right from the start I should not share a hotel room; he wanted me to have a proper night's sleep and not be disturbed by a roomie coming and going. I appreciated the privacy but the downside was I became known as something of a loner – a yoke, alas, from which I have never been able to break free. Loner or not, I was ready now to become a member of the pack.

CHAPTER THREE

RYDER CUP ROOKIE

Where better to test the waters than Le Touquet? The jewel of France's Opal Coast with its sparkling sea, rolling sand-dunes and pine forests was a world and a half removed from the practice ground at Welwyn Garden City Golf Club on a miserable Monday morning in February.

Unusually for someone who habitually sets himself dizzyingly lofty targets, I entered the 1976 French Open with the modest aim of simply qualifying. So uncertain was I of becoming a member of the professional band competing against Tony Jacklin, Bernard Gallacher, Brian Barnes, Neil Coles and their battle-hardened ilk, on the flight over to France I admitted to Angela that if I survived the cut for the final two rounds it would be a feat to rank with winning the English Amateur Championship. Having also confessed as much in an interview with *Golf Illustrated*, I was heartened to receive the following message from Ben Crenshaw: 'Tell that boy to go out and win the French Open and set his sights no lower.

There was absolutely no pressure on me in my first professional tournament at the San Antonio Open three years ago, and Nick should realise this. He should go out and play for his life before he starts to realise, as I did, the enormity of his achievement. He must know and believe he can win in France and think of nothing else . . .'

I did not win in France but I did qualify – after a comic interlude with an Inspector Clouseau-style French taxi driver who had never heard of golf let alone that Le Touquet actually possessed a golf course. I made the cut with something to spare and finished a heartening 38th with rounds of 72, 70, 72, 71 to earn 60 quid. The members at Welwyn Garden City had generously raised £1,000 to assist my venture, but my professional debut proved a nice little earner. In those days you were not allowed to keep your prize money for the first six months in case you wanted to be reinstated as an amateur – except for winnings from international open events, such as the French Open. I think I am correct in saying that I was actually the last player to be affected by this rule.

I banked another priceless £500 from the German Open, and came to the last green in the Swiss Open needing to hole a 15-foot putt to make another couple of hundred. Never count your chickens, or, indeed, your Swiss francs – I proceeded to three-putt and waved goodbye to some serious money. To cheer myself up I bought an enormous double ice cream, which cost an arm and a leg in Switzerland even then, but as I was about to savour my first lick, the damned thing slipped out of the cone and slid down my trousers. Ah well, at least it was double chocolate chip running down my leg this time, not pee, broken eggs or vomit.

That was my introduction to the major league. The pressure to make a putt when a few hundred pounds is riding on it was unlike anything I had experienced when I was the leading amateur in the land. This was a whole new challenge and my sole aim for that first season was to finish in the top 60 on the Order of Merit, thereby gaining exemption from pre-qualifying, which was a serious drain on frayed finances and frayed nerve-ends.

I was the proud owner of a second-hand Ford Capri 1600 GT by then. Pretty flash, eh! Thus did car and driver pass the rest of that summer chugging around the B-roads of Britain and Europe, desperately searching for some obscure golf course where the latest qualifying tournament was being staged.

Fortunately, the travel-weary rookie finished 58th on the money list with a total of £2,239, boosted by a £325 cheque from the 1976 British Open Championship at Royal Birkdale, where I not only made the field by leading the qualifying tournament at West Lancs, but finished in a tie for 28th place with Gary Player, Neil Coles and Doug Sanders. I may have been 15 strokes behind the new champion, American Johnny Miller, but to see my name alongside that of Player, winner of three Opens and nine Major championships in all, was a tremendous boost to a 19-year-old setting out in the footsteps of a living legend.

It was at Birkdale that I had my first argument with that most curious of breeds, the old-school, battle-hardened, seen-it-all caddie. In modern golf, caddies such as my regular partner, Fanny Sunesson, with whom I have shared so much success, are far, far more than mere bag-carriers. Fanny is my personal assistant on the course and has an influence upon me as a golfer and as a person, but to Paddy, the crazy Irishman of Royal Birkdale, Nick Faldo was an intrusive nuisance to be tolerated for the one and only reason that Paddy was being paid to do so.

Locker-room caddie tales are the stuff of legend; for example, 1951 Open Champion Max Faulkner to Mad Mac, when lining up a treacherous swinging putt, 'Will it break left or right, Mac?' 'I believe it's slightly straight, Mr Faulkner . . .'; Harry Vardon, throwing one, two, three blades of grass into the air to gauge the wind, 'Well, what do you think?' Caddie: 'I think it's getting windy and I'd put on a sweater if I were you . . .'

One of Paddy's many idiosyncrasies was to don shoes he found lying about the locker-room, no matter to whom they belonged and even if they were four sizes too big. He would totter to the first tee looking like Coco the Clown. After the third round on the Saturday night, rather than taking my clubs into the clubhouse, he left my bag leaning against an outside wall, whereupon Birkdale was hit by an almighty thunderstorm and torrential rain. When I came out, the water was pouring out of the top of my bag and after a real set-to in the car park, I sacked Paddy on the spot. It was only as he disappeared round the corner into an unknown future that I realised he had made off in a pair of my best shoes.

Enter dear old George Blumberg, a Johannesburg paper magnate, who telephoned me a few days after my return from Birkdale with two offers. An IMG (International Management Group) board member, 'Uncle' George had persuaded Mark McCormack to offer me a six-month trial contract. I would be joining a client list that included Arnold Palmer, Jack Nicklaus, Bjorn Borg, Niki Lauda and, latterly, the Pope – the boy from Welwyn would be mixing with the nobs. Mark and I concluded the deal on a handshake over afternoon tea, during which Mark told me he intended to make £100,000 out of me. That meant he thought I would earn £500,000 which, to a kid with nothing in the bank, represented serious money indeed. Twenty years later, during which tens of millions had passed through our hands, I was still part of the IMG family without ever having put pen to paper to sign a written contract with Mark, which was a measure of the man. Trust was everything to us both.

When I eventually decided to leave IMG, Mark called me four times on my day of departure and, although he never once told me I was doing the wrong thing, simply by chatting he made it patently obvious he thought I was making the worst business decision of my sporting life. When Mark died in 2003, by which time I had returned to the IMG fold, I was invited to speak at his memorial service and, for one of the few times in my life, I choked; I bottled out. When Jackie Stewart made the speech instead, I realised it was a bad call on my part because I would have spoken of our mutual sense of trust. Another regret . . .

During the course of the conversation with George Blumberg he also invited Warren Humphreys and me to go to South Africa to compete on the Sunshine Tour beginning in November. George paid our fares, put us up in his apartment and generally treated us like adopted sons. One of the events on the Sunshine Tour was due to be held at Elephant Hills in Rhodesia, as it then was, but as we were about to leave for Johannesburg Airport, there came news that a number of terrorists had made their way across the Zambesi and been shot on the golf course. After a day of frantic exchanges, George announced, 'The tournament's on.'

'But is it safe?' muttered macho-man Faldo.

'It must be or they wouldn't have invited us . . . and anyway, they've promised to pay all your expenses,' George replied.

At the magic words 'pay all your expenses', which amounted to about 60 quid, any thoughts of terrorist attacks were duly ignored and off we set for Elephant Hills. We stayed in a truly sumptuous hotel overlooking the Victoria Falls, which have to be one of the most amazing natural wonders of the world. I had been to Niagara, which is pretty impressive, but nothing prepares you for walking down a jungle path, feeling the first hint of spray on your face, then emerging through the undergrowth to see the Victoria Falls in all their indescribable splendour.

We had been happily swiping golf balls across the Falls one afternoon in a futile attempt to drive to the other side when we were engulfed in a tropical downpour. Dashing back to the hotel, I made the potentially fatal mistake of running between mummy baboon and her baby. It was only later I discovered you do not do that kind of thing, sunshine; she could have ripped me to shreds if she had thought I presented a danger to her little darling.

I was in somewhat less danger on the course, where we were

guarded by the Rhodesian army – 300 troops with anti-tank guns, armoured vehicles, the lot, lying in wait on the edge of the bush by the fairway. One of the soldiers even competed – rear-gunner Nick Price arrived every morning, changed out of uniform into golfing gear, completed his round and then returned to barracks.

When you drove into the rough, all you could hear was the sound of rifles being engaged. Unblinking eyes stared down the sights at you. You felt like saying, loudly, 'It's OK, I'm a golfer. Look, I've got a little green crocodile on my shirt.' I doubt if I have ever driven straighter. Angel Gallardo was less fortunate when he drove into a bunker and found his ball buried in an elephant's footprint which, under local rules, did not permit him a lift-and-drop. The army lads would join us in the hotel bar every night, leaving their AK47s behind the desk at reception before ordering up their beers. Given the unusual surroundings, I was well pleased to finish fourth.

Thanks to George Blumberg, I now realised that as well as wanting to be a champion golfer, I had acquired the desire to travel, and so, after spending Christmas and New Year with my parents in Welwyn, I returned to Africa in January 1977 to compete on the Safari Tour. My first port of call was Lagos, in Nigeria, where I was invited to stay with the manager of the local beer company who, luckily for me, lived in the biggest and grandest house in town. We had to tee off at six o'clock in the morning to ensure we were back indoors by midday when, so the locals cheerfully informed us, the heat of the sun was so intense it would kill a white man. The 'greens' were brown, rolled sand and oil mixed – it was like trying to land the ball on the bonnet of a Citroen Diane – and the sweat dripped off you.

Lagos is not a place I would particularly choose to visit again, although I was there in a position of privilege as I discovered when the lady of the house took me on a trip to a nearby village. Open sewers ran down the middle of the road through which five-year-olds on their way to school had to wade naked.

'How many of those kids live to be teenagers?' I asked.

'Not many,' came the haunting reply. 'Most don't even make it to the age of five.' I have never forgotten those poignant words or pathetic images.

To be selfish, however, my 10-day Safari Tour was an enormous success and I returned to Welwyn clutching 2,200 US dollars. We gathered round the kitchen table, Mum and Dad and me, and just pushed it around dreamily. We had never seen so much cash stacked up in front of us in our lives before.

During the subsequent weeks leading up to the start of the European season, Ian Connelly constantly tantalised me with the notion that, while less than a year earlier I had been considering remaining amateur in order to play in the Walker Cup, my goal should be to qualify for the 1977 Ryder Cup team due to play the US at Royal Lytham that autumn. All – *all!* – I had to do was finish in the top eight on the Order of Merit and I would become the youngest ever player in the history of the biennial contest.

The new season began both thrillingly and tragically; I finished third in Madrid, winning £1,500, but Grandad Faldo died over the weekend. I had been to visit him the previous week and was deeply moved by the sight of my dad leaning over talking to him even though the old fella was in a coma; to watch your father grieving right in front of you is hard to take at 19, especially since it was the first time I had ever seen him cry. I desperately wanted to hug Dad but we were very much a step-back family; we preferred not to show our emotions, so I just stood behind him at the side of Grandad's hospital bed. I felt incredibly guilty when Dad telephoned me in Madrid because you want to be with your family at a time like that.

Sadly, the same thing happened years later when Uncle Harry died. I was driving home from a tournament with my second wife, Gill, and our baby daughter Natalie, whom Uncle Harry always called his little princess, when I made one of those bad decisions that forever eat away at you. I knew Uncle Harry was very ill, but we were all tired, we were almost home, and rather than drive an hour and more out of our way to drop by the hospital, we decided to postpone our visit until the following day. Uncle Harry died before we could make it to the hospital and I still bitterly regret that decision because he had been such a big-hearted pal to me when I was growing up. I could make up all sorts of reasons for not visiting him that night, but the reality was it was inexcusable.

The intense battle for Ryder Cup places left me no time to wallow in the aftermath of Grandad's death. I finished sixth in the PGA Championship at Royal St George's, and by the time of the Uniroyal Championship at Moor Park in June, qualifying for the team to be captained by Brian Huggett was no longer a pipedream but a genuine possibility. Opening with rounds of 68 and 67, at the halfway stage I was four strokes in front of Greg Norman, but to recall Ben Crenshaw's words, the enormity of my achievement began to nag at me and a lacklustre 73 sent me into the final day one shot adrift of Seve Ballesteros. Still one shot in arrears on the 18th, and boosted by the encouragement from Graham Marsh to 'just knock it in', I sank a mischievous 20-foot downhill putt to secure a play-off against Seve, the first hole of which he proceeded to play in time-honoured fashion. Whereas I unleashed two mighty shots to the back of the par-5 16th green, Seve carved two successive hooks, the second of which cannoned off the foot of a spectator to save it going into the bushes. Seve, being Seve, chipped to within three feet, whereupon a shell-shocked Nick Faldo three-putted, leaving my opponent a tiddler for the title. He tapped in – birdie golf the Seve Ballesteros way – and I drove home feeling a mixture of delight that I had finished runner-up to such a great player in such a high-profile event, and abject misery that I had squandered such a golden opportunity to record my first professional tournament victory.

There was an additional painful experience during the pro-am event preceding the Kerrygold International in Ireland. Playing the 18th, I was idly minding my own business from a distance of 20 yards and maybe one pace in front, when my amateur partner – a huge brute with arms like pistons and a swing like a windmill – let fly with a 7-wood, sending the ball careering off at an angle of 90 degrees. It caught me flush on the cheekbone below my right eye. The last things I heard before losing consciousness were the strangled shout of 'Fore!' followed by a curious 'bong' sound echoing round my head whereupon I collapsed. I was only out for a few seconds but when I awoke my eye had swollen to the size of an orange. I put my hand up to feel the damage and, when I looked at it, I saw that it was covered in blood. I was in total shock and just for a moment I thought my eye had come out of its socket and I was going to be blind. As it turned out, I was lucky and I suffered nothing worse than a black eye for a week.

If that was an unnerving experience, it was nothing compared to an incident in Newcastle when my caddie John Moorhouse and I fell into conversation with a couple of local lasses over a beer and repaired to their flat for coffee. This being in the era before Trivial Pursuit, out came the ouija-board and glass. Fondly imagining ourselves to be men of the world, we played along with the usual 'Is there anybody there?' nonsense when the tumbler suddenly began to move frantically. Spelling out the letters one by one, our 'visitor' informed us she was called Annie and had been the third victim of Jack the Ripper.

'Yawn yawn,' we thought as Annie replied to a few more questions until, almost without realising it, we noticed both of the girls had taken their hands off the glass and it was whizzing around unbidden under John's and my index fingers. I could tell by the look on his face – and he knew by the look on mine – neither of us was pushing the damned thing and we were out of that house like bats out of hell.

Despite having banked over £10,000 – plus having secured a £4,500 per year deal to carry a Glynwed International logo on my bag – I certainly performed like someone who had been seriously spooked in the 1977 Open at Turnberry. Tom Watson and Jack Nicklaus engaged in golf's most memorable gunfight, the young master finally pipping the old maestro by a single stroke with an anonymous Nick Faldo a distant 31 strokes off the pace in joint 62nd place.

As a second-year rookie, I was reasonably content with my earnings and my form, both of which soared to new heights in the 36-hole Skol Lager event at Gleneagles. I beat Craig Defoy and Chris Witcher in a three-man play-off to take the winner's cheque of £4,000 and, more importantly, lift myself to eighth place, above Sam Torrance, in the Order of Merit, a position I held until the announcement of the Ryder Cup team in August.

I think it was only in later years that the 'enormity of that achievement' truly began to sink in; at the age of 20 – a mere six years after swinging my first golf club – I had secured a slot in the Great Britain and Ireland side to face Jack Nicklaus, Tom Watson, Raymond Floyd, Lanny Wadkins, Hale Irwin and the rest of those gods at Royal Lytham. In all modesty, I do not think anyone will ever match the speed of that feat. Tiger Woods has been playing golf since he was in nappies (sorry, diapers). I suppose it was due to a cocktail of time, talent and commitment, allied to that original 'desire for greatness'. I had surrendered so much of my youth to the quest for success, I like to imagine that my first Ryder Cup blazer was a reward for obsessive single-mindedness.

My preparations for the contest had been going splendidly under Ian Connelly's watchful eye at Dyrham Park, when I suddenly began feeling unwell during a pro-am event at Hill Valley, Shropshire. Mum had to drive me straight from the course to the doctor's surgery where the diagnosis was a trapped nerve. Still feeling less than battle-fit but relieved there was nothing seriously wrong – in fact, I was suffering from glandular fever but, although the doctor told my parents as much, they decided not to inform me – I entered the Tournament Players' Championship at Foxhills, Surrey, the following week. I started the first round by going out in an encouraging 33 before being overwhelmed by a feeling of listless exhaustion and stumbling home (literally) in 47 for an embarrassing 80, my worst round as a professional. A second-round 71 fleetingly restored my spirits but when I walked off the 18th at the end of the third round to sign my card for an 83, I knew in my heart that all was not well physically.

On the Wednesday morning before the Ryder Cup, I awoke in Lytham to find my pressure points, fingers, wrists, knees and elbows, covered in an ugly scarlet rash, and presented myself to a doctor who took one look at this apparition and suggested a blood sample. It was the first time I had ever given blood, and I promptly fainted on the floor – it was not the actual needle but the sight of my blood in the syringe that did for me. When I came round, he confirmed I was suffering from glandular fever. 'Attempt nothing strenuous,' he said matter-of-factly. 'Take lots of rest and avoid any stress.'

Avoid any stress? I was due to tee off in the Ryder Cup in less than 24 hours and here I was being blithely ordered to attempt nothing strenuous. As well as feeling drained of any energy, I now felt sick to the pit of my stomach, knowing I could be letting the team down if I did not reveal my condition. There was no rash on my face so I knew I could brazen it out during the final practice session, but what if I was taken really unwell during my match? There were two voices in my head, one telling me I would be fine and that by playing in the Ryder Cup I would be fulfilling one of my boyhood dreams, and another advising me to explain my condition to captain Brian Huggett.

Having been brought up by parents to whom honesty is as necessary in life as bread and water, I duly reported my illness to Brian who, with typical Welsh forthrightness, replied, 'Bugger me . . .' I retired to bed for a couple of hours, woke up feeling a tad refreshed and, pulling the sleeves of our ill-fitting Ryder Cup sweater over my wrists to hide the telltale rash, joined the rest of the team for final practice. I was on the 14th fairway when Brian ambled over and breezily announced, 'You and Peter Oosterhuis are playing together in tomorrow's foursomes. Good luck.'

We were drawn against Raymond Floyd and Lou Graham and Oosty made the decision that I would be first off the tee. I was a bag of nerves the moment he told me and so I decided to go off and calm myself down by hitting 20 extra 5- and 6-irons to warm up. Of course, when I stepped up to the tee I saw instantly it was a 4-iron shot. Needless to say, I promptly missed the green. We were three down after nine holes when, in a dramatic turnaround from everything that had gone before, we won the 11th, 12th, 14th and 15th to go ahead for the first time in the match, and went on to record an unlikely 2 and 1 victory on the 17th green.

'Did you ever think we were going to lose?' Oosty asked me on the way back to the clubhouse.

'Naaah, I was always confident,' I replied, although the truth was that it had been the first time I'd ever experienced my stomach churning for the whole round.

On day two, Oosty and I were paired with Ray Floyd again, this time in the company of Jack Nicklaus, the golfer who had unwittingly inspired me to take up the game, forsaking all others. As intimidated as I was in the great man's presence, I birdied the second to put us one up and, feeling like Popeye after a can of spinach, unleashed a huge drive on the fourth, which came to a halt a good 30 yards beyond the Golden Bear's tee-shot. As I strode up the fairway I could sense Jack's eyes burning twin holes in the back of my neck. 'Don't look back, don't look back' I said to myself over and over, affecting an air of nonchalance I certainly did not feel. Oosty and his rookie partner beat Floyd and the world's greatest player 2 and 1 but the 1977 Ryder Cup had already been as good as lost, the United States ending the second day with a resounding points lead of 7½–2½.

Given how competitive the Ryder Cup has become since 1985, it is curious to reflect that before then, we went into the contest thinking we had no chance whatsoever; we knew we were going to lose from the moment the US team was announced. We were not really a team; we were not organised. Brian Huggett kept everything close to his chest in terms of his pairings. We never knew with whom we would be playing until the last moment. The whole thing was an amateurish adventure. You arrived at Royal Lytham, were handed your sweater, which was either too small or too big but never ever the right size, ordered into line to have your official team picture taken, then you teed off.

Even though the final outcome was beyond our reach, when the draw for the singles paired me with Tom Watson, the reigning Open and US Masters Champion, I regarded the match as an opportunity to stamp my personal mark on the competition. I was determined not to let myself down, especially when I overheard some idle talk variously attributing my two points to the steadying influence of Oosty, Floyd and Graham inexplicably crumbling when three up, and Nicklaus still smarting from his epic encounter and ultimate defeat at the hands of Watson in the Open at Turnberry. Mischievously, I reminded anyone who would listen that 'I've never been beaten in matchplay at Royal Lytham. I won the English Amateur Championship here two years ago, so I'm keen to preserve my record.'

In front of a huge gallery, which registered every emotion in a roller-coaster match, I was two up at the 6th after an eagle three, level at the turn when Watson started hitting spectacular shots from all over the course, two ahead again after 12, and level again when we departed the 17th green for the 18th tee. Normally the ultimate in straight hitters, Watson found a fairway bunker with his drive. A par-4 was good enough to keep my Lytham record intact, and I ended my first Ryder Cup with a 100 per cent record of three points out of three. We had been beaten 12½–7½ but the

British public were desperate for a success story and I was catapulted to stardom.

Unaccustomed to having a radio microphone stuck in my face, I must have sounded as wooden as Pinocchio to the ears of a less-than-spellbound nation. 'Oh, yes,' I intoned, 'it was a great experience and I am really excited.' That was stating the bleedin' obvious – of course I was unbelievably excited. Overnight, I was made to feel like a star. I had been totally in awe of Nicklaus and Watson; they were gigantic legends, yet I had beaten them on successive days, and there was no preparation for how to react. When you play those guys you are happy just to be able to walk in a straight line, never mind hit a golf ball. To beat the two best players in the world was simply incredible.

The one heartbreak of Ryder Cup week was that Angela terminated our relationship; I was madly in love with her but, clearly, she was not quite as madly in love with me. So I returned with Mum and Dad to 11 Redwoods where we gathered round the kitchen table and, one by one, started laughing at the absurdity of it all.

'Well, that was good, wasn't it?' I said, ever the master of the understatement. I was not feeling cocky or big-headed in any way. I had this wonderful sense of accomplishment, that buzz, that glow, that inspires you to take the next rung up the ladder. After Lytham, I determined to practise even longer hours, to train physically harder, to commit myself further because I wanted more. I wanted trophies and titles rather than money. I was also inspired by the idea of stepping on a plane and turning left into the first-class cabin instead of travelling steerage with my knees wrapped around my ears. And don't forget, I still hadn't won a 72-hole tournament yet.

CHAPTER FOUR

MARRIAGE AND THE MASTERS

'Well, it might not be Concorde but it'll do for starters,' I muttered, casting an appreciative eye over the Rolls-Royce sitting in the road beyond the garden hedge at 11 Redwoods. The neighbours' net curtains were twitching furiously. As a result of my efforts in the Ryder Cup, I had been invited to compete in the World Matchplay Championship at Wentworth. The organisers had sent the car to fetch us and so Mum, Dad and I arrived in some style, luxuriating in the back seat like the Queen. We were driven to a mansion on the course, which was to be my base for the duration of the championship and where awaited our own personal cook. Wentworth being somewhat above Welwyn Garden City on the social scale, Mum and Dad – mad spendthrifts that they were – had even bought new specs for the occasion lest they 'let the side down'.

Although we tried desperately not to show it, to Dad and me the biggest bonus was the presence of the chef because, although Mum was by no means a poisoner with a ladle in her hand, she was a graduate of the '101 Different Ways To Cook Mince' school of cookery. If it was not mince it was salad – even in the depths of winter – and not anything fancy like a Caesar salad, either. This was a leaf of lettuce, a chunk of carrot, a slice of cucumber and maybe a strip of cold meat, served with a dollop of salad cream if she was feeling particularly adventurous.

Quite unfairly, Mum's cooking is still a source of rich amusement. My dentist recently discovered there was a narrow line of enamel missing from around my upper teeth.

'Did you suffer from malnutrition or a terrible disease as a child?' he asked.

'No,' I replied, 'just my mother's cooking.'

This fault-line, as I knew perfectly well, had appeared after I succumbed to chicken pox and the mumps in quick succession as a tot, but I nearly bit off the dentist's finger I was chuckling so hard at the memory of Mum's uniquely inventive ways with mince.

My heart goes out to Dad who has been on a diet of one sort or another for the best part of 55 years. When he began displaying the first symptoms of rheumatism – at one time it was so painful he could barely climb out of the car – he was prohibited from eating acid fruits, tomatoes and much else besides, instead of which he had to swallow heavy dosages of molasses. Being firm believers in nature over drugs, my parents will never ever take any form of medication whatsoever; hence Dad eats what Mum decides is good for him.

Once or twice a year, we head for the river. Valerie, my three children, Natalie, Matthew and Georgia, plus my parents go on a fishing expedition on the River Test. Emma is just a bit too young to have experienced this treat yet. Possessed of the sweetest tooth ever, Valerie packs all the naughtiest things possible, including the biggest glazed cream doughnuts she can find. Mum is always put in charge of the fry-up – yeah, the same calor gas stove we used to take to France when I was a kid 35 years ago – eggs, sausage, beans, the lot, while Dad gazes on, longingly. One afternoon, Georgia took a couple of bites of her double-double chocolate chip and whipped cream cookie or some such delicacy, which was as big as she was, and sensibly decided to leave the rest for later. Watching Mum otherwise engaged over a hot primus stove further down the river-bank, I saw Dad's arm flick out like an anteater's tongue and, hey presto!, Georgia's cookie had disappeared.

Whenever he comes to our house for dinner, if Valerie asks, 'Who's for seconds?' he always has seconds; if she asks, 'Who's for thirds?' he always has thirds. For the rest of the week he will be living on strictly controlled rations. Once, I dropped in unannounced just as Mum was serving dinner. Dad had barely lifted up his knife and fork when Mum bore down on him with a serving spoon, snatched away three of his four potatoes, most of his steak and a mound of vegetables for her beloved son before he could even make a start. Thanks to Mum, however, she and Dad, in their mid 70s, are still active and enthusiastic members of the Ramblers' Association, which only goes to prove there is substance to her dietary fads.

Although I lost in the first round, Wentworth was a terrific experience, and Dad certainly ate well. After that, as the new kid on the block and something of a curiosity, I was invited to compete in the Laurent Perrier Trophy in Belgium where, following my victory in the 36-hole Skol Lager event, I won my first 54-hole title, beating Seve Ballesteros in a head-to-head, last-round duel and earning rave reviews: 'Nick Faldo has the class to rule Europe for years,' wrote Michael McDonnell in the *Daily Mail*. '. . . his display was not merely thrilling but also showed clear evidence he is the stuff of champions . . .'

I was also granted entry to the prestigious Lancome Trophy, an exclusive eight-man competition staged on the outskirts of Paris and featuring Arnold Palmer, Gary Player, Seve Ballesteros and Billy Casper. On the eve of the tournament we were all chauffeured along to a high-class photographic studio presided over by a fancy-Dan fashion-snapper called Armand, or something like that, to be photographed for a magazine feature. Armand proceeded to take pictures of Palmer, zooming in on his stevedore's arms, Player in familiar pose, all in black, and Seve, looking dashingly handsome. Then I was hauled in, fresh-faced and with my pudding-bowl haircut of the day. The magazine writer wanted to know what shirts Arnold wore.

'Pickering,' he said.

'And what watch?'

'Rolex.'

'Why Rolex, Arnie?'

'Because they pay me a million bucks.'

That struck me as a perfectly good reason.

'Nick, what shirts do you wear?'

'Anybody's.'

'What watch?'

'Sekonda.'

I was mighty proud of that watch. I'd bought it to celebrate my new deal with Glynwed. Everyone made me most welcome on my first luxury, all expenses paid trip. I remember ringing my parents from the Paris Hilton, a luxury normally beyond my means but affordable on this occasion because the sponsors were picking up the tab. 'They've got pâté here for six quid. I used to pay two quid for my room,' I trilled down the line.

Gary was wonderful to me although I was a complete unknown in his world, perhaps because he, too, had known what it was to struggle. When Gary first started competing in Europe it used to take two days to make the hop, skip and a jump flight from Johannesburg on an old Dakota. He had so little money in those early years he could not afford a hotel room at St Andrews where he made his Open debut, so he hauled on his waterproofs and slept in the sand-dunes. He reached his peak at a time when it was still deemed unsporting to practise, but he was a small man who worked his way to the top through hard work and mental strength; he would climb any mountain and I have always admired him for those reasons. As a South African on the world circuit, he was the frequent victim of anti-apartheid protesters, yet he bestrode the fairways in dignified silence, whatever insults or missiles were thrown his way.

I told him I had been at Royal Lytham when he won the Open in 1974 and that I remembered how he walked off every green and went into a squat, seemingly as though in meditation, just staring off into the distance.

'I wasn't meditating,' Gary explained. 'That's the most uncomfortable position for the human body and I knew if I could handle that physical pain, I could handle any mental suffering on the course.' That is the kind of perfectionist he is.

Having beaten Jack Nicklaus and Tom Watson in the Ryder Cup, I was becoming accustomed to the media spotlight, which now accompanied my every tournament appearance – I must also confess to feeling a sense of gratification at suddenly being the centre of attention – but I was pleasantly surprised nonetheless when Billy Casper paid me the following compliment in Paris: 'Nick has more talent than anyone I've seen out of Britain. He gets a little hot-headed when he misses a shot but, hey, that's youth.'

Thus did I end my first full season as a professional – a Ryder Cup player and in a highly satisfactory eighth place on the European Order of Merit, with two tournament victories (albeit over 36 and 54 holes), £23,978 in prize money, and in possession of the Rookie of the Year trophy. It was presented to me by the dashing Henry Cotton, Open Champion of 1934, 1937 and 1948. Henry also invited me to join him at Pennina in Portugal for a week, where he gave me his personal guidance. It was an incredible experience – practice by day and story-telling by night. One of the fabulous sessions Henry devised involved a nine-hole round where I had to hit two balls at every shot and always play the worst one. That concentrates the mind. And on short shots he told me never to be afraid of letting my right hand go down the shaft of the club. One piece of advice that I didn't follow, however – and I regret not doing so because it would probably have saved me a fortune – was to rent everything. Henry rented his Rolls, his house, everything.

On 1 January 1978, my New Year's resolutions were to win a 72-hole tournament and to garner sufficient points on the Order of Merit to be granted an invitation to compete in the following year's Masters, thereby fulfilling the dream that had sustained and inspired me since watching Jack Nicklaus at Augusta in 1971.

In some ways, I was older than my years, however, and rather than embark on a spend-spend-spend shopping spree, when Dad spotted Tudor Cottage being advertised for sale in a local newspaper, I invested a proportion of my winnings in the house of my carpet-laying daydream, buying it for £60,000 in partnership with my parents.

Originally built as four cottages in the early 1500s, Tudor Cottage had been converted into a fabulous single home straight from the pages of *Country Life* – it had low wooden beams on which I would bang my head until I worked out the geography of the place, inglenook fireplace, Aga cooker and stone slabs in the kitchen, rickety garden gate, a walled garden of wild flowers and was just two doors down from the village pub.

Mum and Dad quickly adapted to village life but I had little time to enjoy my new rural surroundings. After a winter of seriously hard graft under the sergeant-major-like command of Ian Connelly, I finished runner-up – a distant second, it has to be said – to Seve Ballesteros in the Martini International at RAC Epsom, which served to make me even more determined to break my 72-hole duck. Seve was the 'main man' in Europe at the time, winning everywhere he went, whereas I was still a figure on the periphery.

My big breakthrough arrived at the Colgate PGA Championship – the most important event in Europe after the Open – at Royal Birkdale in May. My opening rounds of 70, 68 and 70 meant I entered the final round with a four-stroke lead over Howard Clark. With me possibly on the verge of my first major win, my parents drove up to Southport on the Saturday night, and I not only took them and South African pro Dale Hayes out for an expensive meal, I insisted on paying the bill out of the winning cheque to come.

'God, these youngsters,' said Dale. 'He ain't even won the tournament and he's buying dinner.'

Inside, it was a very different matter, and I awoke on the Sunday morning as nervous as I had been on the starting-blocks at Stevenage Baths what seemed a lifetime ago. Instead of peeing myself, however, I tried out a relaxation exercise I had read about whereby you lie perfectly still for 20 minutes — my first amateurish attempt at meditating, almost without realising it. I lay full length on the bed and, starting at the tips of my toes, then legs, thighs, chest, arms and head, imagined every muscle turning to lead.

This early experiment clearly had a beneficial effect because I sauntered up the 18th, luxuriating in the cheers of the huge crowd on my way to a 69 and a seven-stroke victory margin over Ryder Cup colleague Ken Brown. When I walked off the final green, the first face I recognised was Dad's. We looked at one another and smiled. His sense of pride was tangible.

As befitted my role as the blue-eyed boy of Fleet Street, the scribes waxed eloquently on my endeavours. In the *Daily Telegraph*, the late Michael Williams, a gentleman of the old school, noted I was the youngest British tournament winner since Bernard Gallacher won the Schweppes event, also at the age of 20, in 1969. Pat Ward-Thomas in the *Guardian* described my victory as '. . . possibly the most commanding win ever by a young player in a professional event'. Another writer commented '. . . what sets Nick Faldo apart is his gift for making it all look so damned easy'. Most glowing of all, one reporter said I had displayed '. . . the five-star class of Walter Hagen and Tony Lema in celebrating victory by calling for champagne'. Mum had the joy of cutting out these columns of praise and pasting them into her ever-thickening scrapbook.

Returning to Ian Connelly on the Monday morning, I sashayed into the Dyrham Park pro shop expecting another round of congratulations, only to be met with a good, old-fashioned bollocking. Ian had heard of an incident at Royal Birkdale when I told a spectator who had annoyed me on one hole to shut up or get lost, and Ian had no hesitation in venting his displeasure.

Suitably chastised, I retired to the practice green to burn off any sense of resentment at Ian's criticism. Nothing could temper my feeling of jubilation and relief, however. The relief was at finally winning a *bona fide* 72-hole event, which just happened to be our PGA Championship, although this lack had not been an albatross around my neck. Gerald Micklem, a former captain of the R & A and a mentor from my early days as an amateur, had always drummed into me that you had to blow six tournaments before you learned how to win, but my victory in the PGA confirmed I had no fear of winning.

Content in my role as a loner, I did not form any close friendships with my fellow professionals, but Gerald, one of the most highly respected and beloved figures in British golf, remained a staunch friend until his death in 1988, the year after I won my first Open at Muirfield. I was so delighted to have won it that year so that Gerald could share in the joy, and I have forever consoled myself with the notion that if Gerald Micklem liked you, then, despite what your critics might say, you could not be all bad.

A new friend emerged on the scene in the aftermath of my PGA triumph in the shape of John Simpson, my recently appointed agent at IMG. In those early years John came up with all manner of imaginative deals, including a sponsorship with Robertson's jams. I will leave you to imagine the good-natured ribbing I received in the locker-room when I first appeared with the now infamous Robertson's golly emblazoned across my golf bag and umbrella. When I drew Calvin Peete, the leading black player on the US Tour, in the World Matchplay Championship at Wentworth, it took all my diplomatic skills to explain that the logo was not meant to be offensive.

By the summer of 1978, there was much speculation about whether I would become the first Briton to win the Open since Tony Jacklin in 1969. On the Sunday before driving north to St Andrews, I persuaded Gary Player to join me in a £6,000 so-called winner-takes-all challenge at Welwyn Golf Club. I shot a course record 65 to defeat the newly crowned Masters Champion, who was kind enough to say: 'In golf today, there are many, many potential winners; you can liken the circuit to a stampede of racehorses coming into the final furlong. The real champion is the one who shoots to the front and Nick most certainly has the style, strength and swing to be a genuine thoroughbred.' A prize even bigger than the winning cheque was on offer that day – a £30,000 Rolls-Royce which had been put up by the sponsors for a hole-in-one on the 18th. Being the old pro that he was, as soon as Gary heard about this he turned to me and suggested that if either of us should win the car, that person would give the other £5,000. That way, he explained, we get two shots at it. I agreed and couldn't believe it when my 4-iron tee shot on the last lipped out of the hole.

The real bonus, however, was the arrival of a letter from Gerald Micklem – three tightly handwritten pages of notes and maps outlining the best way to tackle St Andrews, a course I had yet to see with my own eyes, let alone play. It was a survivor's guide to the Old Course, outlining every bunker, every bump, every hollow. I'm sorry to say I later lost this treasure because it certainly deserved a place in the St Andrews Golf Museum, but Gerald's words of wisdom are writ large in my mind every time I walk to the first tee to this day. Gerald said, 'Aim 30 yards left of the green down the first fairway to give you the optimum line into the championship pins . . . on the 7th tee, aim at the 11th tee to bring you down the slope to the pin . . . on 13 you have to decide whether to drive up the 6th fairway . . . on the 17th – the notorious Road Hole – you have the option of driving down the right or look at going left and whack it on to the 18th tee and chip up to the green to make your four.'

It was good of Gerald because when I arrived at St Andrews I felt I was being reacquainted with an old friend such was the detail; it was better than an Ordnance Survey map, even if dear old Gerald's handwriting was of the type usually found on a doctor's prescription and my father had to transcribe the notes into a more decipherable form. We were staying across the Tay Bridge with friends of my parents, so on the Saturday night before the week of the Open, my caddie, John Moorhouse, and I walked the Old Course with Gerald's charts and scribbles to hand. His accuracy was astounding; every pot bunker was precisely where he said it would be, every gorse bush, every hump. 'You must never get mad at St Andrews,' I can almost hear Gerald whisper the words. 'You must be willing to accept exactly what you get. Then you must keep on trying. Keep a clear mind at all times. For there are so many humps and hollows that it is easy to allow your mind to become tangled with frustration. Once you start seeking excuses, St Andrews has got you beaten. It is no good saying this or that is a silly hole, it is no good questioning why a particular hump should be there. Once you start doing that, you can seriously forget your chances of winning. The Old Course must be treated sympathetically. Don't try to fight it, try to understand it.' As the legendary Bobby Jones, who loved this corner of Fife, put it, 'St Andrews is a place you have to study, and the more you study it, the more you learn; of course, the more you learn, the more you have to study it . . .'

Drawn to play with Antonio Garrido of Spain and American Johnny Miller, whom I had seen win the Open at Royal Birkdale two years earlier, I shot an opening round of 71 and, after reaching the turn in 32 in the second round, my name was up there at the very top of the leaderboard at 5 under par for the tournament. Former

US Tour professional Charles Price once observed, 'I don't know if you've ever played St Andrews in the wind, but it has been known to make scratch golfers switch to tennis.' Turning for home on the 10th tee by the Eden estuary, I, too, would have happily swapped St Andrews for Wimbledon at that precise moment, adding an inward 40 for a disappointing level-par round of 72. A third-round 70, however, left me on 213, two strokes behind the joint leaders, Tom Watson and my Ryder Cup companion, Peter Oosterhuis.

I woke up on the Sunday morning of the last round to discover that the magnitude of my achievement thus far had hit home. The thoughts racing through my mind were along the lines of: the Open Championship . . . St Andrews, the historic home of golf . . . the Swilken Burn, across which 'Old' Tom Morris strode a hundred years and more ago . . . two strokes behind the leaders . . . Mum! My tummy hurts.

It was as though I had a vice round my chest, the pressure around my heart was so intense I could hardly breathe. Mum, being Mum, took one look at me lying there in bed, and in her favourite bedside manner frowned at me as though I was a 10-year-old pretending to be ill as a ruse to avoid taking a dreaded school exam. 'Hmm' was all she said on the matter.

Feeling slightly miffed at this apparent lack of parental concern, I rose as commanded, dressed and drove to St Andrews to try to win the Open as a 21st birthday present to myself. Coming to the 17th, I left my approach shot right in front of the accursed Road Hole bunker, with the pin tucked tightly behind. (It's now better known as the 'Sands of Nakajima' after Tommy of that name took five to escape from its depths.) After studying the problem confronting me, I opted for the daring approach and, plucking my trusty old pitching wedge from the bag, envisaged the shot to come. I visualised chipping the ball into the side of the bank, making it curl round the top of the lip and down on to the green.

That was all in the mind. In reality, I struck the pitch too weakly whereupon I dropped the club in anguish, but the ball somehow ran up to the top of the bunker, teetered for a few moments, then performed exactly as instructed and finished two feet from the hole. The crowd behind the green went berserk and I strode off to the 18th tee, intoxicated by the incredible atmosphere of the Open. I wanted more of this.

On the last hole, I drove on to the public road that runs alongside the fairway, played an 8-iron off the road to about 10 feet and holed the putt to finish 4 and 3 from two places where I could easily have taken 6 and 5. Round in 72 for a four-round total of 285, I finished four strokes behind the new champion, Jack Nicklaus, in joint seventh place.

St Andrews has occupied a very special place in my heart since that Sunday afternoon 26 years ago. As Charles Price commented, 'Visiting St Andrews is like visiting your old grandmother. She's crotchety and eccentric, but also elegant, and anyone who doesn't fall in love with her has no imagination.'

As I stood in front of the R & A clubhouse – a golfing pyramid stuffed with ancient artefacts, trophies and memorabilia – watching Jack Nicklaus receive the old Claret Jug for the third time in his career, I knew exactly what he meant when he finished his victory speech with the words, 'There is no place in the world I would rather win a Major championship.' Here, indeed, is paradise on earth. With the shops and houses of the 'auld grey toun' snuggling around the 18th green like a lover's embrace, it is impossible to gaze upon that skyline and not feel the hairs on the back of your neck prickle to attention. When you play St Andrews in the early evening sunshine, there is magic in the air, allied to which the crowds are the most knowledgeable golf fans on the planet. I am mighty proud that ever since that first appearance in 1978, they have treated me with heart-warming affection, except, needless to say, when I represented England in the Dunhill Cup and the chefs would be banging their pots and pans in the kitchens of the hospitality tents behind the 17th green whenever they spotted yours truly coming over the horizon. I love the Scots dearly but that emotion is seldom reciprocated when they are engaged in a sporting contest against the English.

It was a marvellous experience, watching Nicklaus, the King of St Andrews, clutching the Open trophy, seeing the camera flash-lights, hearing the cheers of those marvellous spectators. But most importantly of all, I came away from it all thinking to myself, 'I know that one day I am going to win the Open.'

The remaining months of 1978 were spent in an exhausting contest with Seve Ballesteros for first place on the Order of Merit but, although I successfully defended my Laurent Perrier title in Belgium by defeating Seve at the second extra hole of a play-off, it was he who finished number one in Europe for a third succes-sive year. Two places further down, I was left to wait and wonder whether I had done enough to impress those who draw up the invi-tation list for the following year's Masters.

Before Christmas, I embarked on my first adventure to Australia and New Zealand. I would unhesitatingly add both countries to any round-the-world holiday itinerary now, but back then they were the scene of the most depressing weeks of my professional career to date. Firstly, I made the major mistake of selecting a brand new set of clubs, which turned out to be too short, too stiff and altogether too unwieldy. Not surprisingly, everything went wrong. I played miserably in Melbourne – so miserably I failed to appreciate the sheer beauty of Royal Melbourne – failed to make the 54-hole cut in the New Zealand Open, and set off for home with nothing but memories of a wondrous fishing trip to the highland lakes to sustain me during the 28-hour flight. Then, when we landed at Heathrow, I discovered I was Public Enemy Number One in the Australian newspapers because, among a number of charges levelled against me, I had left without thanking the organisers for laying on the fishing expedition.

It was a stern-faced father who greeted me on my return. He

had so far read the press reports verbatim but was impatient to hear my side of things. I was able to tell him that Pommie-bashing was all the rage Down Under thanks to the publicity generated by Ian Botham. I deeply resented being branded a 'whingeing Pom' when I had been angry at myself for performing so woefully, but I accept I had been foolish and ungracious not to express my unbounded gratitude to those directly responsible for organising such a memorable fishing expedition. I know I said 'thank you' to someone in New Zealand, but presumably not the right person and, young and inexperienced as I was, it was a lesson learned in the art of public relations.

On a far more pleasurable note, in the days before Christmas I agreed to be interviewed by Melanie Rockall, whose father published a jogging magazine. She had discovered that one of the ways I had conquered glandular fever was to put on my running shoes and take to the leafy lanes of Hertfordshire. She came to Tudor Cottage at Ayot St Lawrence, and it was a classic case of love at first sight. So besotted was I that I ended up interviewing her. She was a beautiful girl, humorous, intelligent with a bubbly personality and, mystery of mysteries, for reasons known only to herself, she appeared to like me. I do not know who invited whom out, but the following evening we went to a club she knew with a number of her friends. Melanie enjoyed a social whirl whereas my world revolved around golf, golf and more golf. This unexpected development represented a refreshing change for someone accustomed to such a sheltered existence. Being a sloth compared to this butterfly, I was totally out of my depth and so, when we went dancing later on the night of our first date, I was dressed like the Michelin Man because it was late December and freezing cold outside. As we danced, I began peeling off layers of hitherto unseen clothes – big thick outer sweater, another V-neck sweater, down to a roll-neck complete with Slazenger logo. I was so embarrassed I tried to rip off the little panther; there I was on a nightclub's dance-floor still looking like a golfer rather than John Travolta. I have never felt confident on a dance-floor anyway, although, in my defence, it is difficult to swing to the rhythm like Fred Astaire when you are a lug of six foot three and blessed with all the dancing skills of Fred Flintstone.

Thereafter, we threw ourselves into a whirlwind romance and I duly proposed to Melanie over the ritualistic candle-lit dinner on Valentine's night 1979 – who says I am not a romantic? – just seven weeks after our first meeting. With the benefit of 20/20 hindsight, it goes without saying that we should have taken things at a more leisurely pace and I cannot understand why no one thought to grab me by the neck and say, 'Whoa! Slow down, pal . . .' If any of my children wanted to embark upon the same high-speed march up the aisle, I would strongly advise them to live with their girlfriend or boyfriend for at least two years before committing themselves to marriage.

Melanie was – and, indeed, is – a wonderful woman but she would be the first to admit she was never cut out for the role of a golfing wife, which is no criticism of her whatsoever. On 23 June we were married even though on the very morning of the wedding one thought kept nagging away at me – 'You know this just isn't right, don't you?' But the 1931 Lagonda convertible to be driven by my old carpet-laying pal Ron Marks was booked, as was St Mary's Church, North Mimms, plus the reception, and I suppose I did not want to let anyone down when people had spent so much time and money on the arrangements. It says everything about the cocooned golfing world I inhabited that I had known my bride a mere six months and my best man, John Simpson, for less than two years. Melanie and I were happily married for six months. Unfortunately for both of us, we remained married for four and a half years.

Just as the wedding invitations had been landing on our guests' door mats, the envelope for which I had been praying landed on mine. The tournament committee of the Masters required my presence at their annual shindig to be played over the Augusta National Golf Course.

Before my first jaunt to the States as a professional, I embarked upon a return trip to Africa to compete in the Kenyan Open and in a pro-celebrity event run by the Variety Club to raise money to build schools for local children. We were an interesting bunch, comprising such diverse characters as Jimmy Tarbuck, Henry Cooper, Sir John Mills and the legendary Sam Snead.

Meeting and, even better, being able to talk to Sam is a memory I will forever cherish. To watch him on the practice ground was, in golfing terms, the equivalent of hearing Pavarotti sing 'Nessun Dorma' or gazing upon Michelangelo painting the ceiling of the Sistine Chapel. As a wise man once said, 'Anyone who would pass up the chance to see Sam Snead play golf would pull the shades driving past the Taj Mahal.'

Slammin' Sam rewrote the record books – seven Major titles, including three Masters, 81 US Tour wins (11 more than Jack Nicklaus, 19 ahead of Ben Hogan and almost 50 in front of Tom Watson), joint fourth at the age of 60 in the 1972 US PGA Championship at Oakland Hills behind Gary Player – and so, although two years past retirement age, his sweetest of swings remained prescribed viewing. Whenever he arrived on the practice tee with that John Wayne swagger of his, we would all stop what we were doing to enjoy watching the maestro at work.

'Whaddya wan' me ta hit, boy?' he would ask in that famous Virginian drawl.

'A one-iron, please, Sam,' someone would say, and he would unleash a drive that would soar through the air for miles, to our accompanying wows, oh-my-Gods, and did-you-see-thats.

On one occasion, in an attempt to stump him, the suggestion was made for him to try and hit a high draw with a 1-iron. Of course, he proceeded to hit the shot with sickening ease.

'You think that's impressive,' he then grinned, reaching into his bag, 'wait until you see this' — and he hit a high draw again, but this time off the deck with his driver. No wonder Byron Nelson, himself a US Open, US PGA and Masters Champion, said of Sam, 'He did for the tee shot what Roger Bannister did for the four-minute mile.'

Mesmerised and totally gobsmacked by this exhibition, I returned to my pyramid of practice balls thinking, 'Friggin' hell, do you still have some work to do!'

There were laughs and tears on our African safari. On a visit to a nearby Masai village, Henry Cooper was horrified to see the little kids running around with their eyes covered in flies because the roofs of the houses were built with — for want of a better description — cow shit. Sir John Mills, bless him, who like us all had been suffering from the 'Kenyan two-step' — one step off the loo, one back — turned to the local Masai chief and remarked, 'You should have told me, dear boy. I could have put a new roof on the town hall.'

We were also taken to Mount Kenya Safari Club where I witnessed, for the one and only time in my life, a lion and lioness having wild, rampant, jungle sex 20 feet away. At the climactic moment, he let out a Dolby surround-sound roar that actually reverberrated through the van. I do not know about the lioness, but the earth certainly moved for me. A few hundreds yards down the path we came across another lion ripping off the back leg of a deer with the poor beast still alive; two versions of the jungle's never-ending circle of life.

Rather less memorable was my introduction to the Masters the following month. After all my dreams, all my fantasies, turning into Magnolia Drive and approaching the surprisingly small 'Gone With The Wind' colonial clubhouse was a desperate disappointment; having fallen in love with the image of the place as a 13-year-old, the reality was a stark contrast. The town of Augusta is at best nondescript, and 25 years ago Magnolia Drive was lined by scrubby, stunted trees that had yet to reach the majestic maturity of today. Still, in my imagination it remained one of the most romantic spots on earth, even if my new fiancée, Melanie, failed to appreciate its charms after stepping barefoot on a dead snake during our pre-tournament hand-in-hand lovers' stroll around the course.

Overawed merely to find myself in these surroundings, I was further disconcerted when the first-round pairings were announced and I discovered I would be sharing the company of Billy Casper, Masters Champion in 1970, twice winner of the US Open and a 51-times winner on the US PGA Tour. One of the quickest men on a course, he was a huge presence in every respect. He was also renowned as one of the greatest putters in the history of the game. Gary Player once joked, 'Billy's losing it. Why, I saw him miss three thirty-footers out there today.' I knew our partnership would not be granted the anonymity I so craved.

It is impossible to stand on the first tee at Augusta and not feel a sense of awe: and stepping up beside the larger-than-life Casper before the opening round was a petrifying experience. No matter how much you read or hear about the place, nothing prepares you for its unique challenge, and to be honest I struggled all week to get comfortable there. I was overawed by the club and everything surrounding it, so much so that I was worried that if I walked across the wrong piece of grass I wouldn't be invited back (the Masters was by invitation only in those days). As a tenderfoot, I quickly discovered that I lacked the experience, the know-how, to handle the speed and slopes of the greens. I was not helped in my endeavours by the appointment of a local caddie who, to be blunt, was less than expert although he liked to give the impression he knew it all.

Despite the treacherous putting surfaces, the intimidating shadow of Casper at my side, the massive gallery, and the entire atmosphere surrounding the Augusta National, I started the first round promisingly with birdies on the first and eighth holes to appear, briefly, on the leaderboard – but it didn't last. I thinned my wedge shot on the 14th and it air-mailed the green, hitting someone square on the forehead before crashing back to within 8 feet of the pin. But by that point my bottle had gone and I missed the putt, finally signing for an unimpressive 73, seven off the lead. Augusta takes a long time to digest and it was all a bit too much too quickly, reflected in my eight over par total of 296, 16 strokes adrift of the new green jacket winner, Fuzzy Zoeller of the US.

That summer, Melanie and I were married and I whisked her off on honeymoon to Stratford-upon-Avon for a few days – yes, it would have been nice to laze in a hammock on a beach somewhere under a cloudless sky with an ice-cold beer to hand for three weeks, but the Ryder Cup was fast approaching. I have little doubt the new Mrs Faldo entertained her first serious doubts when, less than a week after our wedding, I was teeing off in the Lada Classic at The Belfry. I would like to say I softened the blow by returning to Tudor Cottage clutching both trophy and winner's cheque, but I could do no better than finish joint fourth with Sandy Lyle behind the runaway winner, Seve Ballesteros.

The remaining summer months were spent in a frantic effort to secure my Ryder Cup place which this year, 1979, would see the first ever European rather than Great Britain and Ireland side, under the captaincy of John Jacobs. The contest was to be played at the Greenbrier, West Virginia, but my crusade to be there was not helped greatly by my joint 19th place finish in the Open at Royal Lytham, won by Seve Ballesteros. I clearly couldn't live up to Arnold Palmer's prediction on the eve of the tournament – 'I believe Nick Faldo will give Britain the home winner the whole nation so desperately craves.'

With my domestic life also less than idyllic – Melanie, quite understandably, found living under the same roof as her in-laws at Tudor Cottage an increasing strain – I withdrew into myself on the golf course, inspiring some press reports describing me as 'self-obsessed, dour and aloof' and stoking up unwarranted rumours of a feud with Sandy Lyle, rather in the manner of the troubled relationship between Seb Coe and Steve Ovett. The suggestion was arrant nonsense but, heck, Fleet Street wanted a goodie and a baddie, and so I came to be projected as the cowboy in black.

My mood was lifted momentarily at the German Open where I shot my first hole-in-one as a professional in the pro-am. The sponsors had donated an £18,000 Mercedes 500SL (which now costs about £80,000) as the prize for an ace, but unfortunately, as in most tournaments, it counted only when scored in the event proper. Discussing the incident with Tony Jacklin I suggested I could do it again and Tony said 'I'm sure I can do that too', so we agreed, in a similar fashion to the deal I had made with Gary Player the previous summer, that if either one of us were to repeat the feat, we would give the other £1,000. Next day, on the same hole of the first round, I struck a 5-iron that had Mercedes stamped all over it until it came to rest half-an-inch short of the hole. Being one of nature's anointed lucky ones, in the third round Jacko holed out and, typically Tony, proceeded to order a salmon pink version loaded up with every extra known to German technology. And I waltzed home with a grand in my back pocket.

By the towering standards I had imposed upon myself – the pursuit of perfection, or as near to perfection as can ever be attained on a golf course – I then endured a dismal run of form, even if I did manage to sneak into the Ryder Cup team in ninth place. As expected, Sandy, Oosty, Bernard Gallacher and Brian Barnes also qualified, and we crossed the Atlantic under the flag of Europe in the company of Seve and his fellow Spaniard, Antonio Garrido.

Ever-gracious, the American non-playing captain, Billy Casper, met our party at Dulles Airport, Washington, and accompanied us on the flight to White Sulphur Springs, West Virginia, where I was bewitched by the charms of the Greenbrier Golf Club. Paradise on earth compared with some of the venues on the European Tour, the Greenbrier came equipped with a five-star hotel and 10-star facilities, including a practice ground to make you drool. Alas, Mark James – the future Ryder Cup captain – and Ken Brown, obviously did not share my pleasure in the surroundings. They were often late, did not want to wear the uniforms, niggled over team pairings, adopted an air of studied boredom throughout the opening ceremony and generally behaved like truculent teenagers. Non-playing captain John Jacobs was surprisingly accommodating and allowed them to remain in our midst. It is ironic that, 23 years later, Mark James of all people should accuse me of not being a team player before the postponed 2001 contest at The Belfry.

Having held the trophy since 1959, the American public was completely under-whelmed by the arrival of a European team. They did not even refer to the contest as the Ryder Cup but as 'the international Ryder Cup matches', although what difference that title made to the occasion was entirely lost on me. The crowds were sparse and the atmosphere lacking. I surrendered my 100 per cent Ryder Cup record in the opening foursomes, Peter Oosterhuis and I losing 2 and 1 to Andy Bean and Lee Elder, both of us finding the greens incredibly fast. But we grew more accustomed to them as the tournament progressed and once again we gelled as a pairing, winning our next two matches. I was delighted with our showing after the disappointment of the first day and was equally proud of my singles performance when I won against Lee Elders after being three down after three. So all in all, it was a good Ryder Cup for me personally, but unfortunately, and more importantly, it was a disappointing one for the team, with fledgling Europe being roundly cuffed 17–11.

Having left the Greenbrier with my haul of three points out of four, I returned to Britain a hero of sorts, but the laudatory headlines were soon to take a sinister turn.

CHAPTER FIVE

BIG SANDY AND THE PSYCHOLOGISTS

Sandy Lyle is unquestionably one of the most popular men ever to bestride a fairway, an uncomplicated (compared with me, at any rate), easygoing soul who, as the BBC's 'voice of golf' Peter Alliss so memorably recorded, won the 1985 Open at Sandwich 'playing in a cloud of unconscious competence'. Unarguably one of the greatest natural talents the game has ever known – his collection of two Major titles is scant reward for such God-given skills – Sandy basks in his reputation as 'a flake'. Adopting that wide-eyed Stan Laurel smile, he engenders genuine affection in locker-rooms across the globe with his carefree manner and air of bemused absent-mindedness.

Asked 'What do you think of Tiger Woods?' before the wunderkind made his debut in the 1992 Los Angeles Open, Sandy scratched his head and searched his memory-bank.

'Never played the course?'

Although the press pack frequently suggested that an intense rivalry existed between us, for my part I have never harboured a shred of envy or animosity towards Sandy, even if our contrasting personalities prevented us from ever becoming bosom buddies. None of my closest friends, as it happens, is a fellow competitor, and many, indeed, don't even play the game.

Sandy's famous absent-mindedness during the Kenyan Open in March 1980, however, was to be the root cause of a rift opening between me and Fleet Street. When 'baddie' crosses 'goodie', there can only be one winner. Hence, I was presented as the villain of the piece in the angry aftermath of the 'Sandy Lyle Incident'.

We were paired together in the first round. After about six holes I noticed a piece of tape on Sandy's putter and I asked him what it was. 'Oh it's great,' he replied. 'It takes the glare off my putter.' And that is where I committed my mistake – I didn't say anything else. En route to the 10th, past the clubhouse, I bumped into an official and asked, 'Sandy has a bit of tape on his putter, can he do that?' All hell was about to break loose. Worsening the situation, in my view, the official waited until Sandy was walking off the 18th before he approached him.

'I'm afraid you can't do that,' he pronounced. 'You changed the characteristics of your club and you are hereby disqualified.'

Sandy left Nairobi as the aggrieved party while Michael McDonnell in the *Daily Mail* sneeringly called me 'a snitch'. Tour veteran Tommy Horton later approached me in the airport departure lounge and said, 'You did exactly the right thing. A rule is a rule and we are all referees for the other players in a tournament.'

On the subject of being a snitch, after I had won my first Masters in 1989 I was invited on to 'The Terry Wogan Show' with Sean Connery and, unwisely perhaps, allowed Terry to slip into my precious green jacket. I did not intend to be disrespectful in any way but Michael McDonnell took it upon himself to track down Augusta chairman Hord Hardin, who was on holiday in Florida at the time, to ask the correct protocol for wearing the jacket. Hardin explained that the reigning champion was allowed to take the jacket out of the Augusta clubhouse during his reigning year and could wear it at his own club. Well, guess what? McDonnell told him that I had just taken it on a television show and allowed the presenter to wear it. McDonnell made a major story out of the incident and I later rang him up to let rip. He closed the conversation by saying, 'I'm your biggest fan and your biggest critic,' which, to me, sounded two-faced in the extreme.

To state my case, this was the first time a fellow professional had broken the rules under my nose. In retrospect, what I should have done is queried the piece of tape with Sandy and asked him to check with an official. But it was me who brought it to the attention of the authorities and in so doing I became the snitch. Unfortunately, something of a grudge seems to have grown out of my actions. Sandy is always quoted as saying, 'Nick Faldo's a marvellous competitor but I wouldn't invite him round for a cup of tea. He never even says "hello" . . .'. That, not to put too fine a point on it, is the biggest crock of shit; for the last 10 years or so, since I first read that quote, every time I have bumped into Sandy in the locker-room, on the practice tee, or wherever it is, I always stop and say hello. We do not see each other nearly as often as you might imagine, but it is totally wrong to suggest I ignore or snub him.

This statement does not anger me, but I do find it genuinely hurtful and, in such a downright likeable individual, puzzling to say the least; I have always admired and respected him both as a fellow professional and as a man and if he really has said 'he would not invite me round for a cup of tea', then why was I invited round to a party at his home in Wentworth to celebrate his Open victory five years after the unfortunate events in Kenya? I was happy to attend and, OK, I admit I envied Sandy his moment of triumph, which is why, when all the other revellers were queuing up to have their pictures taken holding the Claret Jug, I made sure I never laid a finger on it. 'I'm going to hold it properly, one day,' I vowed inwardly.

It was not to be at Muirfield in the summer of 1980, however, where Tom Watson took possession of the treasured trophy with me 13 strokes back in a tie for 12th place. My confidence was clearly growing because before the first round I plucked up the courage to instigate a conversation with the recently crowned US Open Champion.

'Mr Nicklaus,' I opened, wringing my hands with all the subservience of Uriah Heep, 'you played fantastically at Baltusrol to win the US Open, your swing was incredible. If it's not too much of an imposition and you're not too busy, could you possibly consider playing a practice round with me sometime this week?' There was more, much more, in the same grovelling vein before Mr Nicklaus interrupted me with a one-word answer.

'Sure,' he said.

And so the following morning Andy North and I teamed up against Nicklaus and Watson. I may have beaten both during the Ryder Cup three years previously, but here was an opportunity to watch and listen to two supreme masters at work. After six holes in baking sunshine, Andy North espied a Mr Whippy van and enquired, 'Hey, who wants an ice cream?' He came back with four 99s complete with chocolate flakes, which we duly demolished before teeing off at the 7th. Arriving on the 9th tee, I paid for a second round of cones. Jack stumped up for a third ice cream around the 12th, and with only one of our foursome yet to put hand in pocket, on the 15th a theatrically outraged Andy North yelled, 'Hey, Watson, it's your shout.'

'But I don't want another ice cream,' demurred Tom.

'You tight bastard, Watson,' growled North, surreptitiously extracting the necessary coins from Tom's bag before making a fourth visit to the van.

I beat Jack, winning £20, but North lost £40 to Watson, where-upon he raced off to the nearest bank and returned carrying a huge sack containing 40 quid in one penny coins, which he dumped at

Tom's feet. As luck would have it, I was paired with Jack for the opening two days and, man of style that he is, my £20 note was presented to me with suitable ceremony on the tee before our first round. Like an idiot, I stuck it in my trouser pocket and subsequently spent it without thinking, whereas I should have asked Jack to sign it so I could later have had this priceless memento framed. Jack also offered me an even more precious secret. 'At Muirfield, Nick, never play level with the bunkers; always play past them or short of them but never, ever level.'

For his part, Tom Watson may have been careful with the pennies, but he gave me so much insight into what it takes to become a great champion; his striking ability, allied to the sheer strength in those lumberjack's forearms, was second to none. It was the sound of his shots, that special fizz, that rang like a symphony in my ears. You did not watch his 2-irons, you listened to them in flight.

The other sound of which I became increasingly aware was the growing crescendo of marital discord. Melanie had surrendered her burgeoning career as a journalist to become a 'Tour wife', which, especially in the United States, where I began my preparations for the 1981 European season, was a truly miserable existence for any young woman. For four months, we lived out of a suitcase, sending my small collection of golf shirts to the hotel laundry to be boiled and cremated a dozen times or more until they shrank to Action Man size. Having a wife on hand, I foolishly suggested to Melanie that she might like to wash my shirts by hand in the bathtub, which, looking back, transformed her from journalistic young bride into unpaid housemaid. I certainly did not regard her as such, but without doubt, I could and should have displayed a greater level of understanding.

Not for Melanie shopping trips to Bloomingdale's in New York or sight-seeing flights over the Grand Canyon; through her world-weary eyes, America represented one endless concrete mass of anonymous hotels, shopping malls and freeways. You opened the blinds on the window of your latest hotel room and the view was always exactly the same – eight lanes of cars, a parking lot the size of Yorkshire and a Taco Bell Mexican fast-food takeaway if your luck was really in. How those guys can play the US Tour for 20-odd years never fails to astonish me. In Europe, the golfing wife can relax by strolling round Paris, Edinburgh or Rome, depending upon the latest venue, but in America you can swap the suburban sprawl of Chicago for Detroit, Milwaukee for Baltimore, and seldom detect the slightest difference. There are some fabulous postings along the way – San Diego to Los Angeles to Pebble Beach and Florida – but even when you play Hawaii, you never have the opportunity to see the place depicted in the glossy holiday brochures. Life becomes a less-than-glamorous whirl of airport-hotel-course-hotel-airport.

Being a Ryder Cup player, I was allowed five US Tour invitations and made five cuts in a row, which allowed me to compete week after week without using up another precious invitation. Although Tudor Cottage grew ever more enticing in my mind's eye, and despite the deepening frostiness in our marriage, after finishing seventh at the LA Open, I had earned sufficient dollars to secure my card for the following season.

I enjoyed playing in the US, but in addition to Melanie and my problems, there were other concerns brought on by a large number of Americans of the day who made it patently obvious they were less than enamoured of the idea of having so many Europeans cluttering up their patch. Tony Jacklin related an incident during a meeting of the US Tour committee when the guy sitting beside him, whom he had always considered a friend, raised his hand and said, 'We've got to get these foreigners off the Tour.' They regarded us as little more than latter-day pirates who had sailed across the Atlantic with the sole intention of stealing their treasures. The sense of resentment, which I could never understand, reached a peak in the mid 1980s when Seve Ballesteros, Bernhard Langer, Ian Woosnam, Sandy Lyle and I were all right up there at the top of the world rankings, and we even had the audacity to start winning Ryder Cups. The situation was different if you committed fully to the Tour, in which case the US players accepted you far more willingly but, in general, it is only in recent years that we have been made to feel welcome as fellow competitors. It's as though it has been acknowledged that our presence might just add lustre to the US Tour.

Things certainly weren't very friendly at the 1981 Hawaii Open where, after an opening 2 under par-70, I put together a near-flawless 62 to lead the tournament; not that you would have known from the leaderboard from which my name was conspicuous by its absence. All the way round I kept glancing up at the various scoreboards to find 8 under par was 'leading' and thinking, 'Where's my name?' It wasn't until I was actually back in the clubhouse that they grudgingly added my moniker at the top.

The following day I added a 71 and with Hale Irwin shooting a 63 I was left in his dust, which was a brutal lesson in the ways of American golf. If you were winning in Europe and shot a pair of 70s over the weekend, it was doubtful if anyone would overhaul you. In the States, you would need a couple of 66s to be almost certain of victory. Such has been the development of European golf, I am delighted our Tour has become every bit as competitive as the Stateside version. Hence our recent successes in the Ryder Cup.

Back in 1981, we were still being served up as a ritualistic offering to the American golfing gods, especially when they arrived at Walton Heath with the most powerful Ryder Cup team ever assembled – Jack Nicklaus, Tom Watson, Lee Trevino, Raymond Floyd, Ben Crenshaw, Hale Irwin, Johnny Miller, Tom Kite, Bill Rogers, Larry Nelson, Jerry Pate and Bruce Lietzke. The first 11 of those had all won Majors and they descended upon an unsuspecting Surrey at the very peak of their powers. Each and every one, with the exception of Bruce Lietzke, was a megastar, so what did our captain,

John Jacobs, do in reply? Leave out our undisputed number one, Seve Ballesteros, because he had hardly played in Europe due to a dispute concerning appearance money.

Our heroics at Royal Lytham four years earlier had obviously been long-since forgotten because when the announcer read out the formations for the first morning's foursomes following the opening ceremony, including, 'Match Four: Faldo and Oosterhuis to play Nicklaus and Watson', I distinctly heard some old dear in the crowd mutter, 'Ow, poor loves . . .' And poor loves is exactly what we turned out to be, losing 4 and 3. Although I had the personal satisfaction of beating former British and US Open Champion Johnny Miller in the singles, a Seve-less Europe was ultimately pulverised $18\frac{1}{2}$–$9\frac{1}{2}$.

Along with Ballesteros and Lyle, I was in the vanguard of European golf, but even after finishing fourth, second and fourth on the Order of Merit between 1980 and 1982 – during which period I also recorded highly respectable 12th, 11th and fourth place standings in the Open – I knew in my heart and soul I had to drive myself even harder if I was to challenge Seve, let alone Watson and Nicklaus on the world stage. I was winning a tournament a year, allied to a series of runner-up and top ten spots but the all-important breakthrough to the next level continued to elude me, for reasons I could not readily pinpoint.

There being little wrong with my swing, Ian Connelly thought my problem might lie in the mind and so he suggested I visit a sports psychologist who specialised in helping actors and actresses suffering from stage-fright. Terrified by the prospect of lurid headlines proclaiming 'Loopy Faldo Visits Shrink To Have Head Examined', I kept these visits secret for 15 years and more until it became common practice for almost every sportsman and woman.

We discussed my particular form of stage-fright from every angle when, almost by chance, I related a story from my visit to South Africa in 1976 when my good friend Warren Humphreys told me

Sunbathing with my parents at 285 Knella Road, Welwyn Garden City.

A bucket, a bike and a box – who needs a PlayStation?

The Chigwell mafia: (l–r) Uncle Percy, Harry Faldo, Auntie Gwen, Dolly Faldo, Granddad Faldo, Dad, Nana Faldo, Mum, me, Auntie Gladys and Uncle Charlie Faldo.

My first Ryder Cup partner and wingman, Oosty.

En route to beating the Open champion, Tom Watson, one-up, the day after beating Jack Nicklaus.

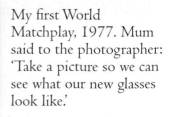

My first World Matchplay, 1977. Mum said to the photographer: 'Take a picture so we can see what our new glasses look like.'

David Foster presents me with the Colgate PGA trophy, my first 72-hole tournament win. To this day, I still use Colgate!

Nick, Jack and Tom.

With Tony Jacklin, our most inspirational captain.

'I can't dance. I can't sing.' Celebrating my singles victory over Jay Haas.

With Bernhard Langer, the consummate professional and my Ryder Cup partner in 1983 and 1985.

Breakthrough! My first tournament win, the 1987 Spanish Open, after the rebuild with David Leadbetter.

The Open, Muirfield, 1987

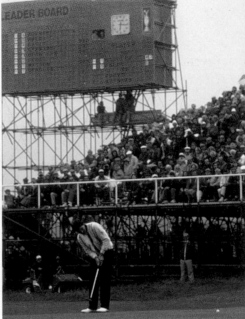

Three to go in the gloom. Can I hang in there?

Right: The 18th green: two putts to win.

'Nineteen eighty-seven Champion Golfer, Nick Faldo!'

enthusiastically, 'Gosh, Nick, you're good enough to win a tournament a year.' As soon as I had recounted this seemingly unimportant aside, the psychologist snapped his fingers and said, 'That's it. That's exactly what you're doing. You're good enough to win one tournament and so mentally you quit after winning one. Now all we need to do is re-programme you into becoming a serial winner.' Subconsciously, Warren's well-intentioned message had become my goal, and so, whenever I won my first tournament of the year, the mind switched off. Hey presto, in 1983, after my re-programming, I promptly became a serial winner with five important victories.

My sessions with the psychologist benefited me in another way in that they strengthened my concentration levels. Taking me on to a golf course and standing 100 yards from the flag, he handed me a pitching wedge and asked what would represent the perfect 10 out of 10 shot.

'To within three feet of the hole,' I replied.

'Right, without even thinking about it, hit me a 10 . . .'

Wooomph, I proceeded to hit 30 consecutive wedges to within 10 feet. He would try to put me off, talking, coughing, whistling on my backswing or, strangely the most annoying of all, just before I struck the ball shouting, 'Good shot!'

Not all my visits to the psychologist were quite so beneficial. Would you believe that on one occasion I visited a lady with a padded room who handed me a tennis racket with which to swat the demons – in effect the press who knew how to wind me up with a few well-chosen words or cutting barbs – off my back. When it came to it, however, I just couldn't do it and made a hasty retreat.

Of far more help was a psychologist called Dr Rene Kurinsky whom I subsequently consulted in South Africa and who taught me to build a coat of armour around myself – what we referred to as my 'iron chest' – as a protection against outside forces. With her help I eventually perfected the popular image of an 'ice man', whereas in reality, strip away that armour and you will find a softie who gets emotional watching *Mary Poppins*. Rene also introduced me to the word 'intention'. It is an amazingly powerful word – with proper intention you are far more committed to achieving your goal. After all, nobody 'intends' to play a bad shot. Years later I was lucky enough to meet Deepak Chopra, and his words in *The Seven Spiritual Laws of Success* really struck a chord: 'One-pointed intention is that quality of attention that is unbending in its fixity of purpose. One-pointed intention means holding your attention to the intended outcome with such unbending purpose that you absolutely refuse to allow obstacles to consume and dissipate the focused quality of your attention. There is a total and complete exclusion of all obstacles from your consciousness. You are able to maintain an unshakeable serenity while being committed to your goal with intense passion.' Now who does that sound like? ·

My children know me as a seriously soppy dad, but the manner in which I chose to play golf – head down, total concentration – was not an act. It was a defence mechanism designed to create a barrier between my world and the outside world. I wish in some ways it *had* been an act because I would be a better person today. Not that I think the public at large have ever regarded me as some sort of robot – the cold and aloof Nick Faldo has always been an invention of those who do not understand me – but knowing what I know now, with my mental strength I believe I could have been taught how to switch in and out of golf. If there is a disturbance on the tee – a kid opening a bag of crisps, say – the amusing way to react would be to stroll over, steal a crisp, ruffle the child's hair, then switch back into golf mode, but I was never taught that so if my concentration was broken, I knew I would proceed to hit a bad drive. I always laugh when I am having dinner with a group of people, some of whom don't know me particularly well, and I later learn that one of them has whispered to one of my friends, 'Nick's a bit chirpy tonight', to which my friend will reply, 'No, no, that's the normal Nick.' It comes as a bit of a shock to some people when they see me mucking around or hear me wisecracking, but it is nice that American professional Peter Jacobsen once described me as 'the funniest Englishman since John Cleese'.

I save the Monty Python stuff for nights with my friends, however. Lee Trevino would greet the click of a camera shutter with a merry quip, but I tended to react with a scowl because by disturbing my concentration the perpetrators were breaking down my defences. I like to think I have learned from my errors but, at the time, I never fully appreciated the wake of resentment I was leaving behind me, or that some people perceived me as being a bit of a bastard for the mistakes I made and the things I said that came out wrong.

Anyway, as a golfer, 1983 was my most successful season to date with five Tour victories and the honour of being the European number one. I was also the first player to break the £100,000 mark in prize money – and nine years later I would be the first to win £1 million in a season. Arnold Palmer achieved the equivalent record in the US. But as a husband, it was a year of total, abject, miserable failure. Before breaking up with Melanie, however, came my divorce from Ian Connelly.

CHAPTER SIX

THE GRAHAM MARSH INCIDENT

Ian Connelly and I had been together for more than a decade and, like any marriage, we had enjoyed a roller-coaster ride along the way. It was Jack Nicklaus who unwittingly came between us, during the first round of the 1983 San Diego Open. I watched the Great One hit a series of controlled fades and draws to the green, landing the ball five, 10 and 15 feet to the left and right of the pin at will. Whereas I shot a solid 71, the Golden Bear was round in 63, convincing me that I would never be admitted into the pantheon of the golfing gods if I did not learn to manufacture such a repertoire of shots.

Nicklaus was a consummate master. Physically, no one has ever hit a 1-iron quite like Jack. Mentally, his concentration was legendary. He would visualise the flight of any shot – a process he called 'Going to the Movies' – before addressing the ball. He was also the ultimate gentleman, sporting in victory, gracious in defeat.

Having been inspired by him as a 13-year-old all those years ago on television in our front room in Welwyn Garden City, studying him from such close quarters in San Diego renewed my belief that, no matter what success I had enjoyed, no matter how much hard work Ian and I had put in during the winter months, I had to push myself even more strenuously if I was to become a champion. In stark contrast to Ian's assurances that my swing was 'a thing of beauty', a photographer armed with a 50 frames-a-second camera showed me footage of my style, which, to my eyes, looked absolutely atrocious. It was one of those classic end of a relationship scenarios because, when I finally returned to England for the forthcoming European season, we parted without a word being spoken. Ian never called me to ask, 'Why aren't you coming for lessons?' and I neglected to contact him to explain my reasons for staying away – another one of my wonderful trademarks of which I am less than proud. Ian has sadly passed away recently but his influence is still with me – even to this day I still use many of the lessons and beliefs which he ingrained in me right back at the beginning of my career.

As one old friend departed, so I came to meet the remarkable George Keogh during a pro-am at Broadstairs. Teeing off at the first, George unleashed an horrendous slice and muttering, 'Bugger that,' unzipped his golf bag, removed what looked suspiciously like a false leg, rolled up his trousers, unstrapped his right limb and fitted the replacement. Returning to the tee, George declared his original drive out of bounds and smacked a beauty straight down the middle.

'That's better,' he growled, 'that's the leg I want.'

It transpired that George was a famous war veteran who had been parachuted in behind German lines during the D-Day landings, suffered a series of bullet wounds to his legs, completed his mission by holding a vital bridge in the company of a private, was awarded the Victoria Cross (which he refused because the private was not similarly honoured) and then joined up with the French Resistance – all this I learned before we had reached the turn at Broadstairs.

George's war adventures were only just beginning. Making his way to SS Headquarters at Trianon Palace on the outskirts of Paris, where we now stay during the Lancome tournament, he hid in the bushes until nightfall before booby-trapping the service line of a Gestapo general's tennis court. Next morning, as he knocked up in blissful ignorance, the explosive device (known as a 'de-bollocker') went off right up the SS officer's shorts, killing him outright. Although George's own war injuries were such that he later had one and a half legs amputated, years later he insisted on returning to parachuting.

'No way,' said the young army doctor. 'I've got nothing against your right leg but, unfortunately, neither have you . . .'

But George was persistent and eventually, having been worn down, in a moment of exasperation, the doctor announced: 'The only way I'll sign the papers to give you the okay is if you climb up on that wall, jump off it and execute a perfect roll.' George duly obliged.

John Simpson, my agent, and I later played a trick on the self-same doctor, by now approaching retirement age. We arrived at his surgery with my right arm tucked inside my sweater and the empty sleeve tied in a knot.

'And what can I do for you, young man?' he enquired gently.

'Well, as you can see, I'm in a bit of a state but I want to become a paratrooper and I hear you're the man who can sign my medical papers.'

He had obviously endured a tiring day at the office because the doc turned to his secretary and asked, 'Have we still got those forms?' Through tears of laughter, John croaked, 'Doc, I'd like you to meet Nick Faldo the golfer . . .'

I reported to Augusta in the spring of 1983 for my second tilt at the Masters (70, 70, 76, 76 earning me a share in 20th place behind the blastedly talented Seve Ballesteros), then on to Texas where I enjoyed a practice round and spent some time with Mark O'Meara who, in commenting on how shut my take-away was, asked whether I had ever tried fanning the club face open instead. I gave it a shot and was pleased with the results. Was that moment the very start of my 'rotation of the arms' swing?

And so to the cafés and boulevards of Paris, the venue for the Paco Rabanne French Open, where the organisers had renamed me 'Mick' Faldo on the starter's sheet. Despite this identity crisis, I won the event after a three-man play-off involving Spanish Ryder Cup player Jose-Maria Canizares and David J. Russell, with the help of a Titleist ball bearing 384 dimples that was in advance of anything available in Europe. This was, of course, the start of one of the biggest changes in the game. With golf ball technology really taking off from around that time, the balls have consistently flown further and further and now more than 20 years later many players are questioning where it will stop. Having been re-programmed as a serial winner, I emerged victorious just one week later in the Martini International at Wilmslow where, in an extraordinary coincidence given the increasing competitiveness of the European Tour, I again beat the luckless Canizares in a play-off, this time at the third extra hole. It was also a victory for my mind. There are a few holes at Wilmslow that are less than inspiring and so I took myself off the course and imagined I was on the practice ground to keep my concentration from wandering.

Like a Las Vegas gambler on a roll, it appeared I could not stop winning and I proceeded to notch up my third successive tournament victory in the Car Care Plan International in Leeds before my three-in-a row streak came to an abrupt halt in the PGA Championship at Royal St George's, closing rounds of 74 and 75 leaving me in 23rd place after I had been only one stroke off the lead at the halfway stage.

I may have been in the form of my life but, remembering the Family Faldo traditional work ethic, I prepared for the Open Championship at Royal Birkdale as never before, playing five practice rounds – two in the company of Tom Watson – and hitting upwards of 300 balls a day on the range, frequently putting in a full working day from nine in the morning until after seven at night. It was July and there was a blistering heatwave. So hot was it in the bedrooms of the Marine Hotel, Southport, that Mrs Tom Watson bought every electric fan in town, which probably numbered about six since the Lancashire coast is unaccustomed to being transformed into the Copacabana. Mr and Mrs Faldo, however, had to make do with a little water-squirter which we would spray above our heads when lying in bed to generate a mist of cold, moist air.

Playing great and putting even better, I compiled rounds of 68 (after starting 6 and 6 to stand 4 over par after two), 68 and 71 and, with nine holes remaining on the final Sunday afternoon, the name Faldo stood at the very top of the leaderboard above all the usual challengers – Watson, Irwin, Trevino, Rogers, Ballesteros, Lyle. But I succumbed to the pressure. I simply could not handle leading the Open. I three-putted the 13th and 14th, made a complete hash of the 16th, totally losing my head and blaming my caddie, Dave McNeilly, for handing me the wrong club, and eventually walked off the 18th tied for eighth place, five strokes behind Tom Watson. (Maybe those air-cooler fans were a shrewd investment by Mrs W.) Devastated, I returned crestfallen to the hotel, harbouring the first doubts that I lacked the swing and technique to win a Major. I was coaching myself to all intents and purposes, and events at Birkdale suggested I was not making a very good fist of it.

Be it the Olympic 100 metre final, taking the crucial kick in a penalty shoot-out, or leading the Open with nine holes to play, you need enormous mental strength and stamina to emerge victorious. To win a golf Major, or indeed to be successful at anything in life, it is my opinion that you must have enormous self-confidence at the very least, but even more important is to have true self-belief. At the age of 26, I was simply not up to the task. I had proved to myself I could lead an Open; I had yet to convince myself I could actually win the biggest prize in golf. Critically, however, I had enjoyed being in that position. It had felt comfortable and while not winning was incredibly frustrating for sure, I did view it as part of my learning curve.

But if I was crushed, how did the hapless Hale Irwin feel? On the 14th green of the third round, Irwin, now a leading money winner on the US Seniors' Tour, had a three-inch tap-in for a par when, probably still mad from leaving it short, with a careless back-hand swipe, his putter struck the ground an inch short and bounced clean over the ball. As Irwin had intended to hit the ball, it counted as a stroke and I wonder if he has had to spend the last 20 years living with the knowledge that he finished runner-up in the 1983 Open to Tom Watson by one, single, agonising shot.

'I prayed Tom would win by two strokes so my air shot would have been irrelevant,' Hale later told me. 'That was probably the most embarrassing, and expensive, putting lesson in history.'

I was still feeling less than buoyant when I teed off in the Lawrence Batley International at Bingley St Ives four days after the heartbreak of Birkdale. I started miserably, so much so that I almost threw in the towel; I pride myself that in over 25 years as a professional, I have probably jacked it in no more than three times, but on that occasion I was ready to pack my suitcase. 'That's it, I've had enough,' I told McNeilly after narrowly surviving the halfway cut. I didn't pack it in, however, and went out and shot 64 and 62 to win my fourth title in six weeks, which only goes to show that sometimes – and I repeat sometimes – when you surrender all hope on the golf course, you immediately relax into carefree abandon and everything mysteriously falls into place.

Then came one of those agonising 'should I, shouldn't I?' family dilemmas that are the curse of every sportsman's life. After finishing second to Isao Aoki of Japan in the European Open at Sunningdale, I still led the Order of Merit but Ballesteros was looming ominously at my shoulder. The potentially decisive Ebel Swiss Open clashed with the wedding of Melanie's brother, Steve, at which I had agreed to serve as best man. Melanie, quite rightly in her eyes, thought her brother's marriage outranked 'just another golf tournament', but I was determined to finish the season as European number one and so, neither for the first time nor the last, I put my career first, made my excuses and departed for Crans-sur-Sierre.

Was I right or was I wrong? Melanie certainly believed me to have been guilty of gross selfishness, and so my sense of jubilation at beating Sandy Lyle in a play-off, having been 11 shots adrift of the big fella at one stage in the third round, and becoming 'King of European Golf' was tempered by the fact that my wife thought I had let her down by not standing at her brother's right shoulder in church. I doubt Steve Rockall ever forgave me either; following Sandy's victory in the 1985 Open at Royal St George's, 18 months after the end of our marriage, he telephoned me to say how sorry he was that I had not been the victor. Strange, until then, he hadn't spoken to me since the break-up and hasn't done so again.

So the new European number one prepared to contest the 1983 Ryder Cup at Palm Beach Gardens, Florida, brimful of confidence, only to discover our PGA was still unprepared. I had been playing in the States for much of the previous two years so I was stunned to discover we were to be given just one pair of shoes for the week and one shirt per day. At the first team meeting I stood up and said, 'Do you know what the weather is like here in Florida in September? It's brutally humid and it rains every afternoon; the course will be soaking wet. We'll need at least two pairs of shoes and three shirts a day.' Sure enough, after our initial practice rounds we all had to troop off to the pro shop to buy another 13 matching shirts. I hated to say 'I told you so', but I did tell them.

Looking back, half the team were convinced we could win – notably Seve, Bernhard Langer, Sandy, Ian Woosnam and me – but the other half were not quite so sure about succeeding on American soil for the first time in the 56-year history of the contest. Ultimately, we fell short by a single point under the inspired captaincy of Tony Jacklin, losing 14½–13½. Tony was the captain supreme. Every night he would come into the team room completely hoarse from his exhortations. We would sit him down, pour him a whisky and ginger ale and insist he relax, having done more than his day's work. 'Oh, but it's the Ryder Cup,' Tony would say. 'Whenever I hear the words Ryder Cup I come over all unnecessary.' Having beaten the Americans to win the US Open, Tony was the first European captain who genuinely believed they could be defeated under a team format.

The final result could so nearly have been the other way around – in the last day's singles, Seve halved with Fuzzy Zoeller after being three up with seven to play; Brian Waites lost to Calvin Peete by one hole; Sam Torrance halved with Tom Kite; and Jose-Maria Canizares halved with Lanny Wadkins, who avoided defeat with a 60-yard approach at the 18th which landed a foot from the pin.

Wadkins's pitch was the stroke that won the Ryder Cup but I also witnessed the greatest shot I had ever seen on any golf course at that time, Seve Ballesteros's 3-wood out of a bunker on the 18th across water to a green about a quarter of a mile away; but because he missed the green by a yard, it has never fully been recognised.

Although I finished with a personal haul of four points out of five, I was feeling suitably depressed at having run the Americans so close only to lose yet again, when Seve burst into the team room. 'We muss celebrate . . . thees ees beeg victory . . . thees ees great day for European golf.' Only Seve could turn defeat into victory and we duly put the Americans to shame with the extent and longevity of our celebrations; from that moment on, we knew we could win.

Like Muhammad Ali and Joe Frazier, or Bjorn Borg and John McEnroe, Seve and I would never become intimate friends; our rivalry was too intense for us to form any sort of attachment but my admiration for him – especially the way he almost single-handedly made us believe the Ryder Cup was within our grasp – is unbounded.

We were fierce competitors but whenever the Ryder Cup came round we would leave our egos at the door and become passionate team-mates. The next week, of course, we were back at each other's throats, in a sporting manner of speaking, and so we never became buddies, which is a great shame because he has always been a hero of mine in a way. Our relationship was born out of respect rather than affection and I wish there had been a bit more affection. I really feel for Seve these days because he is in so much pain, physically with his back and mentally coming to terms with his waning powers. He should not be so hard on himself because no one has done more for European golf than Seve Ballesteros.

Typically, no sooner had I built up a few precious brownie points with the public through my efforts on Europe's behalf, than, through no fault of my own, my image as a 'baddie' was reinforced after a bizarre occurrence against Australian Graham Marsh during the World Matchplay Championship at Wentworth. All square after 33 holes, I had no idea all hell was about to break loose at the 16th of the afternoon round. After driving into the left-hand rough behind a copse of trees, from where I could not see the green, I hit a hook that, as I later discovered to my mortification, ran through the green and into the hand of a spectator who, in an instant of sheer madness, decided to throw the ball back on to the putting surface. Now, television viewers around the world all witnessed this incident in repeated slow-motion replays but, unsighted as I had been, I had no reason to suspect anything was amiss.

When I finally walked on to the green, Graham said, 'I think something's wrong, Nick.'

'Yeah, but what?' I shrugged, totally mystified.

Gradually, the story unfolded and the referee finally announced, 'As the ball was still moving, play it from where it lies.'

Some of the gallery booed. Even worse, a few of my fans had the audacity to cheer when Marsh, understandably unnerved by the brouhaha, missed a three-foot putt to halve the hole. I went on to win 2 and I amid a chorus of, 'Did you see that? It's disgusting. Faldo's a cheat.' When I saw a replay of the full incident on television later that night, I thought, 'Oh, my God. What have I done? I'll be crucified for this.' Obviously, if I had appreciated what had occurred at the time, I would simply have dropped the ball on the spot where it would have originally finished, over the green. In retrospect, after watching the replays, I should have called Graham and invited him to start again from the 16th – play a let – the next morning. Who among us has never wished they could turn the clock back? It was an error of judgement and I find it genuinely hurtful that some people harp on about 'The Graham Marsh Incident' as an example of my supposed win-at-all-costs attitude. For a while after this incident, the authorities utilised a television referee to assist those on the course. If there had been one on that day, he or she would have immediately seen what had happened and could have advised the walking referee accordingly and the outcome would have been very different.

Call me paranoid but I have detected a level of double-standards over the years. Returning from the Johnnie Walker World Championship in Jamaica a decade or so ago, I watched a fellow pro, who had obviously enjoyed a couple of drinks on the flight from Montego Bay to Gatwick, bring the carousel in the baggage hall to a grinding halt by jumping on and off like a wayward three-year-old. Only one newspaperman in attendance made mention of the fact that a large number of people hoping to make connections from Heathrow to the Far East missed their flights because of his antics. The assembled tabloid hacks stood back grinning as if to say, 'He's a character, isn't he?' If it had been me creating this mayhem, I would have been splashed across the front pages the following morning. Perhaps I should have gone out of my way to be more affable, or perhaps I should have buried the hatchet years ago; I guess there is blame on both sides.

The 1983 season ended with me setting a new European prize-money record of £140,076, becoming the first player for over 20 years to win five Tour events and achieving the lowest stroke average in world golf of 70.15. Seve was fourth, incidentally, on 70.53 with Tom Watson ninth on 70.81. Certain sections of Fleet Street were not the slightest bit impressed, preferring the headline: 'Star Golfer Nick in Love Triangle'. Thanks to those moral guardians on the *Sun* newsdesk, on the morning of 9 February 1984, my secret love affair with Gill Bennett was a secret no more.

I offer no excuses for entering into another relationship while still legally wed, except to say our marriage had been inexorably disintegrating before our eyes for over a year and neither Melanie nor I seemed able – or, perhaps, willing – to prevent the inevitable. Golf had come to represent a release from the turmoil at Tudor Cottage and so life on the Tour was a pleasant change from being at home where the atmosphere had become suffocating. I had never argued with anyone before in my life – Family Faldo were not given to confrontation – yet there we were, becoming increasingly embroiled in these awful screaming matches. It was deeply distressing because this lovely young woman with whom I was now trading the most hurtful verbal abuse, was the same person with whom I had fallen so passionately in love only four short years before. It is difficult to remember you once loved someone when domestic battle rages.

I had known Gill Bennett since the previous summer when she joined the IMG London office so I suppose it was inevitable, given the circumstances with Melanie, that out of our friendship grew love. Over Christmas – oh, yeah, I picked my time – I told Melanie that it would be best for each of us to go our separate ways and explained that I was already seeing someone else. There is no gentle way to impart such news but, unlike those not in the public eye, we were not allowed to cope with what was an intensely harrowing situation in privacy.

Gill accompanied me to the Hawaii Open where a *Daily Express* gossip columnist tracked us down to my hotel bedroom via a transatlantic phone link. Pretending to be the butler, in my best Jeeves accent I informed him, 'I am terribly sorry, sir, but I am afraid Mr Faldo is out playing golf at present. I would be pleased to pass on a message on his return.' He did not believe a word of it, needless to say, but at least he had the decency not to call back and harass us, unlike a number of his fellow Rottweilers, as the tabloid hacks glorify in being known.

They would slide the most courteous of letters under the door, send flowers or bottles of champagne, pleading for an interview with one or both of us, then took to stalking us when we refused each and every invitation for 'a friendly chat'. We were strolling through the streets of Honolulu one night when an intrepid photographer started taking pictures of us while walking backwards. Finding it difficult to do two things at once, he crashed into a lamp-post at which Gill burst out laughing and, of course, that was the photograph on the front pages in London – Nick Faldo and his new lover Gill Bennett strolling through Honolulu grinning like Cheshire cats, seemingly without a care in the world. Following our trail to Australia, we were dining in a Melbourne restaurant when – Flash! Flash! Flash! – we had to make good our escape through the kitchen, an incident that was recorded in an hilarious cartoon of the two of us fleeing past the cauldrons of soup.

It was the last message in the world I wanted to send Melanie who, as you can understand, was baying for blood back in Ayot St Lawrence. Although I was happy to be with Gill, I also felt a mixture of sadness, guilt and regret at the break-up of my marriage.

Always an innocent abroad, I think the only person who did not know Gill and I were an item was caddie Dave McNeilly. 'Why's Gill out here so much, then?' he enquired disingenuously when he spotted Ms Bennett on the other side of the ropes during a practice round for the San Diego Open. Thinking on my feet, I spun him a line that she had travelled to America at IMG's behest to assess the caddies with a view to sponsorship deals on their visors, vests and shirts. Dave did not say a word but next morning he turned up on the first tee brushed and scrubbed, wearing a freshly laundered and newly ironed shirt. He had never looked so smart.

Two decades on, Melanie runs a highly successful sports marketing company and has found a level of happiness I was sadly never able to give her. We were married too young and too soon, at a time when I was committed to becoming a champion golfer. True, I was selfish, because that is one of the traits you need if you are to fulfil your destiny, but Melanie was aware of that from the outset. I did not suddenly move the goalposts 12 months into our marriage. When Melanie used to complain, 'You think you're number one and everyone and everything revolves round you,' I would reply in all honesty, 'Guess what? At this moment in my golfing life I *am* number one and everything *does* revolve round me because I'm the one with the career. For now I'm the one generating the money to give us this fabulous lifestyle.' That attitude had a positive effect on my career but a negative effect on my marriage, and I am sorry if it makes me sound insensitive. To be a success in any walk of life means making sacrifices and understandably Melanie did not like my being away for up to four months of the year in America.

It was the same career versus family balancing act that would bring about the eventual break-up of my marriage to Gill. After years of struggle with my golf, I was on the way up and I wanted to keep going up but it is hard to persuade others to come along for the ride. I found myself constantly reassuring them, 'Look, this ain't going to last for ever.' As a sportsman, I knew I had a limited time at the top and I was determined that I would be 100 per cent committed to my sport while that playing window was still open. Knowing that I have given everything I can in a day is important to me, although at times that attitude can be both applauded and decried. There is a story I read once about an owner of a small business who wanted to get the point across that for the company to succeed, all the employees had to give their all. He gathered his dozen or so staff members together and asked each one of them how much they gave the company each day: 75 per cent, 80 per cent, 90 per cent came the responses. The next day he took them all off for a corporate day out parachuting. When up in the plane he introduced the instructor with the words, 'This is Bob. He will be looking after us today. He packed all our chutes and he reckons he was concentrating about 95 per cent on the task.' Sure, I could have handled a lot of situations better and there have been some hideous errors of judgement along the way, but here and now, in my mid 40s, I am content that, in golf at least, I have achieved almost everything I set out to do all those years ago.

As anyone who has been through the trauma of a separation will appreciate, once the lawyers enter the fray the battle-lines have been drawn, and Melanie and I endured 18 months of legal misery before the terms of our divorce were finalised. Financially, it cost me one third of my net worth, but the incessant rounds of haggling and bickering cost far, far more in emotional terms. Ironically, having played the best golf of my career during these turbulent times at Tudor Cottage, no sooner had I found peace and tranquillity in my private life than I entered a slump in form from which I would despair of ever escaping. Fortunately, however, when I was at my lowest ebb, I met the golfing partner with whom I would finally achieve my 'desire for sporting greatness'.

CHAPTER SEVEN

REBUILDING THROUGH THE WILDERNESS YEARS

The azaleas and dogwoods, the redbuds and camellias, the flowering peach and the magnolias had never looked more beautiful or smelled sweeter than they did on my third visit to the Augusta National for the 1984 Masters. Oblivious then of the problems to come, which would torture me for the next three years and more, I took inspiration from the scenic grandeur to shoot 70, 69 and 70 and went into the last round just two strokes behind the pacesetting Tom Kite's score of 9 under par. As former US Tour veteran Frank Beard famously observed about the unique pressure exerted by Augusta, 'Every day, every minute, the greens become a little more difficult to read and the fairways become narrower.' By halfway through Sunday's final round, the greens could have been written in hieroglyphics such was the difficulty I was experiencing in reading them, while the fairways, previously so accommodating, suddenly appeared narrower than a 10 pin bowling alley. Out in 40, having spent so much time in the trees people thought I was a steward, I recovered my dignity if nothing else on the homeward nine, to record a 4 over par-76 which left me tied for 15th place, eight shots behind the latest green jacket winner, Ben Crenshaw.

Also, recalling the manner in which I had disintegrated when leading the previous year's Open at Royal Birkdale, my 'admirers' delighted in dubbing me 'Nick Foldo', which did not do a lot for my self-esteem; nor did the suggestion that I had 'thrown in my hand when the pot got a bit expensive'.

Like football managers who always trundle out the popular line, 'We've learned a lot from this defeat,' I was, actually, learning fast. Watching Crenshaw hole putt after putt after putt from ridiculous distances and unfathomable 'borrows', I told myself, 'At least I now know what it takes to win the Masters. You've got to sink every-thing. It's as simple as that.'

After 14 weeks in America, during which I had played 11 tour-naments, I toyed with the idea of skipping the next event on the Tour – the Sea Pines Heritage Classic at Hilton Head Island – and returning to England, but decided that if the worst came to the worst and I missed the cut, I would be home in a few more days in any case. On the way to the hotel from the airport, I asked the courtesy car driver to stop at a 'liquor store' where I bought a bottle of whisky with the intention of taking a 'wee nip' every night before bed to relax me. Suitably refreshed after a full night's sleep, on the first tee I informed Dave McNeilly, 'It's shit or bust this week. I'm either going to win or miss the cut by miles.' Shooting 66, 67, 68 and 69, I beat Tom Kite by one stroke to record my first victory in America and temporarily dispel the perceived wisdom that I suffered from vertigo whenever I found myself near the top of the leaderboard. What was that I said? After successfully defending my Car Care Plan International title at Moortown, Leeds, I would not win another tournament for more than three years.

I finished a humbling 55th in my US Open debut at Winged Foot, Mamaroneck and although I began our own Open Championship at

St Andrews in encouraging fashion – opening rounds of 69 and 68 elevated me to joint second place on the Friday night – even with the assistance of Gerald Micklem's famous notes, I saw my challenge evaporate with a third round 76. It was infuriating in the extreme, especially so when I returned to form with another splendid 69 on the Sunday afternoon. Having outplayed the entire field for 54 holes, that ruinous third round became even harder to bear when Seve Ballesteros won his fourth Major with a total of 276. To fulfil my dream of winning an Open I had to find a way to allow my game and my mental stamina to last all four days.

Most humbling of all that year, playing with my boyhood hero Jack Nicklaus in the second round of the US PGA Championship at Shoal Creek, I stood on the par-4 18th on 6 under, a nicely poised fourth behind Lee Trevino, Gary Player and Lanny Wadkins. Arriving in the scorer's tent 10 minutes later, I could hardly sign my name my hand was shaking so hard with a mixture of embarrassment and fury – I had committed golfing suicide with a quadruple-bogey 8 at the last.

By the time December came around, and with it the Million Dollar Challenge in Sun City, a little voice in my head kept nagging away at me, 'You ain't got it, mate.' My swing was too willowy, I could not quite 'shape' my shots as I wished, my trajectory was not what I wanted, and so, although I was number one in Europe and had won in the States, I finally accepted that drastic action was required if my 'desire for greatness' was not to remain unfulfilled.

Drastic action was duly taken at the instigation of David Leadbetter. I first came across him working on the practice ground with fellow Zimbabwean Nick Price (runner-up in the 1982 Open to Tom Watson at Royal Troon), during that Sun City tournament in 1984. I knew David by reputation although he was unknown to the public at large. Leadbetter – specialist subject 'the swing' – operated from the orange groves of Florida as a teaching pro, his reputation among golfers having been built on his work with Dennis Watson and Nick Price. Strictly informally, I asked him to cast his expert eye over me to see if he could detect what was preventing me from moving on to the next level. It was not a request delivered in haste for I had already sounded out John Jacobs and Bob Torrance, two of the wisest heads in the game, among others, but when Lead said, 'You've got about half a dozen things wrong with your swing that I can spot, but rather than trying to tackle each one individually, I'd suggest we try to find the one thing that will end up curing them all in a chain reaction,' his words made immediate sense. Rather than being a Band-aid doctor, he was in favour of major surgery and I left that original consultation mightily impressed by his diagnosis. I do not know if it was due to the 'Leadbetter Effect' but I was runner-up to Seve Ballesteros in Sun City, and in my seasonal debut in America in January 1985 I finished joint fourth in the Phoenix Open. Thereafter, however, I went downhill faster than Franz Klammer in the Winter Olympics and by the time I arrived at Muirfield Village for the Memorial Tournament, I could not find the green with a map and a compass, let alone a 9-iron. Spying Lead on the practice tee – where else would he be? – I reintroduced myself with the words, 'Right, I'm all yours. Throw the book at me.'

Oh, how I sometimes wished in the following years that I had ducked that flying tome. To those of you who are students of the 'hit it, go find it' school of golf, what is about to follow may read like a car manual explaining how to strip down an engine and rebuild it back-to-front. But, as Lead eventually transformed me into the world's number one golfer, I would like to share with you the gory details of the 'wilderness years'.

After our initial session on the practice ground, Lead decreed that my swing was too 'willowy' (as I had thought myself) and too steep, my trajectory too high and too weak. 'You're swinging the club on too upright a *plane*,' he told me. 'The whole thing has a big reverse "C" seventies look about it, which is understandable because that's the era in which you grew up. We need something for the 1990s. What we need is better connection between your body and your arms. What we need to develop is a body swing rather than a legs and arms action.'

Lead was correct because when you look at the great champions of the 1970s, Johnny Miller, say, his swing was incredibly 'active', incorporating fast legs, fast hands and fast arms because you cannot have one without t'others. I was cast from a very similar mould and because I had spent so many long hours on the range by myself as a youngster, I had not corrected things along the way. I might have had a lesson from Ian Connelly and then practise on my own so hard that I'd go too far the other way. In effect I would practise through the correction Ian had identified and actually end up over-correcting it. When Lead undertook the task of assembling Faldo Mark II, my swing comprised a lot of lateral movement, whereas the classic compact swings of Ben Hogan and Sam Snead were built round their spines. I was a 'feel' player, which meant there were far more areas in which things could go wrong because the basic mechanics were questionable to say the least.

When you start to break the swing down into its component parts, there are so many to consider and all are interlinked: the foot action, the knee action, the hip action, the chest action, then to the wrists, hands, elbows, arms, shoulders, head. There are at least a dozen or more different aspects of the swing but, put simply, a good leg action provides a solid base on which to turn, the rotation from the upper body generates the arm swing, while a bit of wrist action is needed for controlling and shaping shots.

Lead decided to start with my arm rotation. Before, I used to take the club back very shut, which means the heel of the club moves faster than the toe because of an excess of body movement. We wanted to create the opposite effect, where the toe of the club would move first, followed by the rotation of the arms. I practised that solidly for a couple of months but the problem was that this new style did not fit in with the rest of my swing, which of course had a detrimental impact on my tournament play.

I returned to the orange groves of Grenelefe, south of Orlando, in the autumn, a time of the year when Florida is brutally hot. This is especially so in the morning when there is dew on the grass, still wet anyway from the sprinklers of the night before, and the humidity bounces up at you off the ground – it was like practising in a sauna. Lead would provide me with a bucket of balls, big buckets containing 300 balls, and I would hit five of those every day until my fingers were screaming in pain. Throughout 10 days of this torture, I was also working on a new leg action.

Lead wanted more solidity in my legs (it made me feel like Daddy Woodentop), the theory being that they would then serve as resistance to allow the creation of the torsion in the upper half of my body. Now when you have swung a golf club in a certain style for the best part of 15 years, your muscles can cope with it: but when you suddenly ask those muscles to start performing in a completely different way you are exposing them to a great deal of strain.

Another interesting thing, which struck me only recently, is that we were totally preoccupied with what my body was doing, we rarely correlated that to a target. I just whacked balls into the distance. Yet for everything we do in life we always have a target in view, whether it is throwing a ball, running a race, or starting a business: you always know where your goal lies. To be fair to Lead, these techniques were all so new we were learning off each other, so every time I thought I was nearly 'complete', he would come up with something else. It seemed never-ending; having rebuilt my backswing and leg action, we then moved on to the downswing and follow-through with re-rotation and supernation (arching the wrist on impact). What we were trying to create was a modern golf swing whereby, with the body leading the club head – or 'holding off' in technical parlance – no matter how hard you swing through the ball, you would never have the fear of hooking it left.

As always, the fundamentals of golf stood tall – grip, alignment, posture and balance – and nothing was left to chance. Even my old 'hit it high and let it fly' philosophy was shredded in favour of a far lower, flatter finish. If you study the truly great swings, those of Hogan and Snead, their arms used to fill exactly the same slot on the follow-through as they had on the backswing.

I have not stopped readjusting the various components of my swing to this day, as my body shape changes. As you grow older, you have to become gentler on yourself to continue, which is why Snead was still able to play fantastic tournament golf well into his seventies. I have since developed a single backswing but four different follow-throughs, creating a slight fade and a big fade, a slight draw and a big draw, which for me is the right way to do it because I am then responding to the target.

A number of players have subsequently blamed David Leadbetter for failing to turn them into champions but I trusted him implicitly even though I was earning little or no money from tournaments. Far more demoralising for me, however, as a vote of no confidence, was the losing of sponsorship deals by the day; only Glynwed and the Scottish knitwear company Pringle stayed loyal (Pringle, bless 'em, actually increased my contract). Everyone else dropped me. Whenever my agent John Simpson walked into the kitchen, I would greet him by saying, 'Oh, here he comes, the harbinger of doom and gloom.' I often felt like releasing my frustration by hurling the crockery against the wall, but then I would remind myself that I would have to replace them.

With so many diverse instructions running through my befuddled brain, my form continued to nosedive, if such a thing were possible, at an even more alarming rate of descent. I am often asked whether I would undertake such a rebuild again and, if so, what I would do differently from my time with Lead. In hindsight – and this is in no way meant as a knock at David because we were both experimenting – to undertake the rebuilding of my swing during a competitive season was just short of reputational suicide. If a rebuild is necessary, what I would suggest is that the player disappears for three months and takes with him a sports psychologist and a physiotherapist. With such a team behind you, a lot can be achieved in three months. The key is to assess where you want to get to and then reset the muscles to help achieve that new swing. With the aid of the psychologist it is possible to dispose of the old images of your swing and paint new, positive ones in line with that goal. I would also suggest hitting balls in a much more constructive programme and certainly playing more golf. At least nine holes a day, so you can add feeling to what you are learning. When I think about it now, that's what I did when I was a kid. I'd practise in the morning and go out on the course in the afternoon to see if it was working.

To return to those anguished early days with Lead, the 1985 Sandwich Open was a nightmare. I shot 73, 73, 75, 74 to finish joint 53rd; and I was 52 places behind my old rival Sandy Lyle. I can freely admit to being Lincoln green with envy that Sandy was the first Brit to win the title since Tony Jacklin 18 years earlier. By the time news of Sandy's victory came through, I was already in my workshop tinkering with my putters, having long since departed the course with the rest of the also-rans.

Just when I thought things could not become any worse, they did. Tony Jacklin thought the Ryder Cup would provide the motivation and inspiration to lift me out of my slump and graciously granted me a wild card place on the team, even though my miserable form did not merit my inclusion. It was an act of faith on his part, hoping against hope that I could reproduce my past deeds at The Belfry.

'Nick,' he told me, 'you're going to be my chameleon. I know you can change colours this week.'

Tony was the master psychologist, even dominating US skipper Lee Trevino in the pre-match mind games. Introducing the teams at the arrival banquet, Lee told us how much his team members had won. 'Lanny Wadkins,' he enthused, 'winner of three hundred and forty-seven thousand dollars and eighty-four cents . . .' and so on and so on, closing with the words, 'My team has won a combined figure of six million dollars.' We sat there thinking, 'How much!' Then Tony stood up: 'I would like to introduce my team in alphabetical order – Seve-ri-ano Ball-es-teros . . .' The roar was deafening.

Having taken note of this, at the opening ceremony Lee followed suit: 'I would like to introduce my team in alphabetical order – Raymond Floyd . . .' But Tony had changed tactics: 'Winner of six events, the winner of this, this, this and this, Ke-e-eeen Brownnnn!' *Ken* Brown? Tony made his record sound like Ben Hogan's; neither did he let the Americans forget that Sandy Lyle was the reigning Open Champion, Bernhard Langer the Masters title-holder, nor that in Seve, the European team possessed a winner of both the Open and the Masters, each of them twice.

Alas, the inclusion of Nick Faldo in those illustrious ranks was a gamble doomed to failure. My partnership with Bernhard Langer, so successful at Palm Beach Gardens two years earlier, was a pale imitation and we were thumped 3 and 2 by Tom Kite and Calvin Peete in the foursomes on the first morning, at which point I sadly informed Tony, 'Sorry, mate, but I haven't got it.' I did not play again until the final day singles when I contrived to lose 3 and 1 to Hubert Green.

As history now shows, Europe won the trophy, 16½–11½, the first Ryder Cup victory since 1957. But I could not find it in my heart to join in all these joyous celebrations. As far as I was concerned, the 11 other fellas had won the trophy. I simply did not feel part of the team, having failed to do my bit. And so, while Tony and the lads stood on the balcony at The Belfry spraying the jubilant spectators with champagne and Concorde flew overhead dipping its wings, I sat alone at a corner table in the clubhouse. One of the greatest moments in European golf and there was I, Little Jack Horner sulking in a corner. That hurt because I had had a great Ryder Cup record up until then – 11 points out of 15 and unbeaten in singles. It would have been nice if Tony or someone had come looking for me, put his arm round my shoulders, and said, 'C'mon, my son, get your ass out there, you're as much a part of the team as anyone.' That was when my tendency to be a loner came back to haunt me with a vengeance.

Perhaps it is the effect of time, but the painful memories of The Belfry have been replaced by a golden glow of warm satisfaction. I can remember the night before the singles, when we led 9–7, Spaniard Manuel Pinero hopping about like the proverbial cat on a hot tin roof as Tony Jacklin prepared to exchange line-ups with American captain Lee Trevino. 'I go number one, I wan' Wadkins . . . I wan' Wadkins . . . I wan' Wadkins . . .' he chanted, his voice becoming increasingly strident. Obviously, there had been a bit of history between the two and so, when Tony returned from his meeting with Trevino to announce, 'Pinero will play,' his voice trailing away to a whisper, 'Wadkins,' any lingering doubts we entertained that we could finally beat the Americans evaporated. Manuel won that opening match 3 and 1 and from that instant on, victory was ours.

In the aftermath of my own wretched display, my harshest critics made merry at my expense. Did the fact that I had plummeted from number one in Europe in 1983 to 42nd on the Order of Merit in just 24 months not suggest that I would have been better leaving my game well alone?

David, to his eternal credit, committed a lot of time to me, and because of his skills as a communicator I never harboured the slightest doubt that he was the one man in possession of the key that would transform me from European number one to world number one. During this period, Gill's and my finances were certainly tight and without appearance money, I would have been in dire straits. Given my ineptitude with a club in my hands, I began feeling guilty about accepting such perks, so much so that after missing the cut in the Benson & Hedges, I handed back half of my payment. I also fired Dave McNeilly as caddie at the same tournament because he handed me a wedge with a great wad of mud on it. 'That's it, I don't require your services any more,' I growled. It was not a sacking offence, and had I not been under so much pressure Dave would have escaped with a withering look.

If 1985 had been troubled, 1986 was trouble doubled and then some, although it began in the happiest of ways when I married Gill one week into the New Year, my divorce from Melanie having been finalised. Second time round, there was no open-topped Lagonda, no white bridal gown and no church wedding, simply a secret visit to Stroud Register Office in Gloucestershire, followed by a service of blessing at St Mary Magdalene's Church, Rodborough.

In between visitations to Leadbetter HQ in Florida, where we would assemble my swing like pieces of Meccano only to dismantle it halfway through and begin the process of reassembly all over again, I proceeded to miss six cuts in my first 12 tournaments of the new US season, playing promisingly one day only to hack my way round the next. In the Tournament Players' Championship at Sawgrass – arguably the most important event in world golf after the four Majors – I opened with a 69 to stand high on the leaderboard, then contrived to miss the cut following a second round 78. On to the Sea Pines Heritage Classic, which I had won two years earlier, where I shot 71 and 80, then the Houston Open, where again I was in a challenging position after shooting 68, 69 and 70. I blew that one big time with a 77 in the final round.

Occasionally, I would put together four satisfactory rounds, as in the PGA Championship at Wentworth (third) and the French Open (fourth), encouraging me to travel to Turnberry for the Open with a renewed level of confidence. With the mountains of the island of Arran as a backdrop, par-70 Turnberry is one of the most beautiful championship courses on the planet, but it can be an ugly brute when the wind howls, as it did that July, and so my fifth place finish behind Greg Norman was an acceptable 29th birthday present to myself. I came off the 18th on the Sunday afternoon smiling, a fact not lost on Gill, who commented, 'That's the first time I've seen you smile for two years.'

Was that a light at the end of the dark tunnel? No, it was a high-speed locomotive hurtling towards me. Missed cut after missed cut meant I ended the season a disappointing 135th on the US money list and a mediocre 15th on the European Order of Merit. Blessedly for my sanity, on 18 September 1986, Gill gave birth to the gorgeous Natalie. Sadly, after our split in 1995, I was criticised in print for the fact that we had had Natalie's birth induced. The reason we decided on that course of action was because I had been selected to represent England in the Dunhill Cup at St Andrews and, basically, we desperately needed the money. Also, I was part of a three-man team and, had the baby been born a week or so after the due date, I would have had to withdraw from the tournament to be back for the birth, and it would have jeopardised the whole team. It was a subject Gill and I discussed at some length before reaching a mutual decision. In retrospect, I can appreciate how some might see this chosen path as putting career first and family second; I know every mum wants a natural birth – and every dad for that matter – but, as I have said, we desperately needed the money, and I also wanted to attend the birth of my first child and so a compromise had to be reached.

Natalie's birth was the most precious moment of my life to date. I was dozing in the room next door when the midwife shook my shoulder and said, 'Are you ready to be a dad?' The adrenaline rush was incredible. I was a jangle of nerves as I stood surrounded by doctors and nurses, when out pops this little nugget. I cut the cord, held by consultant gynaecologist John Hughes, and she was just so sweet, so tiny. Her head fitted nicely into my hand and she lay there, her entire body in the crook of my right arm. Natalie cried, I cried, I had never seen anything so beautiful, even if she was covered in purple gloop. The midwife took Natalie away and returned with this glowing little bundle, which she placed in the cot by the side of Gill's bed.

I looked down at her, only 30 minutes old, the original besotted dad, and she was lying there with her hands entwined in the classic interlocking grip. That's my girl. I spent hour upon hour watching her sleep, sniffing her head, luxuriating in the sensation of her tiny paw wrapped tightly round my index finger.

She was also a 24-hour taskmaster what with feeding, burping, nappy-changing, bathing – all of which I adored doing – and at the age of six weeks she flew with us to Japan for the Four Tours event, where she was a monumental hit. My wild-haired, brown-eyed girl caused a sensation wherever she went, especially in restaurants, where she was constantly plucked away by waitresses for a tour of the kitchen staff, which meant we could finish our meals in relative peace and quiet.

Next it was on to Hawaii, from where I was due to return to Japan for the Dunlop Masters. I was physically exhausted. Natalie had a serious stomach-ache and was crying all day and I had not had a full night's sleep for a week. I had actually packed my bags, said my goodbyes and was heading off down the corridor when I thought, 'Sod it, I can't do this.' I called the office in London and told them there was no way I could board another plane. In common parlance, I was knackered. 'Fine, don't worry,' they said, at which point I retired to bed, leaving John Simpson to call the Japanese sponsors in the morning to tell them that I would not be on the plane. Unfortunately John couldn't get hold of them in time and they duly assembled at Tokyo Airport, awaiting the arrival of Faldo-san. Alas, I was still fast asleep in Hawaii. When they checked the passenger list, the Dunlop executives were suitably outraged to discover I had cancelled my ticket and had now booked a return flight to London. The shit hit the fan Japanese style. The office were back on the phone first thing in the morning. I rubbed the sleep from my eyes to hear my agent say, 'Nick, they think you've

deliberately snubbed them. They are insisting you fly to Japan immediately and explain your decision to pull out of the tournament.'
To my way of thinking, that would rather have defeated the purpose
of my not getting on the flight in the first place, but of course
that viewpoint only seemed to fan the flames.

With 90 per cent of the ball market and boasting a billion dollar
golf business, Dunlop are a fiercely proud organisation and the
thought that I had simply given their tournament the two-fingered
salute caused apoplexy in the Tokyo boardroom. As an exercise in
damage limitation, I was advised to write three letters of apology,
a grovelling explanation to the boss, a slightly diluted version to
his number two and a polite note to number three. As it happens,
an even worse insult than not turning up to a business lunch, golf
tournament or other appointment in Japan, is to send an empty
envelope to someone bearing his name. I do not know how it came
to pass, but when the chief of Dunlop in Japan opened his envelope,
he found there was nothing in it: zilch. To the Japanese, as I have
said, this is the most insulting of insults, a sort of 'stick it right up
your jacksie, son' message. A full-blown major diplomatic incident
ensued. The message came back never to show my face in Japan
again, a contract to build a golf course on the outskirts of Tokyo
was immediately cancelled and my character was duly assassinated.
How to win friends and influence people Japanese style. Fortunately,
when I won the British Open the following summer, the head honcho
had to swallow his pride and, though it must have pained him to
do so, issue me with a personal invitation to return to the land of
the rising sun.

After the Japan fiasco, I received a call from John to say he had
arranged an exhibition match for me.

'Oh, that's great,' I said, income of any sort being crucial at the
time. 'Where is it?'

'It's with Christy O'Connor senior.'

'That's very interesting. Strange choice seeing he's been retired for yonks [his last Ryder Cup appearance had been 13 years previously in 1973] but I'm game. Where did you say we were playing?'

Sheepish silence, followed by, 'Northern Ireland.'

'You're kidding. Haven't you been reading the news? There's a new terrorist atrocity there every day . . . Whereabouts exactly in Northern Ireland?'

'South Armagh.'

'But that's bandit country, John.'

'OK then, I'll go if you'll go.'

'Oh, shit.'

So off we went, to be met at Belfast Airport by plain-clothed armed police and driven off at speed to a nice hotel. The journey from airport to hotel was decidedly scary, especially when you saw soldiers coming down the street, cagily crouching from lamp-post to lamp-post as cover against sniper bullets, seemingly oblivious to the crowds of shoppers blithely going about their daily routine. It was a bizarre scene because on the one hand you had the army walking a high-wire while the housewives of South Armagh were acting as though life was perfectly normal.

The exhibition was a resounding success because the Irish love their golf and Christy is a tremendous folk hero. That night we retired to the home of a friend of his who was a priest. We sat in his front room surrounded by our security guards, police from Northern Ireland security and members of the Garda who had come across the border from the Republic in our honour. We were served drinks by a five foot nothing Irish fella, unshaven for about a week and wearing checked trousers, striped shirt, funny patterned waistcoat and a checked jacket, none of which matched.

'An' whit wid ye like, sur?' he enquired.

'I'll have a whisky and ginger ale, please,' I replied.

He disappeared and returned with a tumbler of Bushmills and a small mixer bottle. Not being able to find a bottle opener about his person despite a frantic search of his various pockets, he put the bottle between his teeth and bit it open. I later discovered he was an IRA terrorist who had served his eight years in prison and had been released into the care of our host, the priest, who was to reintroduce him to the civilised world.

John asked the good father where he might buy a bottle of poteen, the illegal Irish spirit.

'Oh, sure, that'll be no problem at all,' he replied, leaving by the back door and returning with a one-litre lemonade bottle filled with the notorious nectar. Our armed police guards were obviously familiar with such transactions because they even smuggled our booty through all the security road blocks on our behalf.

On New Year's Eve 1986, I tried one sip and it brought tears to my eyes. Hard as it was to be optimistic, I had a sneaky feeling 1987 would mark the end of the wilderness years. Maybe the poteen revitalised my system, so that I was ready to start anew.

CHAPTER EIGHT

'CHAMPION GOLFER, NICK FALDO'

January, February, March . . . Australia, Hong Kong, America . . . the months and the tournaments came and went with never a hint of any discernible improvement in my fortunes; in April I returned to the Grenelefe Resort where David Leadbetter and I approached the crusade to turn me into a world-beater with renewed vigour.

'It's not so much knowing why you hit a bad shot,' he explained, as I sent 1,500 balls a day hurtling into the air off the practice ground in an attempt to master a 'controlled fade', 'but why you hit a good one that matters.'

As luck – or bad luck – would have it, my route to the Deposit Guaranty Golf Classic at Hattiesburg, an event for those lost souls who have not been invited to compete in the Masters, took us through Atlanta Airport at the precise moment the plane carrying a number of European players plus the British press contingent touched down. Thus, while they all took a right turn to Augusta, we turned left to catch our connecting flight to the boondocks of

Mississippi. The golfing world was assembling for the Masters, and I was heading for a tumbleweed town in the woods somewhere; I felt grievously humiliated. As Doug Ford observed, 'If you don't get an invitation to the Masters, it's like being out of the world for a whole week.' But it was at Hattiesburg — and how I have come to love the place — that all Lead's teachings over the previous two years suddenly and mysteriously clicked into place. I shot four 67s to finish second behind David Ogrin and, abracadabra!, Nick Faldo was back in business.

I returned to Europe a born-again golfer, recording top-four finishes in both the Madrid and Italian Opens before finally ending my three-year drought in the Spanish Open at Las Brisas, a notoriously difficult course designed by the fiendish mind of Seve Ballesteros. Even Jack Nicklaus, there as cheerleader for his son, Jack Jnr, described the narrow fairways and high-speed greens as 'almost impossible'. Despite Seve's sense of mischief, I shot 72, 71, 71 and 72 for my 14th professional tournament victory, and my first since those far off days of 1984. I was delighted with my performance at Las Brisas but something in the back of my mind kept telling me that I needed just one more win before I could conquer the British Open. Then, out of nowhere, a flash came to me — 'No, I'm alright. I am going to win the Open.'

Muirfield, or The Honourable Company of Edinburgh Golfers to use the official title, is not only one of the most exclusive clubs in the world, it also provides one of the most testing courses on God's earth. As former South African champion Harold Henning said of the rough, 'You need a search warrant to get in, and a wedge and a prayer to get out.' It is often said that whether you would like to become a member or an Open Champion at Muirfield, only the crème de la crème need apply, as a glance down the list of former winners on this links on the outskirts of Edinburgh fully illustrates: Walter Hagen (1929), Henry Cotton (1948), Gary Player (1959), Jack Nicklaus (1966), Lee Trevino (1972), Tom Watson (1980).

My game was honed as never before, to the point that David had told me the week before at Gleneagles that I was swinging the best in my life. On my arrival at Muirfield I had been idly tinkering about with assorted putters and was walking back from the exhibition tent when I looked up and saw the giant championship leaderboard by the clubhouse. I glanced up and it was empty; then I looked up again to see the name FALDO at the very top. It was only in my mind's eye, but I thought, 'Okay, I can handle that.' The positive images kept building up. Prior to the start of the tournament I went off to the Pringle stand to pick out my sweaters for the week. We decided which ones to wear on the Thursday, Friday and Saturday and when the Pringle representative pulled out this yellow intarsia number we all agreed 'Yup, that's the one to win it with on Sunday.' And for once, it wasn't wishful thinking. Needless to say, I've still got that sweater – although keeping my Pringles got me into a serious dispute with the tax man some years later. At one stage I had so many that the tax authorities claimed I could pop out to a car boot sale on a Sunday morning and set up a stand to sell them. I guess I would have needed a pretty heavy disguise to get away with that one. On the Friday I had another image that I would not be leaving the Marine Hotel in nearby North Berwick on the Sunday night; I could 'see' myself sitting at the breakfast table on the Monday morning with the Claret Jug at my elbow, being interviewed live on the BBC 'Breakfast Show'.

Natalie, little angel that she was, was 10 months old by then with a vocabulary of two words – 'get down' – learned from her mum and me every time she poked her nosy little head over the top of her cot in hotel bedrooms around the globe. With the innate timing of a toddler, every morning on the stroke of six o'clock she would awaken us by hollering 'Gitt denn, gitt denn', so yet again I was suffering from serious sleep deprivation.

The adrenaline was flowing, however, and playing with Nick Price and Raymond Floyd, I started the first round with three straight birdies and by the Friday afternoon, despite having to negotiate the worst of the wind and rain, I was lying a handily placed second on 5 under par, one shot behind American Paul Azinger. On the Saturday, wrapped up in my 4-ply cashmere I headed off into the Scottish summer, where Azinger and I shot matching 71s to leave me still one stroke adrift in joint second alongside South African David Frost with the American trio of Tom Watson, Payne Stewart and Craig Stadler breathing down our necks. Alas, as Frost had produced a third round 70, to him went the advantage of part-nering Azinger as the last couple out in the final round, while I was paired with Stadler directly in front, although I was very comfortable with this as Stadler is one of those players who just wants to get out there and get on with it.

Having blown the 1983 Open at Royal Birkdale when I led with five holes to play, I was surprisingly relaxed about the showdown to come. As far as I was concerned, I was a 'new' golfer. Azinger came out like a greyhound from the gate with birdies on the 4th and 5th whereas I covered the outward nine playing strict par golf to fall three behind. It could have been worse, far worse: bunkered on 7, 8 and 10 I got up and down from all three. The one on the 8th was the shot of the week – a sand-wedge into a fierce head-wind some 40 yards from the pin. In all modesty, Gary Player, the King of Sand, would have been hard pressed to better my escape to three feet.

Par, par, par, par – by which time Azinger had bogeyed the 10th and 11th to lead by just one – walking down the 14th, everything became a blur; I could no longer hear the encouraging voices of the gallery, I was no longer aware of my surroundings, I was cocooned in a little world of my own. I could see my shoes and each footstep, but beyond that, nothing. In modern parlance, I was 'in the zone' and I can still remember saying to myself, 'One great shot's going to win it, and one bad shot's going to lose it.' Par, par, par, then the 17th, shrouded in a pea-soup mist, represented my last genuine chance of a crucial birdie; playing a good 50 yards further than its official distance of 550 yards, I had to make a decision as to whether I could clear the cross bunkers in two. In the conditions I chose to lay up, leaving me with a full 5-iron to the green and two putts for par.

The 18th at Muirfield is one of the most challenging closing holes in championship golf, especially so with a capricious crosswind blowing in off the Firth of Forth. At that stage the leaderboard read: Azinger -6, Faldo -5, Davis -4 (the Australian having returned a 69, remarkable in the conditions).

I played an immaculate 3-wood controlled fade from the tee and, to the unique sound of the grandstands cheering you hitting the fairway, it landed between the famous bunkers, leaving me a shot of 186 yards to the pin. But what shot to play? A half 4-iron or a full 5-iron? I chose the latter. Suddenly, I was operating in slow motion – I . . . stood . . . over . . . the . . . ball . . . and . . . smashed . . . a . . . 5-iron . . . at . . . the . . . flag. I can hear the sound of the ball even now as it disappeared into the clouds, accompanied by the drawn-out cries of the crowds like a 45rpm single being played at 33rpm. The 4-iron proved to be the club, however, because the ball landed on the gentle upslope to the green and stopped dead 40 feet short of the hole.

With the adrenaline pumping, I knocked my first putt pin high but five feet off the intended line – so much so that a cricket umpire would have signalled a wide. While waiting to take what I hoped would be my final putt, I glanced up at the leaderboard and saw Davis had finished on 4 under and I suddenly realised that, even though I was still a shot behind, if I didn't hole the putt I would end up tied for the lead. For some reason, at that moment on the 18th green, with Azinger still out on the course, I just knew something was going to happen. But I had to make the putt if it was going to be the moment of my boyhood dreams – in my mind a putt to win the British Open. I read it right-edge, and addressed the ball. As I took the putter away ever so smoothly a little 'Yes' went through my mind. The ball dropped into the middle of the hole and my shoulders slumped as I physically felt the adrenaline course out of my body.

I signed my card and joined Gill and Natalie in the R & A tent to watch Azinger play the 17th and 18th on television but I couldn't do it. I sat between two TVs with my head in my hands. Natalie was climbing all over the TV, pushing all sorts of buttons, as I tried desperately to calm myself in case it should come down to a play-off despite what I'd felt on the 18th. When Azinger took a bogey six at the 17th to join me on 5 under, I went to the top of the leaderboard by virtue of having finished my round. Azinger replicated my drive, but he dragged his 4-iron approach into a greenside bunker and splashed out to 15 feet from a horrible downslope. The words of Peter Alliss on the BBC filled the tent: 'How the next fifteen seconds are going to change one of these young men's lives.' Azinger's putt pulled up three inches short and an almighty groan reverberated from the crowd. Suddenly I was the 1987 Open Champion. I burst into tears and all I could manage to mumble was, 'I've finally done it . . . I've finally done it . . . I'm the Open Champion . . .' David Begg, the chief press officer whom I had known for years, came into the tent and, although he was also in tears, he kindly gave me his best hankie to dry my eyes.

Azinger, Davis and I lined up in front of the clubhouse windows to await those immortal words from Michael Bonallack, a long-time friend and secretary of the R & A, who announced, 'Champion golfer of the year – Nick Faldo.' Apart from cuddling Natalie for the very first time, I had never held anything quite so precious in my life as the Open trophy. As you stand there, luxuriating in the roars of the galleries, you read all the other names engraved on the old Claret Jug and, if you are a first-time winner as I was, you cannot help but wonder, 'Does my name truly belong there?'

There followed the traditional round of television, radio and newspaper interviews, after which the Family Faldo – Gill, Natalie,

Mum and Dad and me — were allowed to begin a serious round of celebrations back at the Marine Hotel. My caddie Andy Prodger, however, did not join us — would you believe it, his mum was expecting the plumber round on the Monday morning to have her boiler fixed and he wanted to be there (now that's a son for you) — but he did succeed in snaffling the 18th pin, which has now become an Open tradition. I do not know what The Honourable Company of Edinburgh Golfers thought of our effrontery, but I'm glad to say I now have three such mementoes among my souvenirs (plus three from the Masters).

Just as I had slept with my red, wooden fire-engine within my line of sight when it became my prized possession all those years earlier, so I laid my head down that night with the Open trophy on the bedside table. I awoke the next morning to see Natalie in her cot on one side of the room bellowing, 'Gitt denn! Gitt denn!' and the Claret Jug on the other. Nick Faldo, proud dad and Champion Golfer of the Year — life simply does not taste much sweeter than that.

The round of celebratory parties continued apace at home in Wentworth where a constant stream of friends and relatives came to gaze upon one of the most precious prizes in sport. Practically every minute of every day for a month afterwards I thought to myself 'Open Champion . . . Open Champion . . .'

It had been a long-haul journey — I had been a professional golfer for 12 years whereas Tiger Woods became a phenomenon in his teens — but golf tends to be a sport in which you have to serve your apprenticeship before reaping the rewards of your endeavours. Perhaps that is why golfers tend to be much more rounded as human beings than some other sportsmen. To use soccer as an example, as soon as they become famous a lot of footballers cannot handle it. Can you name a golfer who has lost the plot? At worst, a few might have a tipple too much, but the megastars and superstars have always kept their feet on the ground.

Three days after my victory at Muirfield, Gill and I were invited to compete in a charity foursomes event at Birkdale where we stepped on to the first tee to hear the announcement, 'Mr and Mrs Open Champion'. After the drama of the Open, it was the perfect light-hearted antidote. Not being a golfer, Gill was permitted to throw the ball out of the bunkers, inspiring one member of the gallery to comment, 'It's golf, captain, but not as we know it.'

It was pleasing to be in demand again – even the Japanese seemed delighted to see me when I made my return to the Dunlop event – and recognition came from the most unexpected of quarters. Practising for the Kapalua Invitation tournament, I was idly working my way through a bucket of balls when this sexy, gravelly American voice wafted across the range – 'British Open Champion – Nick Faldo.' I turned round and thus began my lasting friendship with rock star Huey Lewis, as keen a golfer as he is a fisherman.

Huey came to London that November to play a concert and, as his visit coincided with Thanksgiving, we had a round of golf at Wentworth before returning to the house where Gill had prepared a traditional turkey lunch. It was the first time I had ever seen Gill wearing full make-up at lunchtime, not in her husband's honour I have to say, but because Huey Lewis was coming round.

Years later, when I was world number one, I was staying with Huey at his ranch in Montana when, as usual, I ran out of cash. We drove to a local bank where they asked for identification which, again as usual, I was not carrying. I jokingly said, 'Do you want to see my swing, or will the "boat race" do?' Deeply unimpressed by my swing and not understanding my rhyming slang, the bank teller grudgingly allowed me 50 bucks provided Huey vouched for my good character. I might have been world number one and a big shot around Wentworth way, but in Montana I was a nobody, which is a wonderful thing at times. Huey loved the whole thing.

Curiously, although the Americans speak a form of English, I also came across the language barrier on that trip during dinner at

Huey's ranch. Having been out fishin' all day, Huey and a dozen or so of us returned home laden down with a vast menu of offerings. Advising me to avoid the duck because it was still on the immature side, I asked his housekeeper for salmon. When she duly plonked a plateful of bloodied duck in front of me, I apologised and explained I had asked for salmon.

'Well, yooah sheeit outta lawck, boy.'

'I beg your pardon?'

'Ah sayd, yooah sheeit outta lawck, boy.'

As a working-class lad brought up by the iron-hand of my mother to mind my Ps and Qs at the table, I was somewhat taken aback by this display of rudeness, and casually mentioned the incident to Huey lest his housekeeper should upset a more sensitive soul than I. With a puzzled look, he replied, 'Well, what's wrong with that?' Then it dawned on him that 'yooah sheeit outta lawck' is Montana-speak for 'I am most terribly sorry, sir, but that particular dish has proved unexpectedly popular and the chef, alas, has had to remove it from the menu'.

The new Open Champion had no difficulty understanding a female spectator at Birkdale where I partnered Jimmy Tarbuck, who was having a nightmare round, against future Walker Cup captain Peter McEvoy and former England cricket skipper Ted Dexter in front of a high-spirited gallery who had clearly been supping well in the hospitality tent. On the 14th green, as I was crouching down to study the line of a 12-foot putt, a mini-skirted damsel shouted out: 'Oooooh, Nicky, baby, oooooh, you're the man to get it in the hole . . .'

'Excuse me, quiet please,' I said, mock seriously. 'This is a very important putt.' And I bent down again.

'Oooooah, ooooooah, Nicky, baby, put it in the hole, pleeease.'

Red with embarrassment at her suggestive remarks, I finally struck my putt, it ringed the hole like a roulette ball on speed and hung on the lip.

'Ooooooh! I think I've just had an orgasm!' she shouted.

Quick as a flash, Tarbie surveyed his 4-foot putt, looked over at my gorgeous admirer and quipped, 'Hey, love, if I hole this putt, I'll have one as well.' I will forever be in Tarbie's debt for that one.

Rather more serious, but equally orgasmic as it transpired, was the 1987 Ryder Cup at Muirfield Village, Columbus, Ohio, a course that bears no resemblance whatsoever to its illustrious namesake in Scotland. Designed by Jack Nicklaus, there are 70 bunkers, but water comes into play on 9 holes and, under championship conditions, the greens are faster than an ice-hockey rink. With Tony Jacklin again serving as non-playing captain we arrived in style aboard Concorde; coming in to land, the captain spoke over the intercom to complain, 'Frightfully unaccommodating, these Americans. They won't give us permission to stage a fly-past so I'm afraid we're going to land . . . five hundred feet and counting . . . four hundred . . . three hundred . . . Hold on, they've changed their minds so it's after-burners on and full-thrust!' We did not know it, but down below the Ohio State Band had just launched into 'Three Cheers for the Red, White and Blue' and Jack Nicklaus was just stepping forward to greet us when we went up, up and away again. With the engines roaring at full welly, we soared into the sky at which point the captain's voice came again.

'You won't believe it, but now they want us to fly over Columbus. Shall we find the golf course?'

'Yeaaah!' we chorused.

'There's a course down there on the left,' he announced, banking like crazy. 'Is that the one?'

'Nooooo!'

'There's another on the right . . .' banking steeply again.

'Nooooo!'

Seve Ballesteros, who has never been the happiest of frequent flyers, had endured enough. 'OK. Eeet eees now time to land. Thees eees no yo-yo.'

The captain landed us as gently as a 9-iron settling on the green and, from that instant on, we scored points off the Americans, and not just because we had arrived as holders. We came down the steps, up strode Jack with his hand extended to Tony, and his other hand went round our skipper's back. Seeing the look in Jack's eyes, Tony adopted his 'Del Boy' mode.

'Yup, one hundred per cent cashmere, Jack, feel the quality. Nice bit of *schmutter*, eh? If your team's interested, I can offer you a good deal. Anyway, how are the greens this week?' Slightly taken aback, Jack responded, 'Well Tony, we're going to triple cut and roll them, then double cut and roll them.'

'Yeah,' came back Tony, quick as a flash, 'and then I bet you're going to dust them.'

Having felt like a semi-detached member of the team at The Belfry two years earlier, now, as the recently crowned Open Champion, it was immensely pleasurable to feel I might have some proper part to play this time. When Tony offered me the chance of partnering Ian Woosnam in the fourballs and foursomes, I leapt at the opportunity. As soon as the cavalcade of Cadillacs deposited us at Muirfield Village, Woosie and I headed straight out on to the course to play nine holes of foursomes and discuss tactics.

Off the fairway, you could not find two more diverse personalities but on it our styles of play dovetailed perfectly and we beat Lanny Wadkins and Larry Mize by two holes in morning foursomes, then Hal Sutton and David Pohl 2 and 1 in the afternoon fourballs as Europe ended the first day with a promising 6–2 advantage. In the clubhouse Woosie, ever the serious party animal, proceeded to sink a couple of beers followed by half-a-dozen glasses of red wine with dinner. Although I am strictly a one beer and one glass of wine man, I had no fears on Woosie's behalf. As I used to say to him, 'As long as you've got the mix right, I ain't worried, partner.'

We also had the mix right on the other side of the ropes where the 2,000 strong European 'Barmy Army', despite being outnumbered by ten to one, reduced the American spectators to silence with their enthusiastic, but entirely sporting, support. 'We might as well be playing in Britain,' complained Hal Sutton as the singing and chanting reached a crescendo. Woosie and I hammed it up in the nicest possible way by always ensuring we were the last couple on to the green where we would greet the latest roar with an extra-appreciative wave.

All of this did not rest easily with the American television networks; flushed with our early successes, we assembled round the screen for the first day's one-hour highlights package to discover that not only had the programme been slashed to 10 minutes, but that the only matches deemed worthy of inclusion were America's two victories. Europe's six points were studiously ignored.

There was also skulduggery afoot; before the second day's play, the Americans were equipped with detailed information regarding not only the exact areas where the greens had been watered but also the amount of water used, which represents a huge advantage when assessing where to land the ball. Fortunately, we had a spy in the camp. Howard Clark overheard what was supposedly a secret conversation and was able to furnish us with all the gen such as, 'Thirteenth watered heavily up to the ridge, then rock hard on the upper tier.'

The Americans also tried to counter our supporters. We assembled on the Saturday morning to discover Muirfield Village had been transformed into the capital of the United States – 20,000 Stars and Stripes had mysteriously sprouted all over the course and, even less pleasing to the eye, the wives of the US PGA officials had been dragged kicking and screaming from the beauty parlour to be dolled up like senior-citizen cheerleaders, resplendent in more rhinestones than Dolly Parton. Having no idea who these ladies were, Woosie took one look at them on the first tee and enquired, 'Who the hell are those old birds?'

With half the population of Columbus lined up along the course chanting, 'USA! USA! USA!' we consolidated our lead. Woosie and

I maintained our unbeaten record with a half against Hal Sutton and Larry Mize, after clawing our way back from four down, before hitting sublime form against the American top pairing of Curtis Strange and Tom Kite, birdieing the opening first six holes and winning 5 and 4. In the Ryder Cup, it is always nice to finish off a day's action with a moment of inspiration and this was supplied by Bernhard Langer, playing in the last match with Sandy Lyle, protecting a narrow one-hole lead over Lanny Wadkins and Larry Nelson. With both teams and thousands upon thousands of spectators gathered around the 18th green as the sun went down, Wadkins produced a superb approach to one yard, sending the Americans into another frenzied round of 'USA! USA! USA!' Completely unfazed, Langer unleashed a 5-iron which came to rest inside Wadkins's ball. 'Eur-ope! Eur-ope! Eur-ope!' erupted our supporters and we trooped off to celebrate with the scoreboard reading USA 5½, Europe 10½ and the last day's singles to come. It was a spine-tingling moment but one played out with the utmost sportsmanship, which made it all the more memorable.

The singles are tough because you tend to be so involved in your own match it is all but impossible to remain in touch with what is happening on the other sections of the course. By this stage I was simply running out of steam. After four intense matches the tension had got to me. This is a phenomenon that often seems to occur on the Saturday afternoon or Sunday for players who have been out there for all the other games. It is very difficult to maintain your stamina. I performed miserably against Mark Calcavecchia, bogeying the first hole and never mastering the speed of the lightning-quick greens. I came to the 18th one down, with both of us facing greenside bunker shots. Calcavecchia made his four leaving me an eight-footer to halve the match – exactly the type of putt I had been sinking with my eyes closed all year. On this occasion, it lipped the hole and stayed out. As the Americans gradually whittled down our overall lead, enter another hero in the shape of

Eamonn Darcy, involved in an epic struggle against Ben Crenshaw who had snapped his putter in anger and still holed everything with a 3-iron. Eamonn eventually secured a one-hole victory with a putt on the last that he hit so hard, it would have finished six feet past if it had not dropped into the hole – unbelievable!

We gradually nudged our way towards the all-important $14\frac{1}{2}$ points total and I was sitting with Tony Jacklin when over the walkie-talkie came news that Seve Ballesteros was about to beat Curtis Strange on the 17th. We tore down the 18th fairway to the 17th green, which was jam-packed with spectators, and as I forced my way through the crowd, I put the spikes of my shoe straight through the back of some guy's shirt as he sat on the ground. 'Sorry, fella,' I said, but I didn't have time to send him to the pro shop to buy a replacement on my account. I hope he has come to regard his shredded shirt as some sort of souvenir of the '87 Ryder Cup.

It was a lovely moment for Seve because the American newspapers had been giving him such a hard time during the build-up to the contest, suggesting he was out of touch, had no idea where the ball was going, was playing like a hacker etc., etc. Then we heard Peter Alliss's dulcet tones announcing with exquisite timing something along the lines of, 'They've been saying Seve's not good enough. They've been saying Seve's lost it. They've been saying Seve's finished . . . and here we have Severiano Ballesteros with a two-foot putt to win the Ryder Cup.' No one can celebrate such moments quite like Seve, and he danced round the 17th green exclaiming 'Up your kilt!' or the Spanish equivalent.

If we had imagined that nothing would top winning at The Belfry two years earlier, we were wrong. To retain the Ryder Cup by triumphing on American soil for the first time in the 58-year history of the contest was a feeling like no other. Tony insisted each and every player make his way to the beer tent where all 2,000 European fans had assembled and were calling our names. Supporters and players danced, sang and generally made merry – I even danced on a table –

as the Americans slunk away to lick their wounds. Whether it was the beer or the sense of jubilation, armed with a penknife the entire European team reassembled in the car park where we unscrewed the number plates from the courtesy Cadillacs – they read 'Ryder Cup '87'.

What a fantastic week. I relished the team atmosphere, all of us eating together, drinking together, partying together. The Americans were 12 individuals, even when playing fourballs or foursomes. I understand that Jack Nicklaus, the first US captain to suffer defeat on American soil, gave them such a bollocking, he reduced one or two of them to tears. That is when the Ryder Cup became serious.

Our return to Heathrow was no less emotional; it was like the 1960s when The Beatles used to come back from an American tour. In fact the police, commented 'There's more here than for Madonna.' There were banners, there was cheering, singing, we were greeted like heroes. The undoubted hero, of course, was Seve who, more than anyone, had embraced the European flag. The British and Irish had been reared on the great contests of the past, while Seve was relatively new to it all. His dislike of the Americans, who had never granted him the respect he deserved, undoubtedly helped create the modern Ryder Cup. I can still remember his victory speech in the press tent after winning the Westchester Classic: 'I was very lucky. At the eighteenth hole I hit my drive three hundred and ten yards . . . very lucky . . . next I hit big with a three-iron, high cut twelve feet from the hole, very lucky shot . . . then I hit my putt way out to the right, it swings back and drops straight in hole . . . very lucky to hole that putt and make an eagle.' That was Seve's uniquely mischievous way of dealing with our American cousins.

The season ended with another sweet victory on 'foreign' soil when I joined forces with fellow Englishmen Howard Clark and Gordon J. Brand to defeat Scotland in the final of the Dunhill Cup at St Andrews. Perhaps it is simply because I have won all three of my Open Championships north of the border, but the Scots have always been tremendously supportive of me except, I hasten to add, when I am representing the Auld Enemy.

Perhaps the clans were still feeling a mite aggrieved over the conclusion of our semi-final victory against Ireland when I refused to complete the 18th hole of my match with Des Smyth for the simple reason that I could not see the pin through the fog (or 'haar' as it is known in Scotland). I have photographic evidence to prove that from where I was standing, green, clubhouse and the neighbouring buildings of St Andrews were lost in a cloak of mist, but because this haar swirled over the fairway to a height of about 15 feet, the spectators up in the grandstands could see me perfectly from their viewpoint. 'C'mon, Faldo, get on with it, you wanker,' summed up the general opinion of the crowd.

I refused to get on with it, however, and the announcement that play had been suspended until the following morning was greeted with a crescendo of booing. Although I had every sympathy with the crowd, who of course wanted to see the semi-final played out to a conclusion, if I couldn't see the pin I simply couldn't play.

Into the New Year and Sandy Lyle, the big fella, usurped me yet again by becoming the first Briton to win the Masters. In the form of his life, Sandy arrived at Augusta as the leading money-winner on the US Tour with $607,478 in the bank, following his successful defence of the Greater Greensboro Open title. I had won a paltry $43,320 by comparison. The disparity in our fortunes continued in the Masters where I finished 8 over par on 296 for a share of 30th place, while Sandy secured the green jacket with a 7-iron bunker shot on the 18th that has entered golf's hall of fame. Desperate as I was to become the world number one, I could not even consider myself the British number one when Sandy had now won two Majors against my solitary success at Muirfield.

I had a 'nice' surprise on arrival at the 1988 US Open at Brookline, Boston, when the Americans took to belittling my Open victory at Paul Azinger's expense. 'How can anyone shoot eighteen straight

pars and call himself a champion? A mechanical robot more like
. . .' was the general opinion. Hale Irwin came to my defence by
simply stating, 'I would love to be a mechanical robot on the course
– and by the way, what was Ben Hogan?' Perhaps as a result of such
press comments I was fired up as never before at Brookline. As a
course, Brookline is one of the most challenging on the US Open
rota. As Ben Crenshaw noted, 'It's a throwback to the past because
it challenges your entire game; you have to go through the bag there,
be able to hit every club and every shot. It's a very special place.'

At the halfway stage, Sandy Lyle and I spearheaded the European
challenge on 3 under par, four strokes behind Scott Simpson, but
in the third round, on a day when play was interrupted for over an
hour by the mother of all lightning storms, everything changed
dramatically. By the time night had fallen, Curtis Strange was the
new leader on 7 under par, one stroke in front of Simpson, Bob
Gilder and me.

I was paired with Strange for the final round and our head-to-
head tussle for the title, alas, turned into a mini-Ryder Cup as the
crowd, fuelled by beer, grew increasingly partisan – which is why,
no doubt, someone had the bright idea of staging the 1999 contest,
forever remembered as the Battle of Brookline, in this same bois-
terous part of New England. By the time we strode up the 17th
with Strange still one shot ahead, the course resembled a Republican
Party Convention such was the number of Stars and Stripes and
the raucous chants of 'USA! USA! USA!' Maybe it was the weight
of expectancy but Strange three-putted the 17th to allow me to
draw level. The 18th was a circus. With the stewards unable to
control the galleries, people were swarming all around us as I hit a
4-iron into the sun on to the apron of the green about 25 feet
from the hole. Strange then found a greenside bunker with his
second shot and made very easy work of a high-pressure bunker
shot to within a foot; even so, I now had a tricky, but eminently
holeable, putt to win the 87th US Open.

I read the line of the putt as the right edge but my caddie, Andy Prodger, insisted it was two inches right and I bowed to his customary mastery of the greens. After the crowd had taken an eternity to settle, I struck it perfectly, but it defied Andy by staying two inches right and so Strange and I retired to bed to prepare for the following morning's 18 hole play-off. (Curiously, without having previously discussed the matter, neither Gill nor I had packed our suitcases that morning. Our play-off, it seemed, had been preordained.)

Coming back for the play-off the next day I found it extremely lacking in atmosphere and I'm afraid my game matched the surroundings. As at Muirfield, I played beautifully from tee to green – I missed only four fairways out of 72 during the four rounds proper – but could not persuade a putt to drop, while Strange holed out from all manner of outrageous distances, a 75–71 defeat representing a poor reward for my efforts.

As a measure of compensation, only six days later I won the French Open in Chantilly. At the last, thinking that an eagle might tie me for the lead, I hit a 3-wood to around 20 feet that ranks with the best shots I have ever stuck. I made the putt and as things turned out it ended up being good enough to win outright. Consequently, I was in reasonably confident mood by the time of the 1988 Open at Royal Lytham. Tony Jacklin, still buoyant after the events at Muirfield Village the previous autumn, raised American hackles by predicting, 'I simply can't see beyond a European victory. I'm biased, but I don't think the Americans are as good as us now.' Jacklin's optimism appeared well-founded given a European challenge which included Sandy Lyle, Seve Ballesteros, Bernhard Langer, Ian Woosnam, Jose-Maria Olazabal, not to mention the defending champion, Nick Faldo, who was busily trying to play down his possible influence on events. Secretly, I felt something was missing, that indefinable feeling I had experienced at Muirfield where from day one I felt destiny's arm around my shoulders.

I began promisingly enough, reaching 3 under par after 16 holes, only to find two bunkers on the 17th. I eventually limped away with a double-bogey six, followed by another bogey on the 18th for a solid, if disappointing, opening round of 71. Playing with Seve and Nick Price on the last day I was in the hunt until the 7th where I three-putted and handed the championship over to a two-horse race between them. At the end my 5 under par total of 279 was good enough for third place behind Price, and Seve, British Open Champion for the third time, who in my view played one of the greatest rounds of his life in true swashbuckling style. The tournament concluded on the Monday after a wash-out on the previous day when the Welwyn Garden City members had driven north in a bus to watch me do battle. One headline the next day proclaimed 'Blown to Brits', which I thought entirely unjustified seeing as I had played well. It was just that Seve had played fantastically well. I actually telephoned the newspaper involved to make the point that finishing third in the Open was no mean achievement, after which they took great delight next day in calling me 'whingeing Faldo'. You can't win sometimes, can you?

Second in the US Open and third in the British, I then finished fifth in the US PGA Championship at Oak Tree, Oklahoma, after sharing the first-round lead with Paul Azinger. Four strokes behind eventual champion Jeff Sluman of the US after 11 holes on the final day, I missed four short putts on the final seven holes and told the waiting newspapermen, 'This putter will not be flying home beside me.'

At the inaugural Volvo Masters at Valderrama towards the end of the year I made a supreme effort to finish off on a high by travelling to Spain with the family a full week before the event. On arrival I set out upon true Faldo-style commitment and was given a big boost by Tony Jacklin, who told me at dinner on the Monday evening at his house that no one would be able to touch me after this amount of preparation. He was right and my victory rounded off what had proved to be a great year. Two victories in Europe, eight runners-up spots, including the US Open and second in the Order of Merit behind Ballesteros. Perhaps most pleasing of all in golfing terms was my increasing belief in my ability to control my shots, which I was sure would stand me in good stead for the year ahead.

Topping the whole year off, I was awarded the MBE – not bad for a kid from a Welwyn Garden City council house – following which I was summoned back to Buckingham Palace for a private lunch with the Queen which, the butler informed me, was the first time this had been done for 25 years. I felt very honoured indeed. There had been a major panic in the house that morning, so 'major' I have no recollection of the reasons for the ensuing madcap dash to the Palace, where I arrived tie-less and jacket-less. I had to struggle into my clothes under the jaundiced gaze of the butler. 'One does not normally do this, sir . . .'

There were a few of us present, drawn from all walks of life. We had been led to an ante-room to be served champagne when I heard a scratching noise on the wooden floor outside and six corgis crashed in followed by Her Majesty the Queen. At lunch, I sat beside the governor of Holloway women's prison.

'And what do you do?' she enquired.

'I'm a golfer.'

'Oh, really, are you any good?'

If you are going to be brought back down to earth I guess there is no better place than Buckingham Palace.

CHAPTER NINE

MASTERING THE MASTERS

Something special occurred on 17 March when my son, Matthew, was born in Windsor. Like Natalie before him, the birth was induced, so that I could be there and then travel to America with sufficient time to prepare for the Masters. Matthew's arrival was another unforgettable experience. The instant I spotted the crown of his head appearing with the familiar Faldo circle of hair, I proclaimed, 'It's a boy!' Even quicker off the mark was Natalie, after Matthew had been brought home. Presented with a window covered in what were clearly her sticky hand prints and asked to explain, Natalie immediately offered up Mattmoo as the culprit.

Not that my preparations for the Masters filled me with great confidence, for week in, week out, I played well without stringing four good rounds together. Thus, when I found myself alongside Jack Nicklaus on the putting green at Augusta and he paused to ask me how things were going, I responded:

'Bit frustrated Jack. Things just aren't happening. I'm playing good golf, but I don't know whether to make things happen or simply let them happen.'

In the Family Faldo, this kind of admission is the equivalent of opening your heart to a stranger, but I was desperate to hear some words of wisdom or encouragement from the Golden Bear.

'I know just what you mean,' said Jack, ambling away.

'Jack, Jack,' I felt like shouting to his retreating back. 'I need a better answer than that. That was your cue to provide an inspirational word of guidance.'

No club in the world treats its former champions with more dignity and I was determined to join the Masters roll of honour, which included not only Sandy Lyle and Seve Ballesteros, but Ben Hogan and Sam Snead, Arnold Palmer and Gary Player, Jack Nicklaus and Tom Watson.

Created by Bobby Jones as the most private of clubs for him and his cronies to enjoy a mint julep on the clubhouse verandah, Augusta is one of the holy cathedrals of golf. The flowers are always in full bloom come Masters week, the sky is invariably cloudless and even the water hazards are dyed a perfect blue to make the television pictures even more alluring.

With a restricted field, usually including a dozen amateurs, on paper it should be the easiest of the four Majors. But the intense pressure that accompanies every shot, allied to greens that commentator Gary McCord once described as 'being so slick they must have been bikini-waxed' (Augusta did not request his presence the next day), ensures the Masters is seldom won by anyone outside the game's élite.

Lee Trevino is probably the finest player never to win the Masters and, at the age of 46, he inspired brief hopes of a sentimental victory in 1989 when he took the first-round lead with a faultless 5 under par-67. After all my travails, I was highly delighted to end the first day in second place one stroke behind. Did I say Augusta was invariably blessed with cloudless skies? Friday dawned wet, windy and bearing more resemblance to Georgia, eastern Europe, than Georgia, USA. After 27 holes, however, I was three strokes clear of the field only to cover the back nine in a disappointing 39 and drop back into a share of the lead with Trevino at 3 under, two strokes ahead of a posse of players including Seve Ballesteros, Ben Crenshaw and Scott Hoch.

If anything, the weather deteriorated on the Saturday and I began the third round in suitably gloomy style with a double-bogey six on the first hole. I was in trouble yet again on the par-5 second where, although I was on the green in three, I was over 100 feet away and under dire threat of three-putting for the second time in as many holes. How to explain the inexplicable? Travelling, as the American commentator put it, 'through two time zones', the ball sped unerringly into the cup, a possible bogey six had become an improbable birdie four with what is unofficially the longest putt holed at Augusta, and I battled on through the elements.

When fading light brought play to a premature end, I was still on 2 under par and returned to Augusta early on the Sunday morning to complete my third round facing a 60 yard pitch-wedge across the creek to the 13th green; having practised the required pitch-and-run assiduously, I was full of high hopes, especially when I played the shot perfectly to about six feet from the pin. I proceeded to miss the putt and promptly descended into a downward spiral of bogeys resulting in a depressing 77, which I am not ashamed to say left me in tears. I'd played the first 27 in six under and the next 27 in nine over – but that's Augusta. Having led the Masters, I found myself a distant five shots behind the new third-round leader, Ben Crenshaw. But having studied the draw sheet for the final day's play I said to myself, 'This is still a great opportunity Nick. There is absolutely nobody there I fear.'

On the Saturday evening I had taken two English friends who had come over to support me out to dinner at Michael's Restaurant. There we fell into conversation with two women – typical Georgia gals complete with Southern drawl – at the next table, who had been intrigued by our English accents. Baby Doll (and I kid you not) told us that her companion, the fragrant Mary-Lou, was off to New York the following weekend on a shopping expedition.

'An ah'm tellin' you, Mary-Lou, you gotta be *reee-ahl* careful in that Big Apple.'

'Why's that, Baby Doll?'

''Cos in New York, Mary-Lou, they've got guys who go down on guys.'

'Hmmm, whaddya call those type of guys, Baby Doll?'

'They're called homo*say*xuals, Mary-Lou. An' you gotta be even more careful, 'cos in New York, they've got gals who go down on gals.'

'And what are they called, Baby Doll?'

'They're called *lez*bayans, Mary-Lou.'

'Baby Doll, in New York, don't they have guys who go down on gals?'

'Yes they do, Mary-Lou.'

'So what are they called, Baby Doll?'

'Hmmmm. Precious, Mary-Lou, precious.'

On the Sunday morning, despite my miracle putt on the second hole the day before, I had been less than satisfied with my putting and selected a new putter for the fourth round that afternoon, which I believed would give me more ooomph on the greens. I departed from the first tee with a 'good luck' from Larry Mize ringing in my ears but I couldn't help but think, 'Fat chance,' whereupon I proceeded to knock in a 30-foot birdie putt on the first, a 12 footer at the second, one from 15 feet at the fourth, and from 20 feet at the seventh as the pace-setting Crenshaw, five ahead of me at the 11th, began to wilt under the pressure of leading the Masters. On the 16th I made the first of possibly the three best putts of my life when I holed out for an astonishing birdie two with the ball approximately 15 feet from the hole, but – and this is no exaggeration – with ten feet of break to take into account, meaning I was putting almost sideways. Then, walking from the green to the 17th tee, I spied, waiting for me at the side of the green, the unforgettable Baby Doll.

'Well, hi there, precious,' she winked.

Her timing was perfect as it helped relieve the pressure and, bless her, Baby Doll has been there every year since then, now in the company of her most recent husband, greeting me with a slight nod and a silently mouthed, 'Hi there, precious.'

On the 17th, with visibility poor due to the grey clouds and light rain, I faced a very difficult approach to the green, pulling the shot to the left of the pin and leaving a vicious left-to-right 35-foot putt up and over the infamous ridge, which would have been daunting on the practice green let alone the 71st hole of the Masters. I switched into autopilot and hit the putt a tad hard I confess, so when it disappeared into the hole – you might remember if you have seen it on TV – I had a look of total disbelief on my face. Did I describe it as being a 'tad hard'? Scott Hoch later informed me, 'If you'd missed that putt, you'd have finished fourth.' But I didn't miss.

On the 18th, I was sheltering under my umbrella preparing to hit a 4-iron to the green when a raindrop came through my brolly right on to the thumb of my glove. Now, the thumb is the anchor of my grip and suddenly I was standing there with a digit feeling like slippery blotting-paper. I knew I couldn't risk changing gloves on the 18th, so I gripped tighter than I had ever gripped it in my life and produced a perfect shot, which even gave me a birdie opportunity. The spectators around the 18th green were in strangely talkative mood – maybe because they did not relish the idea of yet another European victory at their beloved Augusta – not overtly noisy, just as though everyone was chatting to his or her neighbour. 'Oh, just get on with it, Nick,' I thought to myself and struck a great putt that turned right across the face of the hole. For a split second I thought I might have just done enough to win it but the ball pulled up just short.

I signed my card and was whisked away by security into the Bobby Jones Cabin by the 10th tee, where once again I was thrown into the caldron of mixed emotions as I awaited the outcome played out live on TV.

One by one, however, the chief contenders slid out of the reckoning. On the par-3 16th, Ballesteros pulled his tee-shot into the pond, then Reid's challenge died in a watery grave on the 15th. With Hoch having bogeyed the 17th, he and a rejuvenated Crenshaw both needed birdie 3s on the last for outright victory, or a 4 to join me in a play-off. And then there was one – Crenshaw bogeyed the last, Hoch made his par and I prepared myself for a sudden-death shoot-out against an opponent notorious for his outspokenness. For once, Nick Faldo was the goodie.

The ideal tee shot on the 10th at Augusta – the first extra hole – is a strong draw round the corner, on to the down slope to give you full advantage. I, however, skied my tee shot to a less than ideal position on a severe down slope, leaving me 200 yards or more from the flag. I struck a towering 4-iron only a few feet off line, which caught the right-hand edge of a greenside bunker and rolled agonisingly into the sand, whereas Hoch hit a good approach to within 25 feet. I remember the next few minutes in a series of freeze-frames: I splashed out to 15 feet; Hoch struck his first putt two feet past the hole and instead of putting out – and I guarantee he would have holed it – he decided to mark his ball; I missed my first putt and tapped in for a bogey five, leaving Hoch standing over a 24 inch tiddler for the title; I stood by watching helplessly, insisting to myself, 'I can still win this – it doesn't look bloody good, but I can still do it.' As the world now knows, Hoch missed his putt which was a left to right, but given the circumstances, it was very difficult just to dolly it into the hole. It lipped out and rolled a good five feet past and I certainly did not want Hoch to miss his return, for no one likes to win a Major courtesy of an opponent's mistakes. Full credit to Hoch – who must have been feeling that someone had tripped the trapdoor beneath his feet – for holing out with an air of serenity, and so we moved on to the 11th. I was unaware of it at the time but on television there appeared a caption informing viewers I had bogeyed the hole in all four rounds.

I drove down the right side of the fairway and had to take a drop after landing in casual water. It was now past seven o'clock and from where I was I could hardly see the flag 200 yards away, hidden as it was in a shroud of dark mist. With the wind and drizzle blowing in from the right I unleashed a 3-iron into the gloom, which was arguably the best long iron I'd ever hit. Not that I knew that at the time. All I saw was it turning slightly left and then I lost sight of it. I only discovered the result when I was sixty yards from the green – it was that gloomy, although for TV viewers it probably didn't look too bad.

Hoch had missed the green way off to the right and had pitched on to eight feet, leaving me a long putt to win the 53rd Masters.

'What do you reckon?' I asked Andy Prodger, as I studied the line.

'It's all a blur to me, guv.'

I stood over the putt and the tension in my hands and arms was very evident. 'Just relax those hands,' I said to myself. A week before a touring pro and good friend called Mike Hulbert had simplified my putting to left hand back, right hand through, and so I rehearsed that over in my mind and then hit the sweetest putt of my life. The ball broke as anticipated, hit the hole and my arms went into the air. 'Jesus Christ,' I thought. 'I don't believe it.'

Winning the Masters meant the world to me. Even now, 15 years on, it is difficult to find the words to describe my feelings. If I achieved nothing more in life on the golf course, at the age of 31 I had now won the two greatest championships of all. You dream of such a thing happening one day and when it does, it is all but impossible to comprehend.

A word here about Scott Hoch, who, for years afterwards, would carry the label 'Hoch – it rhymes with choke'. He departed Augusta that night in tears after telling his wife, Sally, 'I feel I've let you down – I've let you down, I've let my parents down, I've let your parents and my friends down. I'm sure as hell glad I don't carry a gun.' Although he has since gone on to become a Ryder Cup regular, I doubt if Scott Hoch has ever fully exorcised the memory of that two-foot putt on the first extra hole. As a wise man once said, 'Defeat is worse than death because you have to live with defeat.'

While Hoch was sliding despondently into his car, I made my way through the throng to Butlers Cabin where, as tradition demands, the 1988 champion, my old mucker Sandy Lyle, was waiting to make the ceremonial presentation of the green jacket.

'Sorry, Nick,' said Sandy, 'it's a bit short in the sleeves.'

'Don't worry about that,' I grinned. 'It's the colour that counts.'

With the Ryder Cup in European hands, the sight of a Scot holding open the green jacket for an Englishman to put on must have been a painful one for Americans.

After the customary appointments with television and newspaper reporters, it was on to the formal champion's dinner in the club-house. John Simpson and I (Gill being back home in the UK, looking after baby Matthew) sat round the table with Augusta chairman Hord Hardin and his wife. I was uncertain about whether I should play Hilton Head the following week as previously arranged or, as the new Masters Champion and father of a newborn son, return to England. John decided to intervene on my behalf. He asked Hardin, 'We've got a bit of a dilemma here. Do you think Nick should stay or go?'

There was a long pause while Hardin digested both his food and the question. 'Well,' he finally drawled, 'I reckon Sandy should stay an' play,' at which point his wife had to give him a nudge and remind him, 'Hord, it's not Sandy, it's Nick. Nick won this year.' Classic Hord Hardin after three large whiskies.

I did go on to play and eventually I returned to Ascot to be greeted on the front doorstep by a giant basket containing two dozen bottles of Moet & Chandon vintage pink champagne and a giant teddy-bear with a card reading: 'Congratulations, Gill and Nick, from Elton John.' My mind immediately went back to my English Amateur Championship victory 14 years earlier in 1975 when my erstwhile girlfriend, Angela, and I used to sit in the pub in Lytham listening to Elton singing 'Don't Let The Sun Go Down On Me' on the jukebox. We subsequently met up when Gill and I went to Elton's concert in London and he invited us out for dinner. Elton had just come out of rehab but insisted on ordering wine for us although he stuck religiously to mineral water. As well as pouring the claret, he poured out his heart to us. As someone who treasured his privacy, it was fascinating for me to hear Elton describe his former bizarre lifestyle. Later that year I invited him to the World Matchplay Championship at Wentworth and advised him to wear something inconspicuous. He turned up in a green and black striped suit which, for Elton, was 'inconspicuous'.

Back in Europe, I won the Volvo PGA Championship, the Dunhill Masters and the Peugeot French Open in successive weeks, although I was disappointed to finish joint 11th in the British Open at Royal Troon, six strokes behind American Mark Calcavecchia.

The Ryder Cup was equally disappointing because with all Europe expecting – make that 'demanding' – an emphatic win at The Belfry, we retained the trophy courtesy of a 14–14 draw when, in fact, we should have triumphed in style. We assembled in strangely lack-lustre mood, the reasons for which I've never really been able to explain. We were desperately seeking inspiration and it duly arrived in a speech by US captain Raymond Floyd. 'I want to introduce you to the twelve greatest golfers in the world,' he began. We returned to the team room chirruping, 'Ooooh, Seve, Open Champion but thirteenth best player in the world . . .'

Floyd's infuriating words acted as the perfect boost and Ian

Woosnam and I picked up where we had left off at Muirfield Village two years earlier, by winning 2½ points from our first three matches. Unfortunately our unbeaten run came to an abrupt halt when we were beaten 2 and 1 by Chip Beck and Paul Azinger in the second day's afternoon fourballs, a match in which the Americans were in inspired mood, covering the 17 holes in something like a combined 13 under par. Even so, Europe went into the singles with an encouraging 9–7 lead. I will never fully understand what went wrong that final afternoon, but after Jose-Maria Canizares beat Ken Green on the 18th to ensure Europe would retain the trophy, the do-or-die spirit we had displayed in previous years mysteriously deserted us. Gordon Brand Jnr, Sam Torrance, Woosie and I were all still out on the course, yet not one of us could secure the priceless half point that would have clinched outright victory. I was as desperate to beat Lanny Wadkins as Woosie was to defeat Curtis Strange, but unfortunately we both found water on the 18th. As I have said before, after a long, hard week, come the Sunday it is my belief that we were simply running on empty.

The World Matchplay Championship was looming but before that I had a date with a young lad terminally ill with leukaemia who had written to 'Make a Wish' asking if it would be possible to play a round of golf with me. He was a fantastic kid, even if he thought tearing around in the buggy was far more fun than actually hitting golf shots. Spotting a police car driving by through Wentworth Estate, I flagged it down and said, 'Could you do me a favour? Just nip down the fairway and arrest that kid for driving like a hooligan.' Throwing themselves into the joke with a vengeance, they went racing down the 16th fairway with flashing lights and blaring klaxon to the lad's total amazement.

It was over lunch after our round that the boy's plight really hit home when, with his mouth full of painful ulcers, he had to swallow 66 pills to keep himself alive; it was one of those moments in life that gives you a bit of a jolt. On the Saturday night before my

36-hole final against Woosie, I decided I would donate half of my prize money to a children's leukaemia charity. 'Oh, to hell with it,' I thought. 'I've never been one to do things by halves, I'll give all of it away.' Two down with seven to play, I proceeded to shoot six under for those last few holes, eagling the last to win by one. Keeping my promise I handed over the first prize of £100,000, by far the largest cheque in European golf. After that, I launched the Faldo Charitable Trust, a gesture some then cruelly dismissed as a public relations exercise. By now, you would think I would have become inured to such criticism. Then again, the carpers were never privileged to meet that unforgettable lad and his bottle of 66 pills.

Later that year, during a conversation with my secretary, she casually mentioned it was the little fella's birthday and, on a whim, I jumped on a plane to Liverpool and turned up unannounced on his front doorstep. 'Happy birthday,' I said when he opened the door and the look of surprise – and, I am proud to say, delight – on his face made the whole journey worthwhile. His parents sent out for a Chinese takeaway by way of a birthday celebration and I passed the evening squatting alongside him on the carpet, playing with his toys. Children, bless 'em, come out with such amazing remarks. His sister, who had given him her bone-marrow to prolong his life, was carrying on as small girls do, when up he piped in his wonderful Scouse accent, 'Sisters! Don't they just drive you up the wall, eh?'

Back in London at a film awards ceremony, I met another rock idol of mine, Phil Collins, who had been nominated for his role in *Buster*, the biopic of the Great Train Robber, Buster Edwards, and we got on well. Just to show you how charitable I can be, I even arranged tickets for all the press guys when we were in Chicago as Phil Collins happened to hit town. As a real treat, Phil used to invite me to rehearsals at Bray Studios in Berkshire on occasion; to stand behind the guy while he was playing absolutely blew my mind. (Confession: in my mid 20s, I actually bought a drum-kit, which I would beat the hell out of. Its purpose was therapeutic rather than musical.)

At Christmas time 1989, I acquired two unexpected presents – the BBC Sports Personality of the Year award, and a new caddie, Fanny Sunesson.

CHAPTER TEN

DOUBLE MAJOR

Since time immemorial, caddies have been a breed apart, a law unto themselves. Jack Nicklaus once said of his sometime bag-carrier, Angelo Argea, 'He'd rather go to the beach. I think the only reason Angelo puts up with caddying is because he has to eat. Basically, Angelo has been retired since he was twenty-one.' One of Jack's favourite yarns concerns a practice round at Royal Troon in the company of Tom Weiskopf before the 1973 Open. On one of the par-3s, Weiskopf hit a soaring tee-shot that bounced once and dropped into the cup for a hole-in-one. Arriving on the green, Nicklaus looked over at a laconic twosome, idly sitting on a wall, cloth caps pulled down over their eyes, and enveloped in a private cloud of roll-up cigarette smoke.

'Did you see Mr Weiskopf's shot?' enquired Jack.

'Aye, that we did, son,' came the reply.

'Well, don't you think it was worth a round of applause?'

'Why? He was only practising, wasn't he?'

'Jungle Jim' used to be a well-known figure on the European circuit, partly because of his liberal use of the 'F' word but mostly because he was the oddest-looking bugger ever to bestride a fairway. He had no teeth, and was rumoured to sleep rough in the bushes and generally acquired a reputation as the wild man of the caddies' hut. On one occasion, I was partnering a young rookie who had made the mistake of employing the battle-hardened Jungle Jim and the unnerved kid opened his round with five straight snap-hooks. Jim's comment, 'What did you have for effing breakfast? Effing bananas?' didn't help.

A popular caddie was 'The Prof'. Whenever we played in the Benson & Hedges at York, he would find a cheap room in one of the university halls of residence. He was idly minding his own business over a pint or five in the uni bar one evening when a genteel, professional voice at his side enquired, 'I say, old chap, what are you reading?'

'Greens,' came the reply.

Over in America, Fulton Allem was enduring a miserable round at Hilton Head, dropping shots all over the place and missing a series of short putts. After three-putting the 13th, Fulton snapped the head off his putter and stormed off to the 14th tee where he proceeded to smash the marker before looking round frantically and demanding, 'What else can I break?'

'How about par,' muttered his bag-carrier darkly.

I had first teamed up with Andy Prodger in 1980 at the Italian Open. I had actually contracted another caddie for the tournament but our relationship was abruptly terminated when I arrived on the Tuesday (he had been *in situ* since the Saturday night at a local camp-site) and asked him where the practice ground was. 'Don't ask me,' he replied with a couldn't-care-less shrug. I was about to pull my own trolley when Andy approached to offer his services and we worked together on and off for the next few years. A shy Londoner, Andy was not what you would call loquacious on the golf course. He saw his job as turning up on the first tee at the appointed time, handing me the right club and keeping his mouth firmly shut. At times, these were the perfect credentials, but there were occasions when I could have done with more support and advice and little was forthcoming.

In between, I also employed the peerless Dave McNeilly, an Ulsterman with more than a touch of blarney who is currently on the Tour with Niclas Fasth. I first met Dave, a total eccentric in the nicest possible way, in America in the early 1980s. Although totally different in personality, we seemed to hit it off and I made arrangements to engage him full-time on my return to England for the Dunlop Masters at Lindrick.

'Oh, do you do yardages?' I asked, almost as an afterthought, when I spoke to him on the phone.

'Yes, indeed I do.'

'Do you have a wheel?' I continued, referring to the device caddies use for measuring exact distances.

'. . . eh, no I use public transport.'

Dave, honest soul that he is, was forever getting hold of the wrong end of the stick.

'We'll need to get a video,' I informed him on the practice ground one morning while working on my swing.

'Oh, yeah,' he agreed enthusiastically. 'Have you seen *Jaws 2*?'

With the aid of McNeilly's unique services, I finished runner-up to Bernard Gallacher at Lindrick and the 'dream team' was up and running. When the mood was upon him, there was no craftier craftsman, but he didn't always get it correct, as at the 1983 British Open. While out watching play he spied Arnold Palmer on the 18th green, making a 12 foot putt. Lo and behold, later on I had the self same putt to move right into contention. Normally forbidden from reading the greens, suddenly Dave was at my shoulder.

'What are you thinking?' he asked.

Surprised, I replied 'It goes left to right.'

'No, no, no it's right to left,' insisted Dave. 'Palmer had the same putt and I saw it.'

Heeding his advice I set up to putt just as a spectator bellowed 'Come on bulldog Nicky.' I resettled and promptly missed the putt, left to right of course, earning Dave one of my death-look stares. Headlines the next morning read 'Big Mouth Puts Faldo Off' and on seeing that, Dave dropped the paper next to me with the words 'Right headline . . . wrong person.'

Back in Europe for the Martini International, I stood on the first tee waiting to begin my final round and up bowled McNeilly — who had been mysteriously absent from the practice ground that Sunday morning — with a black eye and cuts all over his face. I did not say anything at the time, but after winning the tournament, I drew Dave to one side to ask what the hell had happened. He told me — and McNeilly had the knack of telling the biggest porkies with a completely straight face — he had picked up 'some bird' in the pub and was enjoying a romp in the bedroom when her husband came home unexpectedly and Dave had to make good his escape by jumping out of the window stark naked.

As with any of McNeilly's tales, I cannot vouch for the veracity of this narrative because he had a habit of making things up to suit the circumstances. Like the time I supposedly noticed the sole of his shoe was flapping and ordered him to buy a new pair of trainers. 'I know, guv,' goes the Friends of McNeilly version, 'but I haven't got enough money.' Reaching into my wallet, I reputedly produce a fat wad of notes held together by a thick rubber band. I remove the rubber band and hand it to Dave saying, 'Here, try that.' Totally fictitious, but Dave has been dining out on the 'rubber band incident' for years and the press have regurgitated it every time they wish to have a swipe at me. I later discovered this incident was first enacted in a Charlie Chaplin movie, which predates me by a few decades or so.

After my adventures and misadventures with various caddies, Fanny Sunesson emerged as the ultimate class act.

Although we had won five tournaments in tandem, including the Masters, I felt something was missing from my working relationship with Andy Prodger. As I've said, Andy was a very, very quiet lad and although his club selection and yardages were invariably spot-on, our communication was lacking, and consequently I reached the conclusion we simply did not 'click' and resolved to find a new companion.

I had seen Fanny around the circuit and had always been impressed by the level of professionalism she brought to her craft. Born and raised in Karlhamn on the outskirts of Gothenburg, she was first introduced to golf by her parents. She had a handicap of 2 and briefly considered becoming a professional on the women's tour before embarking on a full-time career as a caddie.

Whether it was because she was a woman in a predominantly male world, she was not always treated with the respect she deserved and, after assisting Jose Rivero in qualifying for the 1987 Ryder Cup at Muirfield Village, was understandably miffed when the Spaniard opted to employ his brother in her stead during the contest itself. Fanny was then employed by Howard Clark, who is a changeable character, easygoing one day, an unforgiving taskmaster the next.

Walking back with Fanny from an Annie Lennox concert in Melbourne shortly before Christmas, I popped the question: 'Do you fancy working for me next year?' to which she replied, 'Let's talk about it.' She might have been expecting to be offered a two-month trial, but I handed her a typewritten sheet saying, 'Right, here's my schedule for the coming year.' Her chin dropped at that point.

We arranged to meet up at David Leadbetter's new training camp at Lake Nona, Florida, in early January and she reported for work on the first morning, typically bright-eyed and bushy-tailed.

'I appreciate it's not part of your normal duties, Fanny,' I greeted her, 'but I've forgotten to pack a toothbrush. Do you think you could nip back to the hotel and buy me a new one?' Ever-attentive to detail, Fanny arrived back brandishing a choice of two toothbrushes.

'I do not know whether you wanted the hard bristols or the soft bristols,' she explained in that melodic Swedish singsong accent.

I gestured with cupped hands in front of my chest, 'No Fanny, *these* are Bristols.'

Quick as a flash, Fanny shot back, 'Well, you don't want the soft ones then.' In that instant, I knew I had found my ideal golf partner.

Fanny was thrown straight in at the deep end because three months later we arrived at Augusta where I was to defend my Masters title on a course she had never seen except on television, which, strangely enough, was to our mutual benefit. During our practice rounds, I would explain hole by hole exactly how I wanted to play it. This really cemented my game plan and helped take my mind off defending the title.

Fanny was the first woman pro-caddie to work the Masters, which brought its own difficulties – in those days there were no doors on the WCs in the caddies' locker-room. Neither of us probably realised the impact we were making and over the years we have become an instantly recognisable pair; even from 500 yards away, when we come over the crest of a hill, everyone immediately knows it's Faldo and his caddie and it takes a very special personality to deal with that constant level of attention.

Like me, Fanny is a dedicated professional, painstakingly providing me with yardages – at least nine holes, preferably 18 in her eyes – even before I embark upon my first practice round. Fanny does not merely walk the course, she undertakes a route-march complete with Walkman blasting out whatever music has attracted her interest at the time. Now, as someone who cannot even add up a set of simple figures if there is any noise to distract me, just how

Fanny can have Jon Bon Jovi screaming into her ear while totting up yardages with uncanny accuracy is a phenomenon that never fails to amaze me.

Before every tournament, no matter how important or relatively minor, we have to go through the same rigmarole each and every week.

Fanny: 'What time do you think we should start practice?'

Me: 'Oh, how about nine o'clock.' Just for a change.

Fanny: 'And where should we meet?'

Me: 'Hmmm, let's say the putting green.' What a surprise.

We have had that conversation every week for the past 10 years but occasionally, just occasionally, I throw Fanny a curve ball. Before the 1994 Open at Turnberry, we flew into Prestwick Airport from Ireland in a small private plane.

'What time do you think it gets light in Scotland?' demanded Fanny.

'About five o'clock in the morning at this time of the year.'

'Well, I'll whizz out and do the first nine before breakfast.'

'OK, but come back after nine and we'll have breakfast together.'

'Does the ninth hole come back to the clubhouse?'

As it happens, the 9th at Turnberry, one of the most famous holes in golf, is not at the end of the world, but you can definitely see the end of the world from the tee. I could not look Fanny in the eye when I said, 'Yeah, of course it does. No problem at all.'

Off she galloped into the morning mist, pony-tail bobbing, Abba or something echoing in her ears until she reached the 9th green where she popped her head up out of her little shell and espied an old-fashioned Scottish greenkeeper.

'And where is the clubhouse, please?' asked Fanny, peering around the wilderness.

'Ach, you stupid wee lassie,' replied the worthy, pointing at the hotel away on the distant horizon. 'It's yon great big thing you can see high up on top of the hill.'

Some time later, I was merrily scoffing my kippers and toast when the doors to the magnificent dining room of the Turnberry Hotel were thrust back on their hinges and in marched a bedraggled Fanny. Past the regiment of waiters and waitresses, through the maze of linen-draped tables, beneath the chandeliers, she bore down on me still trailing the wheelie measuring device in her wake.

'Morning Fanny.'

'You bastard! Do you know it is one thousand eight hundred and seventy-three yards from the ninth pin to your bloody breakfast plate?'

For a seriously intelligent woman, she has an uncanny knack of coming out with what I term 'Fannyisms'. Playing in the Dunhill Classic in Bali, we discovered the ball was flying far further than normal.

'Do you think it's the altitude?' she asked innocently. Looking out over a million square miles or so of Indian Ocean, I kept my expression deadpan.

'It's a little known fact, Fanny, that in this part of the world the sea is at five thousand feet.'

With barely a pause, she blithely continued, 'I'm going surfing out there tomorrow.'

'Surfing, Fanny? Those are the most shark-infested waters in the world.'

Trusting soul that she is, Fanny related our conversation to the hotel manager the next day and came back in high dudgeon.

'I spoke to the manager and he assured me there are no sharks out there.'

'Fanny,' I replied patiently, 'if he had said otherwise it would kill tourism at a stroke.'

'Hmmm, you're right.'

So another day went by without Fanny taking to the ocean on her beloved surfboard. On day three she broached the subject again.

'I have now discovered there's not millions of sharks out there, there's only a few.'

'It only takes one, Fanny, it only takes one.'

I kept her out of the water for three days before she discovered it was perfectly safe.

Quite inadvertently, Fanny has got her own back on me many times along the way, such as the occasion in Japan where, after putting out on the 9th in a practice round, I asked her to go and buy me a sandwich while I made my way to the 10th tee. She returned empty-handed.

'So where's my sandwich?'

Her eyes as big as saucers — a sure giveaway whenever Fanny has something to hide — she stammered, 'Eh . . . ah . . . er . . . they were sold out.'

'Oh, fine, OK,' I said, playing along with this charade. 'What do you reckon it is from here? A seven-iron?'

'Yeah, a seven-iron.'

I dipped into my golf bag to retrieve the desired club and put my hand into what felt like a bowl of cold custard: withdrawing said hand, I found it dripping in mayonnaise. Apparently, Fanny had bought my sandwich but as she reached for her yardage notes, she had dropped my lunch into the bag, coating my golf club grips in a gooey mess. With previous caddies I might well have exploded but seeing Fanny standing there looking at me guiltily, I had to laugh.

The Swedes possess an unfounded reputation for having had a sense of humour bypass, but not Fanny. Like many athletes, I have a habit of chomping a banana on the course for instant energy. At the Johnnie Walker Classic in Singapore one year, we were barely off the 1st tee when Fanny enquired, 'Do you want a banana?'

'No, I'm fine just now, thanks.' On to the 2nd hole.

'Don't you want a banana yet, Nick?'

'No, I'm all right for the time being.' At the 3rd, 4th, 5th, 6th, 7th and 8th, Fanny asked the same question until, finally, on the 9th hole, to keep her quiet if nothing else, I said, 'OK, give me a ruddy banana.' Reaching into the bag, she produced a banana the size of a miniature yellow submarine. 'Thank God,' she said, 'I've been carting that thing about long enough.'

Fanny is the first caddie with whom I have formed a genuine friendship, and that is vitally important when you are spending 12 hours a day in someone's company. As a woman, she has the gentle touch, which meant a lot to me when I was going through my divorce and she was always there to lend a sympathetic ear. Dave McNeilly was a great character but his eccentricity could be distracting whereas my relationship with Fanny is more like a partnership.

Like any number of partnerships, we later undertook a trial separation. We are two distinct personalities on and off the course, and there are times, therefore, when we become very close, then very distant. Sometimes all the little things Fanny does work perfectly, other times they annoy the hell out of me, but looking back over our 10 years together, our disagreements have been absolutely minimal. It has been a pleasure to have her in my corner.

With Fanny making her Major debut at my side at the 1990 Masters, I arrived in Augusta to the realisation that, 'Hey, I'm not here just to play, I'm here to defend,' a feat previously achieved by Jack Nicklaus only, in 1965 and 1966. It was a vision I carried with me during practice and all through the tournament.

My defence began in unspectacular manner with opening rounds of 71 and 72. Far more spectacular – for both good and bad reasons – was the form of little-known American Mike Donald whose first round of 64 was followed by an 82 and a swift car ride to the airport departures lounge. A third-round 66 left me in third place, three shots behind tournament leader Ray Floyd, at the age of 47 bidding to become the oldest champion in Masters history, and one stroke adrift of the unheralded John Huston.

Unlike 1989 when I began my final-round charge by holing a 30-foot putt for a birdie, I took a humbling double-bogey six at the first, after finding a fairway bunker with an errant drive, then hitting my 6-iron well short of the green, followed by a poor chip and three putts. Walking down the second fairway, I felt I had to respond immediately to get back on track, and almost through sheer willpower I made a four for my birdie, making up somewhat for my disaster at the first. It was only the second hole but I really felt it was the turning point of the round and I continued the momentum by adding further birdies on the 7th and 9th to move back into contention. However, my hopes of adding a second green jacket to my wardrobe appeared to have disintegrated on the par-3 12th where my tee-shot buried itself in the back left bunker. There were two possibilities. Quite simply, a career bunker shot or total disaster with the water staring me in the face across the green. The only way I can describe the awkwardness of the shot is that if you are ten yards from the pin with a normal bunker shot you can plop the ball up to three yards short of the hole and it will roll the remaining distance. On Augusta greens, however, you have to some-how get the ball out the bunker only three yards because it will roll the remaining seven. Fortunately I played the deftest little thump, the ball came out and scuttled across the green, stopping on the fringe, only inches from heading down the slope to watery disaster. I duly holed the putt for a very welcome three and kept my title hopes alive.

'Thank God I don't have to play that hole every week,' I commented to Jack Nicklaus, my playing partner, as we made our way to the 13th tee.

'Heck, I've been playing that hole for thirty-five years,' replied the Great One.

'That's older than me, Jack,' I exclaimed, to which there was no response from a stone-faced Nicklaus.

Even so, with six holes remaining I was still trailing Floyd by four shots; a birdie four on the par-5 13th reduced the deficit to three, I clawed back a further stroke on the par-5 15th with another priceless birdie and moved within one of the leader with a two on the par-3 16th. I ended with par at 17 and 18 – 18 with a very slippery two putts from the back edge for a round of 69 – and when Ray three-putted the 17th and made a brave four at the last, making easy work from the right-hand bunker, we were tied for the Masters. I was facing a second successive sudden-death play-off for the title.

Unlike my previous year's opponent Scott Hoch, in Raymond Floyd I faced an opponent who lived life as hard as he partied, and here was the most enthusiastic party animal on the US Tour.

'Raymond has done it all,' Lanny Wadkins said of his long-time Ryder Cup colleague. 'If Ray was playing in Miami on a Sunday and he heard there was a party that night in Dallas, he'd think nothing of chartering a plane.' That may explain why, when asked to describe the colour of his eyes in a magazine questionnaire, Floyd replied, deadpan, 'They're usually red.' As a golfer, however, Floyd was but one rung below the very best of all time. A past winner of the US Open, US PGA Championship and the Masters, I could not depend upon him wilting in the heat of head-to-head battle as Hoch had done a year previously.

Just as in '89, I hit a slight pop-up tee-shot off the 10th tee and found myself in the same greenside bunker in two. I played a great bunker shot out to five feet, leaving Ray with a chance to take the title. But he left his putt short. I holed my five footer to take the play-off to the next hole. I obviously can't be sure, but it felt to me as though Ray was surprised at my up and down, which in itself gave me a great lift. Two thoughts were running through my mind on the brisk walk to the 11th tee; one, I had been given a print by the artist depicting the scene of my triumph 12 months earlier and golf has an uncanny knack of exacting revenge, and two, I could not bear the thought of losing and being required to hand over my jacket. After hitting our tee-shots, Floyd made a comfort stop in a rest room near the 11th tee and, consequently, had to hurry to catch up. Perhaps it was the memory of that missed opportunity on the 10th, or maybe he was in a rush having kept me waiting for a few minutes, but he pulled his second shot left and as I watched the ball arch through the air I thought, 'Bloody hell. What's he done.' The ball entered the lake with a sickening plop and it was advantage me but I still had to make a great shot to make my four as Ray certainly wasn't going to just give me the title. I played a half 8-iron to a little less than 20 feet below the hole. Ray was in the drop zone and after his chip on to the green I mentally gave him his putt for a five, meaning I had two putts to win. Knowing that, I played the perfect lag putt four inches past the hole and on tapping in, I raised my arms in triumph in a mirror image of 1989.

As I was being driven back to Butlers Creek to receive my second green jacket, more than anything I wanted to receive it from Jack Nicklaus (I most certainly could not present it to myself), as I have said the only other player to have enjoyed back-to-back victories at Augusta. Although I quietly gave voice to this notion, my suggestion was ignored and Hord Hardin stepped forward to make the official presentation. They already knew my measurements, so at least the jacket fitted this time.

Even at the moment of your greatest triumphs, your heart goes out to those such as Scott Hoch and Ray Floyd, who came so close only to have victory denied them. 'You can't imagine how much winning the Masters would have meant to me,' explained Floyd later, blinking back the tears. 'To be the oldest . . . to win another Major at forty-seven . . . nothing has ever affected me like this. At this stage in my life, how many chances are you going to have? If you're a kid of twenty-five and you lose a big one, you still believe in yourself, you still believe you're going to have a lot more chances. You don't feel that way at the age of forty-seven.'

Ever the reluctant dancer, I had rashly promised Fanny a twirl round the floor should I be in the position of hosting a celebration party, a promise I felt duty bound to honour until I saw Fanny dance, that is. The only way to describe her idiosyncratic gyrations is to imagine someone with chewing gum on the soles of their shoes trying to escape from a bin-liner, after someone had put itching powder down their neck. Consequently, I still owe Fanny that victory dance.

Dishearteningly, the *Daily Mirror* used my latest triumph to engage in an act of character assassination. I quote: 'Nicholas Alexander Faldo began life in a small council house in Welwyn Garden City. Sadly, it remains quite big enough to stage the party when he goes home in his green jacket. The friends of Faldo are few . . .'. I considered that piece of 'journalism' insulting in the extreme. Contrary to the evidence of the *Mirror*, I do not walk this world alone and friendless. Sure, I have made mistakes and committed errors of judgement along life's way, but who among us has not?

Precisely why Fleet Street should choose to find a negative slant to a British victory remains a mystery. I can still see the look of utter bewilderment on Paul Lawrie's face as he recounted the tale of the morning after his Open victory at Carnoustie in 1999 when a hack accosted his young son through the hedge of their garden in Aberdeen. The reporter's opening gambit was not, 'You must be very proud of your dad' but 'Have you ever seen Daddy hitting Mummy?' I was as speechless as Paul.

Hale Irwin subsequently gained a measure of revenge for the Golden Oldies at the US Open at Medinha where I felt I made a spirited challenge even though I was totally out of sorts with my driver and played most of the week with a 1-iron off the tee. I was right there until the 72nd hole, where I lipped out from 20 feet, which would have earned me a place in the following day's 18-hole play-off between the 45-year-old Irwin and Mike Donald. My four-round total of 281 (72, 72, 68, 69) left me a single stroke behind in third place. I was so upset I locked myself away in the clubhouse loo and as I sat there feeling morose, I vowed, 'I am going to win the British Open.' The fact Irwin went on to win the title with a lacklustre 74 only heightened my sense of 'what if?'.

Then it was on to the home of golf – where else but St Andrews? – for the 119th Open Golf Championship, a tournament stretching back into the mists of time, to 1860 to be precise when Willie Park won the inaugural event at Prestwick. The Open is always the most precious date on the golfing calendar, especially so when it is staged at St Andrews in front of the most knowledgeable crowds in the world – the Scots.

The Open was to begin in distasteful manner when, under a banner headline proclaiming 'Faldo Is A Plonker!' Scott Hoch, who barely knows me from Adam, took it upon himself to discuss not only my supposed lack of popularity, but also the fact that I had given him so little credit in the aftermath of our Masters play-off, all of 15 months previously.

Honestly, a boy could become paranoid, but I did not take Hoch's criticisms to heart because his outspokenness has not endeared him to his fellow professionals on the US Tour. I preferred to think his words were either exaggerated or taken out of context. All credit to Hoch, a couple of years later, (by this time I had won four Majors), he approached me to apologise and say that, in his opinion, I was now right up there with the great champions, which was a very gracious thing to say given our history.

It is nice to know the Royal & Ancient has a sense of humour. It was inevitable, I suppose, that the opening two rounds found me paired with, you guessed it, Scott Hoch – not that Hoch was foremost in my mind. From the moment I arrived in the auld grey toun, I knew that, given the form I was in, I had but one man to beat – Greg Norman. At the Monday night dinner for past champions, which is only held at St Andrews, the first person I bumped into outside the clubhouse was the Great White Shark. We shook hands and I stared him in the eyes like Muhammad Ali used to do in the middle of the ring, as if to say, 'Let's shake hands and come out fighting.' *Ding! Ding! Round One.* Only, unlike Greg, I didn't quite come out fighting. After my opening iron shot I headed down the fairway thinking about the pin position just a few paces over the Swilken Burn. My second shot should really have been a 9-iron, but taking Lead's advice from earlier in the day about the risks of spinning back into the water I decided on a small 8 until the wind suddenly picked up and I ended up going for a 7-iron . . . which I proceeded to hit 30 yards past the pin. 'Relax NF and play,' I told myself. 'You are going to win this.' What I'd give right now for that level of self-belief.

Greg had a blistering round that day and when I found myself on the 18th tee I glanced up at the leaderboard to see him leading on six under, with me on three under. I genuinely thought I could shoot level 67s that week at St Andrews and if I was going to start the way I intended to continue, I knew I had to do something a bit special. I unleashed a 300-yard drive down the fairway, leaving me 40 yards to the pin and visualising the shot that would give me my goal of a 67, I played an 8-iron chip-and-run which broke right off the first bank, then left off the next bank, ran through the Valley of Sin, along the ridge to the left and into the hole for an eagle two. Even Scott Hoch was moved to mutter 'Great shot'.

Day two dawned with the great sweep of sand in St Andrews Bay bathed in glorious July sunshine. As the early starters began their second rounds in idyllic conditions, a number of players were playing leapfrog at the top of the leaderboard – Payne Stewart, Ian Woosnam, Jamie Spence, Mike Reid, Craig Parry, Nick Price – but by far the biggest galleries were awaiting the arrival of Norman and Faldo on the first tee. Playing three groups ahead of me, Norman compiled a second successive 66 while I birdied the 2nd, 5th, 6th, 7th, 10th, 15th and 16th for a near-flawless 65 and a share of the lead with the Australian on 12 under par.

Going head-to-head with Norman on the Saturday afternoon, and four strokes clear of Payne Stewart and Craig Parry in joint third place, there was the whiff of cordite in the air; our duel had become a gunfight and I have never felt so determined to be the last man standing. I came out all guns blazing. This was a defining moment to stamp my authority on the day's play. I birdied the par-4 first, holing a 16-footer, which Greg failed to match despite being two feet nearer the hole. First blood to me on a day I expected we would be exchanging blows. Deciding to abandon the tactics that had served him so well during the first 36 holes, Norman pulled his driver from the bag for the first time in the tournament on the 2nd, finding the rough and then three-putting for a bogey five to slip two shots behind.

Three ahead at the turn, I moved even further in front on the 11th with a birdie three courtesy of a 15-foot downhill putt. Continuing to forsake his previous tactics, Greg began attacking St Andrews with abandon. My strategy was to play short or long of the bunkers but never, ever level with them, as I had been advised all those years ago, whereas Greg began finding sand. My round finished on a high when I recovered well after bogeying the 17th with a wedge on the last to two feet for a birdie. Greg, one of golf's true gentlemen, was as gracious as ever as he trudged off the 18th green after an error-strewn round of 76 to face an undoubted grilling from the media. When the smoke had cleared, my 67 granted me a sturdy five-shot lead over his fellow Aussie, Ian Baker-Finch, plus Payne Stewart and Ian Woosnam.

It was a curious situation in which to find myself. With such a commanding lead, I knew there would be a temptation to adopt a defensive approach, which was against my natural instincts, but there was certainly no need to take unnecessary risks and squander shots; plus there was the intense pressure of leading the world's greatest golf tournament, even by a fistful of strokes, on the world's most famous golf course. There are Opens and then there are St Andrews Opens.

The hours before the final round of a Major when you are in contention are like no other. I rose early at the Old Course Hotel, played with the kids, ate a hearty breakfast, wandered across to the practice ground with David Leadbetter, then returned to my room for a power nap before a lunch of Scottish salmon. It is important at such times to establish a routine to keep your mind on the matter in hand, to remain positive, to visualise great shots, to rehearse the round to come. Eventually, I made my way through the hordes of well-wishers towards the first tee for the appointed time of my date with destiny – 2.48 p.m. As the past winner of three Majors and with that five-shot cushion, I felt relatively relaxed until I paused to exchange a few words with American Doug Sanders, the man who had famously surrendered the Open at St Andrews almost 20 years earlier to the day in 1970, when he missed a 'gimme' on the 18th and lost the subsequent play-off against Jack Nicklaus. Would fate be as ruthlessly cruel to me?

Facing another wicked pin position on the 1st – just over the burn on the front left corner – I had a perfect yardage for my 60 degree wedge and struck an aggressive shot to two feet and knocked in the putt for a birdie three, which not only increased my advantage to six but sent a message to my pursuers saying, 'Hey, I'm all right, guys.' St Andrews seldom lets you pass by without subjecting you to the odd little drama and Payne Stewart emerged as my chief threat, closing to within two shots at one stage. Walking down the 14th and in her first Open, Fanny, who has a habit of going off at the most unlikely of tangents, suddenly asked, 'Are you thinking about getting a dog?' Of course, I laughed. She was trying to keep me calm.

I was very keen to get my cushion back and a 5-iron to eight feet on the 15th gave me a birdie and left me four shots ahead with three holes to play. If it was not quite time to stop and smell the flowers, at least I could bask in the acclaim of those wonderful St Andrews crowds as I stood on the 17th tee with my advantage restored. God must have been in seriously mischievous mood the day he designed the legendary Road Hole, the most devilish 461 yard stretch of turf on the planet. Here I quote from the *World Atlas of Golf Courses*:

Having driven blind over the hotel wall, the golfer faces a long second shot to the green – the most feared in golf. Raised on a plateau four feet above the fairway, it is long from left to right, narrow from front to back and set diagonally to the fairway. At the front left-centre of the green is the small steep-sided abyss called the Road Hole Bunker, biting into the green so severely there are putting surfaces on either side of it. In the 1978 Open, Tommy Nakajima of Japan hit two lovely shots to the front of the green, putted into the Road Hole Bunker, took five shots to escape, and eventually scored 10.

Sounds daunting? Oh, the Road Hole offers even more fun and games. Should you overhit your approach to the green, there is every possibility your ball will run straight through the green, down the slope, over a rough pathway and come to rest slap bang up against a stone wall. Tom Watson lost the 1984 Open to Seve Ballesteros in this exact manner, inspiring him to comment, 'The reason the Road Hole is the toughest par four in golf is because it's really a par-five.'

That is precisely how I chose to play it. You have to guard against taking a double-bogey or more, so you can either approach it from way right or even hit it far left on to the 18th tee if the pin is placed behind the Road Hole bunker. On this occasion, I chose to leave my second shot deliberately short and took three putts from 50 feet for a five. My past Major wins had all been head down, full concentration. This time I could enjoy it. I drove off the 18th and as I crossed the Swilken Bridge I deliberately scratched my spikes on the stone, thinking that I wanted to leave my mark next to the scuffs of both Tom Morrises and all the other past St Andrews champions. I also found time to wave to the spectators cramming the balconies of the houses that run alongside, as I soaked up every second. And why not? To stand in the middle of the fairway facing a straightforward wedge to the 18th green at St Andrews, surrounded by the packed grandstands, and gazing towards that magical clubhouse knowing you have won the Open Championship, is surely an experience to be savoured. As we made our way through the crowds who had spilled out from beyond the ropes to encircle the 18th, I said to Fanny, 'Take a good look at this. We may never see anything like this again.'

My rounds of 67, 65, 67 and 71 (18 under par) represented a new Open record, but the statistics were an irrelevance. As the Red Arrows screamed past overhead, I handed the trophy to Fanny to hold while I cuddled Matthew and the look on her face was something to behold; after being in the job just six months, she had 'won' two Majors as a member of Team Faldo. 'It's nice to have my baby back,' I told the cheering crowds as I nodded at the trophy in Fanny's hands.

My thoughts immediately turned to the US PGA Championship at Shoal Creek, Birmingham, Alabama, and the possibility of becoming the first man since Ben Hogan in 1953 to win three Majors in a single year. Looking back to the 1988 US Open when I lost to Curtis Strange in a play-off, my record in the four Majors was: 2nd, 3rd, 4th=, won, 18th=, 11th=, 9th=, won, 3rd=, won. As the newly installed world number one, I was eager to emphasise my authority. If the tournament had been played in Birmingham, England, who knows? But in the ovenblast heat of Birmingham, Alabama, I wearily struggled home in a tie for 19th place, a far-off 13 strokes behind Australian Wayne Grady.

Away from golf, the sporting highlight began with a telephone call from world rally champion Ari Vatanen of Finland.

'Do you have a crash helmet?'

'No-ooo.'

'Do you have a firesuit?'

'No, of course I don't have a firesuit.'

'Oh, that's OK, we're roughly the same size, you can borrow one of mine.'

'Why? Where are we going?'

'Bagshot Army Assault Course, to the tank training ground.'

I reported for duty as commanded. Through the trees, Ari announced his arrival by making his car perform triple doughnuts and what-not, its engine screaming in protest. They strapped me up in the passenger's seat whereupon Ari turned to me and, in his curious singsong Scandinavian accent, explained, 'You are being in charge of the gauges . . . the pressure gauge, the temperature gauge, you are making sure we do not overheat.'

Ari's mission that morning was to break the gear-box because only by wrecking some component of the car do the engineers discover exactly how to make them stronger. I had been expecting a leisurely jaunt through the countryside, but Ari set off like the proverbial bat out of hell, deliberately aiming for every boulder and pot-hole he could find, all the while moving up and down the gears with maniacal abandon. Sure enough, the gauge lights started twink-ling away merrily and a small fire broke out in the engine, meaning we had to trudge back to the paddock.

'How are you enjoying it?' asked one of the mechanics.

'Oh, it's fine. We haven't started going quick yet,' I lied. Ari fixed me with a gleam in his eye.

'There I am, driving at eleven tenths and he is not thinking we are going quick yet . . .'

How I came to regret my merry quip. They strapped me in again and this time the head mechanic leaned through the window, squeezed my shoulder and whispered, 'Good luck, pal.' This time we went off like a NASA space-shot, careering around the course until we arrived at a series of three right-hand corners, all three of which Ari negotiated in one, giant power-slide with the back wheels scrabbling for purchase on the edge of a ditch. Driving blind through bushes, we then came back on to the single-track dirt road with a long downhill straight, which Ari took at 110mph plus. Coming to a small kink in the road, he slid the car sideways and I was looking at the ditch I was about to fly into when Ari grabbed my knee. I turned to look at him and he was sitting there, one hand on the wheel, looking straight into my eyes, not the road, grinning. 'Everything OK?' Honestly, my stomach really did hit the roof.

Ari and I became firm friends after that day together and we subsequently had a great 'boys' day out' when I flew a helicopter to meet him at a tyre-testing session in the Welsh forest on a stretch of track he knew like the back of his hand but which, to me, looked impassable in a tractor never mind in a Mitsubishi. This time Ari was being serious, flying off at full race speed over humps, going airborne into blind bends, all the while trees flashing by the window an inch away. We came over the brow of the next hill straight into the sun at which point, the road went black. Ari feigned panic and shouted, 'Nick, you will have to be helping me here. Is it right or left here . . . quick, quick, left or right . . .' It was another of the great Vatanen wind-ups because as I was still spluttering for words, he casually took the corner as I held my breath.

Sadly, Ari, who was a great believer in family values, later found it hard to sympathise with my domestic situation and I have not seen or heard from him since, which is a great shame because he is such a fantastic guy.

Another driving experience which left its mark — literally — was a sponsorship deal I signed with Jaguar who kindly gave me a Daimler Double Six for my personal use. The morning my gleaming new car arrived, we all piled in — Grandma and Grandpa, Gill, Natalie and Matthew, and me behind the wheel — for one of our famous fishing expeditions. I parked in a field full of horses who, clearly impressed by my new set of luxury wheels, immediately trotted over and began licking the chrome bumpers. We chased them off and departed in search of trout and a suitable spot for our barbecue. On our return, we discovered our four-legged friends had lunched on the bonnet of the car, carving great gouges in the bodywork with their teeth. Very embarrassingly, I had to call Jaguar the next day requesting an insurance claim form.

'What have you done, Faldo?' came the voice down the line.

'Some horses chewed up the car,' I replied.

'Oh, yeah?'

Open Champion, Masters Champion, world number one, and two healthy children. Could 1991 top that? – I doubted it.

CHAPTER ELEVEN

'FROM THE HEART OF . . .'

If success at golf could be measured in money terms alone, then 1991 was memorable for the fact that it marked the season I first banked one million dollars in prize money, but it was the number of Majors I could say I'd won in which I was interested. The money was appreciated of course – I am not a completely misty-eyed romantic – but winning the great championships had become my chief motivation. I was grievously disappointed therefore, to surrender my green jacket, albeit to my Ryder Cup sidekick Ian Woosnam. Having ordered shepherd's pie and sherry trifle for the pre-tournament champion's dinner, Larry Mize, sitting at my side drawled, 'Gollee Nick, ya'll be turning me into some kinda Englishman.' I glanced at him and thought, 'Not with that accent I won't, mate.' My game then proceeded to be as equally stodgy as my choice of dinner with my 6 under par total of 282 earning me a share of 12th place.

I managed no better than joint 16th in the US Open at Hazeltine,

Minneapolis, where Payne Stewart was victorious. Just thinking about Payne Stewart today fills me with great sadness. His untimely death in October 1999 robbed the golfing world of one of the true characters of the Tour. Not only did he dress and speak flamboyantly, he also played flamboyantly. I would class his putt at the 18th in the final round of the US Open in 1999, which he holed out from 15 feet or so to win from Phil Mickelson, as one of the greatest putts of the decade. His composure under such intense pressure was remarkable. I remember noticing that throughout those dramatic few moments he continued to chew his gum at exactly the same pace: what incredible composure. He is greatly missed.

During my time in the US that spring there was one highly notable memory, even if most of my golf was instantly forgetable. I was invited to a White House reception hosted by President George Bush in honour of Margaret Thatcher who was due to receive the Medal of Freedom. I had already visited Number 10 on a couple of occasions so it was nice to renew acquaintance with the Iron Lady at the official dinner. At the risk of becoming a serial name-dropper, I can tell you that I sat with television chat-show host Barbara Walters to my right, Mrs Thatcher to my left and the President directly across the round table. President Bush was the latest in a long line of White House residents who were also passionate golfers and possessed a vast repertoire of yarns involving his predecessors. Did you know, for instance, that when asked why he had given up golf for oil painting, Dwight D. Eisenhower replied, 'Because I take less strokes with a brush.' I was keen to glean some Oval Office secrets from the President but he was far more interested in seeking my opinion about whether he should 'switch to a broom-handled putter'.

I returned to Europe after the US Open for the Carroll's Irish Open. Martin Hardie, a friend in the press tent, warned me that the *Sun* had sent one of their Rottweilers, as they call the news hacks, to file a 'Faldo Is Finished' article. I confess I had not won a tournament since the Johnnie Walker Classic in Hong Kong eight months before, but the previous year I had won two Majors, so I considered this particular journalistic exercise a bit premature. As I understand it, the *Sun* had originally requested the vastly experienced sports writer Frank Clough to pen the desired article and, when he refused to put his name to such nonsense, he was summarily sacked. If that's true, Frank deserves great credit for sticking to his principles.

Anyway, the Rottweiler in question doggedly tailed me everywhere from a distance of about 10 paces, trying to sniff out a suitably controversial angle. The best he could come up with — and if this passes for news I am glad I chose another line of work — was an incident in which a security guard initially refused me entry to the clubhouse when, studying everyone at chest height to inspect their accreditation, he noticed I was not wearing my pass. After a pause of two seconds, he looked up, recognized me and immediately apologised, saying, 'Sorry, Nick, I didn't realise it was you,' and let me enter. That snippet was the fruit of the intrepid reporter's efforts for the whole week; he made no mention of the fact that I went on to win the tournament.

Far more worrying was a threat we received through the post concerning my daughter, Natalie, shortly before the 1991 Open at Royal Birkdale, which the authorities took very seriously indeed. A number of details contained in this vile three-page missive were alarmingly accurate and so, on the advice of the police, we packed Natalie and Matthew off to a secret location with their nanny. I competed in the 120th Open with an armed guard and 24 hour security, complete with a large German Shepherd dog patrolling the grounds of the house we had rented in Southport. Abduction of one's children is an ever-present dread of every so-called celebrity parent. Eventually, of course, you have no alternative but to resume normal life, but the fear of an attack on your loved ones is something that haunts every showbusiness or sporting personality.

With my every thought centred on the children's well-being, I stumbled around Birkdale like a zombie. I offered no challenge whatsoever to new champion Ian Baker-Finch of Australia, lagging behind all the way and ultimately coming home in equal 17th position, one place worse than my finish in the US PGA Championship the following month at Crooked Stick, Indiana. (The tournament was won by the unheralded John Daly.)

I was fast running out of opportunities to salvage something from this relatively humdrum season, and by the time the '91 Ryder Cup at Kiawah Island, South Carolina, hove into view, I was also running out of form at precisely the wrong moment. The Americans have an expression, 'If you don't bring it with you, then you sure as hell ain't gonna find it when you get there', and so it proved. Europe's new captain, Bernard Gallacher, had given some thought to splitting my previously successful partnership with Ian Woosnam, whose form had also faltered since his Masters triumph in April, but eventually decided to stick with the tried and trusted formula. With the benefit of hindsight, that was probably a mistake.

In the past, if Woosie was playing well and I was struggling, or vice versa, the stronger of the two could inspire the other through sheer willpower but, with neither of us living up to our reputations, in the opening-day foursomes we were beaten by one hole by Payne Stewart and Mark Calcavecchia, then annihilated 5 and 3 by Ray Floyd and Fred Couples in the fourballs. The old double act, which had won six points out of eight beginning in 1987, now became Ryder Cup history. Bernard then gave me the choice of partnering either Colin Montgomerie or David Gilford. I asked who was playing the better and when he answered that David was the in-form player, I was happy to join forces with him for the second-day foursomes as Europe sought to reduce the overall deficit of $4\frac{1}{2}$–$3\frac{1}{2}$. Unfortunately David and I were to be of no assistance to the team, suffering a 7 and 6 mauling at the hands of a rampant Mark O'Meara and Paul Azinger. An outpouring of criticism suggested that I had been insufficiently supportive of the rookie

Gilford on his Ryder Cup debut. He was shy and less than talkative and, in retrospect, I daresay I should have offered David more support and a friendly word of advice. But in the cauldron of the Ryder Cup, when you are fighting your own demons on the course as I was, it is difficult to provide your equally despondent partner with a stout shoulder. As the junior member, David was probably expecting me to take the anchor role but I was simply not up to the task – if one of us did find the middle of the fairway, the other missed the green; when one of us chipped to five feet, the other missed the putt. I was so down on myself, what I needed was a Woosie or a Langer to take me under his wing rather than try to assist someone else when my own game was falling apart.

I was also lambasted for failing to support the rest of the team on the Saturday afternoon when, in fact, I had spent five exhausting hours with David Leadbetter on the practice ground and course because I felt I had already let the guys down and did not want to do so again come Sunday's singles.

Although Seve Ballesteros and Jose-Maria Olazabal were the only two players to perform consistently well, the European team was not without fighting spirit and, through defiance more than anything, we started the final day's singles level at 8–8, full of renewed determination. Although I was riddled with self-doubt – I awoke at four o'clock in the morning and passed the rest of the night pacing my bedroom floor, my heart pumping furiously – Bernard Gallacher displayed his faith in me by putting my name at the top of his singles line-up. I was drawn to play Ray Floyd which was a great draw for me as I knew I could beat him in the strong coastal wind. Three up after three, I eventually won by two holes and joined Bernard in the role of cheerleader.

Bernard's decision to send me out first meant a lot to me. I'd been having a terrible time on the golf course throughout the whole year and although I now realise that what you have to do is to let all the negative feelings go if you are to change your form, at the time I was feeling very fragile and frustrated. I didn't understand then that life – and, in the same vein, your playing form – really does come in swings – hence the title of this book. Having ups and downs is totally natural, but of course when life is on a down it is very hard to understand that there will be an up. So Bernard's decision was a real boost. I guess he put his faith in me to provoke a positive reaction because when you have to go out and perform for a team it is different from just playing as an individual, especially after a bad week. With all these feelings going through my head, plus the fact that Floyd wasn't playing so well either and the wind was in my favour, I'm pleased to say I did go out and perform.

As the record shows, ultimately we succumbed 14½–13½ when Bernhard Langer missed a six-footer on the 18th against Hale Irwin, which would have guaranteed our retention of the trophy. Bernhard, of course, was not 'the man who lost the Ryder Cup', his missed putt being no more crucial to the final outcome than the defeats suffered by Woosnam and me on the first morning, and it says everything about his character that he recovered his poise to win the German Masters the following week.

It was an unsatisfactory Ryder Cup in many ways, not least in the 'War on the Shore' attitude of certain members of the US team, still basking in the gung-ho atmosphere of victory over Saddam Hussein's forces in the Gulf War and seething with anger that they had not succeeded in beating Europe since 1983. As a sporting contest, the Ryder Cup surrendered its dignity and unique charm that September when winning became the be and end all of everything. For Bernard Gallacher, his Ryder Cup debut as skipper was nothing if not a baptism of fire.

A decade and more on, my perceived lack of support for David Gilford is still being used as evidence that I am not a team player. In fact I have played 40-odd Ryder Cup matches, and tied the record for foursomes victories, yet I am castigated to this day for that one miserable match. To me, that is baloney. Perhaps my mistake

Ryder Cup, Muirfield Village, 1987

Right: Me and the mighty Woosie.

Below: Sam Torrance and I celebrate winning in America with two thousand of our best buddies.

PHIL SHELDON

DAVE CANNON/GETTY IMAGES

PA

Natalie said: 'You can tell by the look on my face that I hate golf.'

PHIL SHELDON

ASSOCIATED PRESS

Above: Victory at Augusta, 1989. Thanks to the weather, the ceremony was indoors, as Sandy Lyle hands over the green jacket.

Left: The moment of sheer joy: sinking my putt on the 11th during the play-off with Scott Hoch in the 1989 Masters.

PHIL SHELDON

The Masters, Augusta, 1990

Left: Fanny, a Major rookie, in our first Masters together.

Main: The best bunker shot of my life: 12th hole, last round of the Masters and I'm plugged in the back of the trap, playing towards water.

PHIL SHELDON

The Open, St Andrews, 1990

Opposite top to bottom

An eagle chip in to move from 3 under to 5 under at the end of the first day to set the momentum going for the rest of the week.

With the Open secure, the crowd is desperate to get as close to the action as possible.

The Red Arrows fly past while I hold the precious Claret Jug.

Elton John wearing Wentworth green, 1990.

PHIL SHELDON

PETER DAZELEY

'Nothing to do with the swing, Fanny. I just like it when you hold my knees.' David Leadbetter looks on.

A dream come true. Meeting the legendary Ben Hogan at his home club of Shady Oaks in Texas.

Rock star Huey Lewis's replacement caddie, 'Fanny Faldo,' at the Pebble Beach Pro-Am.

lay in not taking David aside after our match, or even six months later, to explain my predicament. The loss of the match was most certainly not his fault. We were an untried and unproven partnership thrown together by circumstances and the chemistry just was not there. So much went wrong – while walking along swinging my club I even contrived to hit Fanny on the chin, at which point she understandably burst into tears. With the benefit of my greater experience and maturity, I know I should have had a quiet word with David while we were out on the course and my failure to do so provided my critics with further evidence of my so-called aloofness. Although it is far too late in the day, I hereby apologise to you, David, even though deep in my heart I am convinced that I would have been unable to help anyone that particular morning.

I reached the heights by a different method when I took helicopter flying lessons during a six-week break while suffering from elbow and wrist injuries. Taking the controls of a flying machine was something for which I had had a notion since my first flight as a passenger. I was using helicopters increasingly frequently, either to make a flight connection or because it was the quickest way home, and I thought that if I knew how the machine worked, at least I could put the thing back on the ground in the event of an emergency. I enrolled for lessons at Fairoaks Aerodrome in Chobham where I was fortunate to have Ken Summers as my tutor; an ex-Navy instructor, he is considered to be one of the very best in the business. Right from the first lesson, he had me performing emergency engine-off landings. This is a real eye-opening, not to mention terrifying experience. You are tootling along quite happily in the clouds and the voice in your ear suddenly commands, 'Engine off,' and you have to glide home. If you perform this manoeuvre properly, the rotor blades keep turning at the right speed and you touch down as softly as a snowflake, but get it marginally wrong and you come down to earth like a brick.

When he was satisfied I had learned, if not wholly mastered, this technique, Ken taught me spiral auto-rotation in which you descend, as you would expect, in a spiral, followed by a backward descent whereby you tip the nose up and come down in reverse. During one session, Ken ordered me to land on a 20-yard square on the ground by spiral auto-rotation, which I negotiated perfectly. 'Very good,' he conceded, taking us back up again. Within the square was another smaller square measuring two feet by two feet, on which Ken, show-off that he is, landed the chopper with absolute precision. I had to have some riposte to that.

'You see that hanger over there?' I asked him, nodding at a building over 300 yards away. 'And do you see the door?' which was open about 10 feet. 'Well, I could hit a one-iron through that from here.' Each of us has our own particular talents.

I continually impress upon my students in the Faldo Series how important it is to find a hobby that completely engrosses them away from golf, something on which to concentrate the mind other than swings and tempo. Flying a helicopter certainly concentrates mine. As in golf, you frequently feel you are operating the controls in ungainly boxing gloves such is your clumsiness, but the first time you can hover rock steady 10 feet off the ground without the instructor whistling 'A Life on the Ocean Waves' in your ear is a heady milestone.

So, too, after about 12 hours of tuition, was my first solo flight. I very much doubt if Charles Lindbergh felt as nervous as I did when I looked through the cockpit window to see Ken Summers standing on the tarmac giving me the thumbs up and clearance for take-off. It took all my strength to raise my own thumb in acknowledgement because it was a seriously scary moment. I completed my first solo jaunt around the airfield with my eyes glued to the dials. I did not dare to look out, so concerned was I that all the little hands on the gauges were pointing exactly where they should be.

Having managed to take off and land without any mishap, by the time I reached for the skies again I was Jack the Lad, roaming above the fields singing the James Bond theme tune, '*Dan-dula-dan-dan. Dan-dula-dan.*' At 700 feet, however, I entered a tiny bit of cloud that gave the chopper a real jolt, causing 'Biggles' to utter an expletive probably completely unknown to the boyhood hero.

Day two of my solo flying career and suddenly through the earphones crackled the voice of the control tower. 'Incoming traffic from east – west at seven hundred feet.' 'Wait a minute,' I thought, 'I'm at seven hundred feet! And anyway, where the hell's east – west? If I'm heading south that means he's to my left, no my right, no, left . . .' at which point a light aircraft whistled narrowly overhead.

With plenty of time to fill while my various arm injuries healed, I also embarked on a fishing trip to the Swedish lakes with my doctor, Mike Loxton. Each day we fished until suppertime, smoked our catch of trout over a wood fire, then returned to the lake until about midnight. It wasn't always trout I caught, however. While casting across a pool one day my line snagged on something behind me. Looking round, I discovered my hook embedded in the side of a rather put-out cow. I'd only recently bought a hand-made rod and so when the cow, understandably, set off in high dudgeon I raced after it, rod still in hand. It was fifty yards before the hook came loose and as I stood there panting, rod still intact thank goodness, I realised I was happy that this was the one that got away. Nevertheless, if you want to understand the meaning of the word 'bliss', I suggest you undertake such an expedition. I also advise you to find a companion as entertaining as Mike who, as well as being a gifted doctor, is a tremendous artist. Whenever someone approached me for an autograph, Mike would whip away the proffered book or scrap of paper and add an instant character sketch. This worked well until we arrived at the head of the foreign exchange queue and the damsel behind the grille asked me for my signature. Mike studied the lass with her piano teeth and thick glasses and, as I handed him the slip of paper, he whispered, 'Maybe not.'

When not scaring the pants off myself at the controls of a heli-copter or barbecuing trout in a Swedish pine forest, I was working assiduously on my game with David Leadbetter. After the disap-pointments of the previous season and with the 1992 Masters looming, I embarked upon a mini-rebuild, focusing on getting every-thing right for that first Major of the year. At the end of 1991 David had also given me a book called *Being Happy* by Andrew Matthews and I loved it and still do. It is all about setting goals and targets, so every week I set specific aims during the tourna-ments leading up to the Masters to improve one particular facet of my game. I improved each and every shot and arrived in Augusta jubilant, knowing that my sense of 'feel' had never been keener. Many is the year I would have been reasonably satisfied to finish 6 under par in the Masters, but with Fred Couples winning on 13 under, I was despondent at being out of the running.

I need not have been so harsh on myself. Returning to the European Tour, I successfully defended my Carroll's Irish Open title, and compiled seven top-five placings in eight events, which represented the ideal tonic before the US Open at Pebble Beach. It is said that when the gods come down from on high for a round of golf, it is Pebble Beach they choose to grace with their presence. Robert Louis Stevenson once described this very spot as 'the most felicitous meeting of land and sea in creation'. With the Pacific rollers crashing against the towering cliffs, it is unarguably a photog-rapher's paradise but when the ocean wind is blowing, it can be a golfing hell. Take the 6th hole, a 515-yard par-5 requiring an inch-perfect approach to the green raised on a plateaued peninsula above Carmel Bay. 'If you're five over par when you arrive on the sixth green,' advised Lee Trevino, 'it's the best place in the world to commit suicide.' Others have been equally scathing in their condemnation. 'It's like fighting Rocky Marciano – every time you step on the course it's a cinch you'll take a beating,' 1956 Masters champion Jackie Burke; 'Pebble Beach is Alcatraz with grass. I've heard about unplayable lies, but on the tee?' sometime 'swinger' Bob Hope; 'It's the leading argument for indoor golf,' US sports writer Dan Jenkins.

I found the conditions on the course ever changing. It felt as though the USGA was on a mission to test the players' patience. The greens alternated from rock hard to soft throughout the tournament and, with a view to creating even harder lies, the sand in the bunkers was fluffed up and the rough around the greens raked. I departed with mixed feelings; my rounds had been both heavenly and hellish, comprising a rollercoaster 70, 76, 68 and 77 for a 3 over par total of 291, which made me joint fourth behind Tom Kite's admirable winning aggregate of 285. It might all have been so very different but for two incidents in the second round. On the 9th, I hit my approach into a bunker and the ball disappeared under the 'fluffed' sand like a mole scurrying for cover. Five holes later, I played my third shot right off the green and into a tree where my ball decided to nest. I summoned a rules official and asked, 'What do I do now?' He told me I could either declare the ball lost and be playing five from there, or, if I could identify the ball, I could deem it unplayable and although I would still be playing five I would be able to drop it green side. 'Well, I'll have a bit of that then,' I said, proceeding to shin up the cypress tree, just as I used to do in my youth in the woods around our home. On reaching the top, I was clinging precariously to a swinging branch like Tarzan when I yelled out, 'Where the hell's Jane when you need her?' The search was fruitless and, having been right in contention after the first round, I had to battle hard in the second just to make the cut.

Still, you do not finish in the top four of any Major without playing well. The French Open the following week was a key turning point. I was obviously very disappointed to lose despite holding a two-shot lead with five holes to play but at least I was able to analyse what had gone wrong in those closing holes. I realised as I played the 15th that the problem was with my iron play. Without going into details – the technical term is that I wasn't 'holding off' my wrists at impact – the key point is that I knew what was amiss. I couldn't do much about remedying the flaw there and then but after the tournament I practised endlessly to get things right with my irons and, coupled with help from Simon Holmes, it certainly worked. Simon assisted me in perfecting the setting of my wrists on the backswing and during practice I would take aim at a lone telegraph pole. Throughout the sessions it was my intention never to hit the ball left of the target and by the end of the week I was getting so accurate I could almost take the paint off the right-hand side of the pole.

I booked into the Greywalls Hotel in Gullane on the Saturday night at the start of British Open week at Muirfield in a mood of high expectation. I could sniff a distinct air of homecoming in the stiff Scottish wind and just the fact that I was returning to Muirfield made me feel like the defending champion after my success there in 1987. With the wind whipping in off the Firth of Forth at a good 40mph, I decided to play just six holes rather than a full practice round, and work on my half-shots into the gusts, experimenting with various trajectories and different fades and draws. I discovered that the softer I could make my backswing and through-swing, the more control I could achieve; by choking down on my irons, I could squash the ball off the turf to stop it flying too high into the wind where it could be buffeted off line.

It is precisely that kind of attention to detail in preparation for a Major that can make the difference between victory and a place in the chorus-line. During practice the next day, Fanny and I also marked every hump and bump in our yardage book from 40 yards short of the greens. I knew that if the pin was back right on the 10th, say, I could go down the left and it would kick in towards the flag.

Although I might have felt like the returning champion, Muirfield was not in a particularly hospitable mood, welcoming me 'home' with a bogey five at the first where I drove into a fairway bunker;

but there is something about this strip of land that never fails to inspire me and I regrouped with an eagle three at the par-5 5th which really settled my nerves, before birdies on the 8th, 9th, 10th and 13th gave me an opening round of a 5 under par-66, two strokes behind American pace-setters Ray Floyd and Steve Pate. I was playing fantastically well, supremely confident that I could shape any shot to my will, but there is always room for improvement and so, instead of heading off to the hotel to relax, I came off the 18th and put in a full shift on the practice green, accompanied by Fanny and David Leadbetter. One of my practice drills that week was hitting drivers off the deck which you can only really do with a perfect tempo. The reward came on a bright and breezy Friday when I came to the par-5 9th one under par for the round and facing a 240-yard 3-wood approach into the stiffening wind. Knowing the green was out of range, I realised that if I could play a low draw and land the ball on to the small mound front right, the ball would kick forward towards the hole. Striking it perfectly, the ball landed on the downslope of the hump, just as it had done in my mind's eye a few seconds previously, and rolled up to four feet for a crucial eagle – just recompense for all the hard work Fanny and I had put in during the previous days. Suitably inspired, everything I tried came off in the most spectacular fashion and four additional birdies on the homeward nine brought me a 64 and a 12 under par halfway total of 130.

My second round of the 121st Open was amazing; no matter what club I held in my hand, it felt right. Never before had I experienced that feeling throughout an entire round of golf. This, too, was the Open, where every shot is recorded for posterity, and I could not have felt more content.

On the Friday night, I retired to bed with a three-stroke lead over Scotland's Gordon Brand Jnr and American John Cook. A cast list of stars – Jack Nicklaus, Colin Montgomerie, Fred Couples, Tom Watson and Seve Ballesteros among them – had already departed the scene after missing the cut. Saturday was a curious day on the ancient links. Steve Pate came from nowhere to draw level on 12 under for a brief spell before falling back into the pack; Gordon Brand Jnr's challenge faded with a succession of bogeys; Cook could make no impression on my lead. With birdies on the 12th and 17th, I ended the third round with a four-shot advantage and, in the opinion of the press, the fat lady had sung and packed away her music sheets.

Come Sunday afternoon, the pressure was enormous; I was fully aware that if I didn't win with four shots in hand over Cook and Pate it would be seen by some as an abject failure. All the old 'Nick Foldo' jibes would resurface and my previous Major victories be discredited. On a piece of paper, which I stuffed in my pocket and read and re-read throughout the final round, I wrote the words YOU ARE PLAYING FOR YOURSELF.

As in the first round, I dropped a shot on the first after driving into the sand but thereafter produced near-flawless golf for 10 holes without sinking a telling putt. Still three in front of Pate and Cook with eight holes remaining, the first notes of the fat lady tuning up to sing again were heard. However, I proceeded to bogey the 11th, pulling a wedge shot into the left-hand bunker, and even when I three-putted the 13th, I said to Fanny, 'Don't worry, I'm OK. I'm not choking.' I don't think Fanny was totally convinced, however, because I proceeded to hit a 1-iron into the bunker for yet another bogey on the 14th. 'I'm all right', I insisted. Glancing up at the leaderboard, I was not surprised to discover I now trailed Cook, who had made up six shots in as many holes from the turn, by two strokes. Suddenly I was facing the biggest crisis of my sporting career; relinquishing the Open after amassing a seemingly impregnable lead would leave a scar that might never properly heal. On the 15th tee, I said to myself, 'OK, forget everything, good or bad. Let's forget the whole week. What's done is done. There are four holes to play. Let's make them the best four holes of your life . . .'

I realised that the main pressure had transferred to Cook, un-accustomed to finding himself leading a Major with just a handful of holes remaining, and I felt if I could exert some more pressure on him, anything was still possible. With 164 yards to the 15th green, Fanny and I agreed on a half 5-iron, keeping the ball low into the wind. I aimed at the top of the ridge in the middle of the green and with the ball landing as I intended, it broke right and fed down to the pin, finishing three feet from the hole – exactly the type of shot I had practised the previous Sunday. The roar of the crowd confirmed my expectation that I had executed the shot to perfection and the resultant birdie three moved me to within one shot of the lead. I still needed a measure of assistance from Cook, who spurned a glorious opportunity for a birdie four on the 17th by missing from three feet, whereas I, in the pairing immediately behind, birdied the same hole to claw level after one of the best drives of my life. With a right to left wind, I spotted a letterbox in the tented village and aimed directly at the speck of red to draw the ball back in to the middle of the fairway. I was still faced with a tough 4-iron to the flag, half hidden by the front-right hill, and I knew that if I missed the green right I would never get up and down, but I nailed it with precision, 20 feet pin-high. If I can make this putt, I said to myself, it will give me the cushion I need going up 18. But, alas, I left it a foot short. I then heard the groans from the 18th and I assumed Cook was in trouble.

On the 100-yard walk to the 18th tee, with every step I took I whispered 'four to win, four to win', so certain was I in my own mind that Cook had succumbed to the pressure. In fact he had, slicing his second shot into the crowd to the right of the green for his bogey five while, chest heaving, I hit the best 3-iron of my life, a shot Gary Player later described as 'the greatest shot I've ever seen you hit'. It was an extremely aggressive shot in the circumstances, and my heart was thumping harder than ever before as I prepared to take it, saying to myself, 'Just take it back slowly.' The shot flew straight at the stick, just running off the back edge of the green, leaving me a tricky down-hill putt with the Open title at stake. To be honest, I mishit my first putt but the ball trundled its way to within 12 inches. As I tapped in for my third Open Championship, I felt I had just gone 12 bloody and bruising rounds with Mike Tyson, so physically and mentally drained was I. It seemed I had the Open won, lost it when I was taken right to the edge, then finally won it back again. The tension over those last four holes had been colossal, far more intense than anything I had ever experienced, and I literally fell into Fanny's arms, my legs gone and with the tears streaming down my cheeks.

After accepting the trophy from Michael Bonallack, the subse-quent 'dream sequence' is enshrined in the 'What Happened Next?' category of questions so popular on quiz shows. What did happen next was the sight and sound of Nick Faldo breaking into an un-rehearsed rendition of Frank Sinatra's 'My Way'. I have to confess that Ol' Blue Eyes I am not.

'Nick's singing isn't what it used to be,' muttered my mum loyally. 'That's the problem,' whispered Dad by way of reply. 'His singing is *exactly* as it used to be.'

Having reduced Muirfield to tears, I went into my stand-up comic routine, thanking the hugely supportive crowds 'from the bottom of my heart' and 'the press from the heart of my bottom.' How can I explain such a seemingly inexplicable remark? Throughout 1992, Fleet Street's criticism of me and my methods had intensi-fied. My apparent disregard for David Gilford in the Ryder Cup was still the subject of repeated scorn, I had blown the French Open from a winning position a month before the British Open, and I had arrived at Muirfield to discover reams of newsprint proclaiming Faldo should do this, Faldo should try that, so-and-so accuses Faldo of this, that and the other. Even Peter Alliss, whom I had always respected as a commentator, joined in the furore, suggesting I was obviously 'practising wrongly'. To the best of my knowledge, Alliss had only ever watched me once on the practice ground during a tournament; how did he know what Leadbetter and I were up to during the winter?

In my defence, I was speaking immediately after winning my third Open, still in semi-shock after the emotional wringer that is Muirfield; being bloody-minded or plain stupid, I wanted to say something that would have an impact. Unless you have been a victim of their occasionally poisoned pens, you have been spared the terrible power of the press; there they sit at their lap-tops, hitting the send button and relaying all manner of criticisms to three million readers or however many it is. But when I made one little tongue-in-cheek jest at their expense, they simply could not handle it.

I regret mangling 'My Way' but I refuse to apologise for thanking Fleet Street 'from the heart of my bottom' because the comment was offered as a light-hearted dig and should have been accepted as such. Many of my fellow professionals fully endorsed my senti-ments, especially the Americans who could not begin to compre-hend how a British player leading the Open could be trashed so venomously in the following morning's tabloids.

It had been suggested to me that I chose the wrong venue for my vaudeville act and that I should have waited until the official media interview in the press tent to crack my gag. But the press don't criticise me in a private tent, do they?

Even after all these years, it is nigh on impossible to explain to outsiders the mental torture I endured that Sunday afternoon in 1992. Knowing that I could have lost the title after having one hand on the trophy was a horrible sensation to carry with me over the closing holes when I could feel the spectators willing me to victory from the other side of the ropes. Towards the end, it became a battle of the mind, but as poor John Cook discovered the unbear-able pressure can eventually defeat you. It is no wonder that by the day's end I was worn to a frazzle.

Fortunately, despite my indiscretions during the prize-giving cere-mony, a number of people for whom I have the utmost respect graciously chose to pass comment on my virtues as a champion rather than my lack of prowess as a cabaret singer or comedian: 'Nick Faldo is the greatest golfer this country has ever had, the most complete professional I've seen since Ben Hogan. He is in a similar mould to Hogan; he gives the impression of being very aloof but that is because he's so single-minded. He has devoted himself to the game,' said Michael Bonallack, secretary of the R & A. 'Nick is the champions' champion,' opined Lee Trevino. 'To dominate as he did, when the standards are so very high is absolutely fantastic. Yet it really comes as no surprise because he is so single-minded and determined,' weighed in Tony Jacklin. And how about this for a tribute? 'Nick is potentially Ben Hogan. He is the player who attracts more awe and respect among all the golfers of the modern era. Somebody once asked Tommy Bolt if he thought Jack Nicklaus was as good as Hogan and Bolt replied, "Nicklaus watched Hogan practise, but I have never seen Hogan go out to watch Nicklaus practise." Well, Nick's on his way to becoming the Ben Hogan of modern golf – the ultimate professional,' commented the late Mark McCormack (well, he would say that, wouldn't he?).

I regard any comparison with Ben Hogan as the ultimate compliment because ever since Ian Connelly invited me to sit beside his electric fire in the pro shop at Welwyn Golf Club and regaled me with tales of Hogan's deeds, I have been in awe of the great man. The record book shows that he won nine Majors – four US Opens, two Masters, two US PGA Championships and the British Open on his only appearance in the tournament at Carnoustie in 1953 – but bald statistics cannot begin to explain the aura that surrounded this most intriguing of champions.

Born in Dublin, Texas in 1912, Benjamin William Hogan was the third child of Clara and Chester who, clearly intent on bestowing an air of majesty upon their first two children, had christened his elder brother Royal and his sister Princess. When Ben was nine, his father, a sometime car mechanic and blacksmith, shot himself in the head while depressed at being unable to find work during a financial slump. Ben was forced to quit school and earn some much-needed cash. The suicide of his father coupled with his lack of formal education were the defining experiences of his life.

Hogan was introduced to golf when he got a job as a caddie at the nearby Glen Garden Club, where he would practise between paper rounds, taking care to stay out of sight of the members. In 1931, at the age of 19, he embarked on a career as a professional with exactly $75 in his pocket to pay his way. When the money ran out – as it swiftly did – Hogan supplemented the family income with a variety of jobs including casino croupier, petrol pump attendant, oilfield worker and waiter. He was living on chocolate bars and oranges, and staying in the cheapest motels with his wife, Valerie, when he finally won $400 by finishing second in the 1938 Oakland Open. Financially secure for the rest of the season, Hogan never looked back after that success although it was another eight years before he won his first Major, the 1946 US PGA Championship, then a matchplay event at Portland.

From the age of 14 when I bought my first golf book, *Ben Hogan's Five Fundamentals of Golf*, the game's bible, I have idolised Hogan for a number of reasons – the purity of his ball-striking, his ice-man image, his dedication on the practice ground – but most of all, perhaps, because here was a perfectionist with whom I can immediately identify. As his protégé, Gardner Dickinson, a clinical psychologist who once gave Hogan a carefully camouflaged IQ test and rated him 'genius level', recalled, 'He used to order box-loads of balls and inspect each and every one with a magnifying glass. Ben would reject every ball that had too much paint on the dimples. Now that's what I call a perfectionist.' Further evidence of his acute attention to detail was provided by long-time caddie Clyde Starr, who revealed, 'It takes him three hours to go nine holes in practice; he'll even memorise the grain of the grass.'

In 1949, Hogan and Valerie were driving home to Fort Worth

from a tournament in Phoenix when their car was struck by a Greyhound bus attempting to overtake a slow-moving truck. Throwing himself across the front seat to protect his wife from the impact, Ben suffered a broken pelvis, shoulder, rib and ankle, narrowly escaping death but spending the next month in a full body cast amid fears that he would never play golf again. Not only did Hogan prove medical opinion wrong, but he won the US Open at Merion 18 months later and went on to amass a further five Majors in the next three years.

Such was Hogan's steely domination of his era that he inspired respect rather than admiration among his peers, refusing to offer coaching tips and, following the example of Howard Hughes, becoming something of a recluse in later years when he routinely rejected every request for a television, magazine or newspaper interview.

I had long since surrendered any dream of meeting this enigmatic figure when, after taking a call on his mobile phone during a car trip to London to attend a Genesis concert, my agent John Simpson turned to me and said; 'I'm about to tell you something that'll blow you away.'

'Sounds intriguing, what's that?'

'Ben Hogan wants to meet you. He's told Dave Marr [former US Ryder Cup player turned BBC commentator] the only young professional he would like to spend any time with is Nick Faldo.'

'Then what the hell are we doing driving to London? Let's get to Fort Worth now!' I exclaimed.

And so, a week later, I arrived in Texas for a rendezvous with Ben Hogan. The meeting, arranged by Jody Vasquez, who caddied for Hogan at his home club of Shady Oaks in the 1960s, had been kept secret and, so clandestine was it, we had code-named our visit 'Operation Terry Wogan' (rhymes with . . .) for fear a reporter would get to hear of it. Given Hogan's obsession with privacy, that would have resulted in instant cancellation. Was I excited? I woke up in my room at Jody's house at four o'clock on the morning of our date and sat at the writing desk filling four pages of A4 paper with questions about the swing, coping with pressure and how to practise and strategise.

On the stroke of 10 o'clock, carrying my battered copy of Hogan's book, I walked into his office at his golf equipment company's headquarters to find golf's most famous recluse sitting in a leather chair behind the desk. Now aged 80, with the passage of years Hogan had become mellower and more approachable but, alas, was fast losing his memory and I had no idea what reaction to expect. Although he needed repeated promptings – he did not have a clue exactly how many Majors he had won – we chatted for hours, with me even asking the dumb question, 'What is the secret of winning a US Open?' With a gentle smile Hogan replied softly, 'Shoot the lowest score.'

After discussing everything from posture to swing to course management, the old fella was clearly becoming tired with the effort and so I stood up to take my leave. To my absolute delight I was then invited to join Mr Hogan for lunch at Shady Oaks.

I almost fell over. Thirty minutes later, there I was sitting beside the legendary Ben Hogan at his private table in the Shady Oaks grill room where the conversation turned to his care of his hands, training, exercises, the number of balls he hit in practice and so on. Occasionally, the memories would come flooding back and he told me of the time he was practising at the Colonial Golf Club when he complained the turf was too tough to strike the ball properly and so they re-seeded the whole course especially for him.

Over coffee, I invited Hogan to come outside and watch me hit a few balls to which he replied, 'I reckon you know what you're doing.' Right to the end, Ben Hogan remained steadfastly reluctant to share his secrets. We went down to the locker-room to say our farewells and pose for a prized picture for my photograph album when the famed ice man gripped my hand like a father bidding a fond goodbye to his son and said, 'Boy, you come back and see me again sometime.' I am not ashamed to say that witnessing this so-called cold-blooded golfing assassin so moved brought tears to my eyes.

Why Hogan should have blessed me with such an audience is hard to explain, but I would like to think it was born out of a mutual respect. I was told that he still watched golf on television in a desultory manner but whenever I came on the screen his interest perked up, which was a massive boost to my ego. He had no idea Fred Couples had won the Masters earlier that year, 1992, yet he could talk at length about my Open victory at Muirfield. I do not know if he felt any genuine affection, our meeting was too brief for that, but I think he was pleased I had made the pilgrimage and I regret that I never took up his invitation to make a return visit.

Maybe that is why I became such close buddies with Sam Snead during his final years; just to be able to spend a little bit of time with a great man such as him is a priceless golfing memory. Like Ben Hogan, Sam was a sporting god. I had been acquainted with him for some years but it was at the Masters in 1996 that our friendship blossomed. Walking out of the clubhouse to meet David Leadbetter on the practice ground, I was assailed by Sam's gravelly tones.

'Faldo, what the fuck are you doin' with this guy Leadbetter? He doesn't know what the fuck he's doin'. You don't need no fucking coach. Leadbetter's never been there, how's he goin' to tell you what you're doin' right or wrong?'

He gave me a five-minute roasting in front of Bob Goalby and a few of the other old boys, whereupon, of course, I went out and won my third Masters. Sam being Sam, he laughed long and hard when he was proved wrong, bought me a beer and even spent some hours with me on the practice tee the following year.

'It would be nice to think,' I told him, 'that I'll still be out here toddling round at the age of eighty-five.'

A couple of years later I made a special trip to Greenbrier, Sam's club from his boyhood, and spent a wonderful two days practising and sharing fabulous stories. One sticks in my mind. Some golf-mad Japanese were visiting and they had heard about Sam's pet bass but they didn't believe anyone could have a tame fish, so Sam went over to the pond and wiggled his fingers in the water. Almost immediately the pet bass came across and when Sam held his fingers out, the bass clamped on to them and Sam was able to pull the fish clean out of the water. According to Sam, the viewing Japanese were suitably impressed.

Those meetings with Hogan and Snead remain as priceless to me as any trophy; to be accepted into their company is to be recognised as a great champion and I am proud and privileged to have shared time with both gentlemen.

Returning to 1992, the summer had turned out to be quite incredible. I had an amazing run of three tournament wins, four top four places and one eighth place. At the US PGA I was right in there with a chance to possibly pick up my second Major of the year until my third round 76 let me down, although I did make a very spirited charge on the Sunday afternoon which left me in a four-way tie for second place, three strokes behind Nick Price. You do not need to be a member of MENSA to work out that a third round level-par-71 would have been sufficient.

Compensation of a sort came at the World Matchplay Championship at Wentworth where I was in brutal from, playing 105 holes in an aggregate of 38 under par, culminating in an 8 and 7 destruction of American Jeff Sluman in the final. By this time I had been reinstated as world number one, a reign that was to last 81 weeks, from my Open triumph until January 1994, a statistic in which I have the utmost pride.

I am frequently asked what importance a golfer places upon the world number one ranking. I cannot answer for Tiger Woods, who is the current king, but I rather enjoy the notion of dandling the grandchildren on my knee one day in the far-off future and telling them, 'Oh, yeah, Grandad was the world's best.' To have been the undisputed world champion is a treasured memory to take into your later years. At the time, every tournament I entered, I was favourite to win, which was a tremendous psychological advantage whenever I teed off.

I was also voted 'World Athlete of the Year', an award that lay hidden at the back of my trophy cabinet until Christmas 2001 when my son, Matthew, and I watched that year's ceremony in Monte Carlo on television in the lounge of our home in Old Windsor.

'Isn't she amazing?' said Matthew breathlessly as Serena Williams collected her award.

'Hang on a minute,' I replied, rummaging through the cabinet. 'Ah, here it is. World Athlete of the Year – Nick Faldo.'

I think that was the moment it dawned on young Matthew that his dad used to be right up there with the best of them. And only a few months ago, little Georgia, now eleven, asked me to help her with a questionnaire for school. She had to fill in information about her dad.

'Why did you choose to be a golfer? At what age did you start? What's your greatest achievement?'

'I was world number one for two years.'

Georgia faithfully wrote down 'World number one for two years,' then looked up, eyes popping. 'You mean in the world?'

'Yeah.'

'What, the whole world?'

'Yes, Georgia, the whole world.'

'Oooow!'

I am glad to report I performed like the number one player in the whole world at the year-ending Johnnie Walker World Championship of Golf in Jamaica, a tournament featuring a specially invited 16-man field that read like the *Who's Who* of the game. Sadly, this tournament has now disappeared from the golf calendar, which I regard as a great pity for here was an event to rank with anything outside the four Majors. Johnnie Walker, one of golf's most thoughtful and generous sponsors, deserved more from their commitment but the Tryall Club in Montego Bay deteriorated and what could have developed into a glittering climax to the season was allowed to fade and die. It is a great shame as it was one of the most magnificent and enjoyable tournaments in the calendar and it could have been there for a lot longer.

At the time, however, I regarded the Johnnie Walker World Championship as just that, the world championship, and my victory in Jamaica took my number of victories in 1992 to six after successes in the Irish Open, British Open, Scandinavian Masters, European Open and the World Matchplay Championship. Not for the first time, my victory was achieved after a head-to-head duel with Greg Norman, set up by my fantastic third round of 65 in a Caribbean gale. On the first tee of the last round, Greg's caddie Bruce Edwards said, 'C'mon, Greg, final round of the year – let's make it a good 'un.' So saying, the bugger went out and shot an incredible 63 and so, having had a healthy lead, I needed to birdie the last to have any chance of forcing a play-off. My drive sailed straight down the fairway while Greg's found a left-hand bunker. I hit my second to 15 feet behind the hole and Greg played a fantastic 9-iron out of the bunker to about five feet, pin high on the right. My putt broke right to left, but there was also a wickedly strong grain in the grass left to right. Adding to the difficulties, it was downhill and there was a strong breeze flapping at my trouser legs. I still don't know how I made it – sheer willpower in the hopes of keeping my chances alive. Greg, of course, still had his five footer for victory but it was no forgone conclusion. From where he was, he faced a right to left break, and the strong right to left grain into the bargain, a combination that makes you feel like you are going to snap hook it as soon as you hit it. Greg did miss to the left and, clearly discombobulated, he bogeyed the first play-off hole, which probably explains why Johnnie Walker remains my favourite tipple.

Golf aside, there are so many other moments to treasure from that year. Through my friendship with Elton John, I was invited not only to the concert, but also to the rehearsals for the 'Freddie Mercury Tribute' evening, which was a wonderful privilege. I perched on a speaker and sat there in open-mouthed awe, like any rock fan, listening to Queen and the rest of the guys going through their paces. Just as he did at the actual concert, George Michael came on stage to sing 'Somebody To Love' and blew everyone away. Brian May stood spellbound at the climax, put down his guitar and muttered, 'That'll do, then.' You could feel the hairs standing up on the back of your neck as George struck the final notes.

Equally memorable in an entirely different way was the tour of bonnie Scotland I undertook in the company of my mate Del Dingley, a club singer with his own band. Following my Open triumph at Muirfield, we headed off in a Mercedes SL500 convertible (the first one delivered to Britain), ignoring five-star hotels in favour of friendly B and Bs in the Highlands and Islands. It was a wonderful way to relax. Every time Del and I thought we had found the most beautiful spot on earth, we would come over the hill and find an even more spectacular view. In between fishing and visiting all those beautiful sandy bays, we decided on a round of golf at Royal Dornoch where word soon spread that the reigning Open Champion was in the area. By the time we stomped up the 18th, a 'gallery' of about 100 people had gathered. Del, although out of his depth in terms of golf that day, is a showman who loves a stage, and was in his element.

On the Isle of Harris, we were driving through the most glorious countryside when I casually mentioned, 'God, it was so easy for those old golf architects. Look over at that hill where the sand's breaking through. You can just imagine a pin over there, can't you?' The words were hardly out my mouth when Del broke in, 'There is a pin. What the hell's this? Look, there's more pins . . . all over the place.'

We pulled up by the side of the road – a little single-track affair flanked by a hedge – and found a sign saying: 'Isle of Harris Golf Club. Honesty Box – £2.' The rain was teeming down, there were sheep on the greens, but we were in heaven. Coming up the ninth and last, we spotted a grotty concrete shed where they kept the club's only lawn-mower. Not having two quid in change, I popped a fiver into the honesty box, signing it first with the message: 'This is towards your new clubhouse – Nick Faldo.' I am delighted to say they framed the banknote and the local members still play for the Faldo Fiver every year.

I subsequently took a trip somewhat further afield when I was among those invited to Brunei by the royal family to play in a series of exhibition matches and provide coaching lessons for Prince Hakim, the then 18-year-old nephew of the Sultan. Here was one lucky kid because whatever he wanted to do – golf, shooting, polo – his dad, Prince Jefri, would import the best sportsmen money could buy to act as teachers. We were put up in a sumptuous hotel and offered the best food, with the one drawback being that we were expected to be on call 24 hours a day – which is how David Leadbetter came to be summoned at two o'clock one morning to accompany Prince Hakim to the floodlit 18-hole golf course, that being the best time to play golf out of the fierce heat of the sun.

The various palaces had to be seen to be believed, resplendent with every toy known to man. On my first visit, Prince Jefri's car park was a modest two-storey affair crammed with BMWs and Mercedes at ground level, and wall-to-wall Rolls-Royces on the first floor.

'How many do you have?' I asked, giving up counting.

'I have seventy-seven Rolls-Royces,' came the deadpan reply, 'and two hundred and fifty cars in all.'

When I returned the following year, the car park was five storeys high, housing 1,200 luxury cars of every model and shade. Even Prince Ballait, who was then only 13, had Aston Martins, Ferraris, Bentleys and Jaguars, all in yellow with red leather interiors because those were his favourite colours. Oh yes, the family also owned a fleet of private jets to rival British Airways.

Being a prince, whenever Hakim played a practice shot he would simply drop his club and wait for his caddie to step forward, clean the face of the club, and pop another ball on the grass. I tried to interest Fanny in performing the same tasks for me, a suggestion which, I need hardly say, went down like the proverbial lead balloon.

Every staff member carried two mobile phones – at least one had better not be engaged when the Sultan was calling. At 5 o'clock in the afternoon of the day we were leaving one of the phones did indeed ring and we were asked to hang on as the Sultan wanted to play golf. That was the only time I felt like a hired help as it meant we missed our flight home. Fortunately, however, I had met, and later became friends with, one of the Sultan's business associates, Raffy Manoukian, who kindly flew us back to Heathrow in his G4, complete with Baccarat crystal glasses, Spode china and gold cutlery. Yet amid such great wealth, the like of which I had never seen before, the in-flight meal we all happily tucked into came not from the splendid galley on board but from Brunei's finest Chinese carry-out. We were quite a sight, eating our $20 take-away while sitting on the most incredibly expensive crocodile leather seats. In addition to all this luxury, there was of course a butler, Ernie. Now Ernie, it transpired, slept on the floor and in the middle of the night his wife got up to go to the loo. Poor Ernie was still fast asleep when his wife emerged so she quietly closed the door and headed back to where she was sleeping without disturbing him. Unfortunately, and unknown to her, she had shut Ernie's hair in the loo door. Breakfast time duly arrived and we sat waiting for Ernie to appear with the food but there was no sign of him. Eventually his wife went off to find out what the problem was and discovered him still lying on the floor, no longer asleep but unable to move on account of his trapped hair and too embarrassed to call for help. You couldn't make it up.

The gifts handed out to the various visiting sportsmen, as you can imagine, staggered belief. I was given what turned out to be an extremely expensive Frank Mueller watch (the caddies received Rolexes) which I duly reported at British Customs where the officer took one look and asked, 'How much do you think that's worth?'

'I've no idea, mate,' I replied – it was only later I realised its full value.

'Well, what shall we say – about six hundred quid?'

'I suppose that sounds about right.' As it turned out, that valuation was way off the mark.

I have been back to Brunei on a number of occasions. On one trip Prince Hakim, knowing I was a keen, if failed, drummer, offered to show me his drum kit. Needless to say, it was a fabulous set-up. Prince Hakim, who is a great fan of Elton John, had received lessons from Elton's man with the sticks and duly became an accomplished musician. The room he showed me contained three full-sized drum-kits assembled in front of a 10-foot screen, where the prince would don earphones and watch one of Elton's concerts while drumming away frenziedly. What with his cars and his drums, I could be seriously envious of his boys-toys.

Although Prince Hakim had his own Mizuno workshop to make clubs to his personal specification, it was as a marksman that he made his name, winning the Pan-Asian Games under the tutelage of a German Olympic coach who was a dead ringer for Schultz out of *Hogan's Heroes*. Bernard Gallacher and I were out on the range with the Prince on one occasion when Bernard broke his rifle and the two cartridges shot out backwards nestling in Schultzy's open shirt and singeing his chest hairs.

'Vould you mind breaking your gun to the right and not back-vards?' he implored through gritted teeth, all the while beating out the smoke rising from his chest.

As the New Year of 1993 dawned, I was eager to garner even more treasured moments. It was to be an agonising wait.

CHAPTER TWELVE

LEAVING FOR AMERICA

A wise man once described an optimist as someone who has never had much experience. I should have been sufficiently experienced to know that golf has a nasty habit of exacting revenge on starry-eyed optimists.

The new year began in perfect manner with a hard-fought one-stroke victory over Colin Montgomerie in the Johnnie Walker Classic in Singapore. I battled Monty throughout the last round, played in brutal heat, eventually clinching victory with the most curious of winning putts, which gave lie to the old adage that 99 per cent of all putts left short don't go in. That was the one that, against all the rules of nature, actually did go in. Twenty feet away from the hole on the last green, it looked short all the way but, bizarrely, just kept rolling and rolling towards the hole. Three times the ball seemed to stop and three times it regained momentum, finally reaching the lip and hesitating on the very edge before disappearing from view.

It reminded me of an earlier incident with Seve Ballesteros at Portmarnock where, I swear, Seve made the ball change direction with his mind; his putt was missing by an inch to the right and yet he willed it into the hole. The American illusionist David Blaine could not have pulled off that particular now-you-see-it-now-you-don't flash of magic.

Even more precious than my victory in Singapore was the birth of our third child, Georgia in March, a week before I was due to depart for the Masters. I enjoyed a wonderfully precious moment picking Natalie and Matthew up from school and taking them to the hospital to meet their beautiful little sister. The photograph of them sitting on the bed holding tiny Georgia is one of my most treasured possessions. Atlanta Georgia was far less memorable than baby Georgia that spring, when I contrived to mix the sublime with the ridiculous during four rounds of 71, 76, 79 and 67 to finish in a tie for 39th place, 16 strokes behind Bernhard Langer, who, much to America's chagrin, provided Europe with a sixth consecutive green jacket.

Nonetheless, I played consistently well throughout the season, winning the Carroll's Irish Open for the third successive year (beating Jose-Maria Olazabal in a play-off), en route to claiming second place on the Order of Merit behind Monty, the new European number one, who had played 24 tournaments against my 14.

Of all the events in my diary, nothing gives me more pleasure or provides more entertainment than the Irish Open. No matter the venue, no matter the weather, 40,000 passionate golf fans line the fairways, generating an atmosphere unrivalled anywhere in the world. Portmarnock in particular remains a personal favourite, as much as anything for the characters you stumble across. One guy cut a hole in the fence so he could slip in without paying but, not content with this ruse, he then decided to earn some pin-money by charging other spectators to use his private gate. On another occasion, at Royal Dublin, I was standing with promoter Joe

Flanagan gazing across to the famous causeway when he spotted an ambulance doing a roaring trade as a courtesy bus, ferrying people between the car park and the course. Having watched the ambulance collect and deposit three busloads, Joe eventually confronted the driver.

'How long have you been working this wee fiddle?' demanded Joe.

'Fourteen years,' came the unabashed reply.

'Oh well, you might as well carry on then,' said Joe, appreciating this pay-as-you-go ambulance service was now part and parcel of the tournament's tradition.

However, as always it was the Majors that dominated my thoughts. My tally of five was still two behind Arnold Palmer's seven, let alone Jack Nicklaus's collection of 18. Despite Nicklaus's supremacy, if anything, it is Palmer who remains the game's most towering personality. There has never been such a popular figure in golf. As the brilliant American sportswriter Jim Murray was moved to comment: 'Golf was a comparatively sexless enterprise before Palmer came along. His caveman approach took audiences by storm. He was Cagney pushing a grapefruit in Mae West's face, Gable kicking the door down to Scarlett O'Hara's bedroom . . .' Palmer was a graduate of the 'hit it, go find it, hit it again, go find it again' school of golf and the huge galleries he attracted across the globe became known as Arnie's Army. Even Nicklaus was in awe of his reputation. 'I don't think there will ever be another Arnold Palmer,' admitted Jack. 'He can hitch up his pants, yank on a glove, light up a cigarette and people will start oohing and aahing. When I hitch up my pants, no one notices.'

In order to savour the unique atmosphere Palmer generates whenever he arrives at the first tee, like a prize-fighter entering the ring, I asked him to partner me in the par-3 tournament at Augusta, which traditionally precedes the Masters. The effect of his presence, especially among women of a certain age, was something to behold. As we made our way to the second green, a group of ladies interrupted his march down the fairway to request an autograph. The golf course being Palmer's office, he declined their invitation and strode on, ignoring the proffered pen and paper. His admirers displayed nary a shred of resentment at being so snubbed. 'Oh my God,' they trilled in unison. 'Did you smell him?' When one sniff of a man is enough to send the girls into a swoon, that is what I call sex appeal. In my view golf would not be the multi-million-dollar entertainment industry it has become in the third millennium but for the emergence of Arnold Palmer at the start of the 1960s.

If I was hoping some of Arnie's magic would rub off on me in the US Open at Baltusrol two months later, I was to be sorely disappointed. I finished in a humbling tie for 72nd place, 17 strokes behind the unexpected American winner, Lee Janzen. My performance was the worst in a Major since I had fail to survive the halfway cut in the 1986 US PGA Championship seven years previously.

However, on my return to Europe, my victory in the Irish Open put me in good heart for the 122nd Open Championship. Fanny and I arrived at Sandwich a week early to chart my campaign once again with military precision. After weeks of sunshine, the course was rock hard, and we made our preparations accordingly. As is probably apparent by now, I am a stickler for detail but it has paid off, and at Sandwich that year I plotted and planned as never before, noting the correct trajectory and how much run we could expect on each hole, 30 yards here, 50 yards there. The fifth, for example, burnt to a cinder as it was, would take a 6-iron off the tee and another 6-iron over the hump from the fairway. Thus did we have every hole mapped out – so what happened? On the morning of the first round the Kent coast was struck by a mighty cloudburst and the whole character of the course changed within an hour.

Even so, my confidence soared after opening rounds of 69 and 63, which gave me a two-shot lead at the halfway stage. I lost the tournament, though, in the third round when I could do no better than match the par of 70 – the pin placings having clearly been decided by the most fiendish of imaginations – which left me in a tie for the lead with American Corey Pavin. In any normal year, my final round of 67 would probably have been enough to bring me a fourth Open title, but that Sunday afternoon in July Greg Norman was in majestic form, his blistering 64 relegating me to a frustrating second place by just two strokes. For four hours Norman produced the golf of the gods and try as I might I wasn't able to close the gap – I even lipped out on the 11th for a hole-in-one. If the weather hadn't changed it might have been a different story, but Royal St George's was the one that got away.

There was an additional sense of frustration in the US PGA Championship at the Inverness Club in Toledo, Ohio, where I compiled four sub-70 rounds – 68, 68, 69, 68 – only to miss a play-off berth against Norman and Paul Azinger, the eventual champion, by one tantalising shot. But for a triple-bogey seven on the 13th, it might well have been champagne all round and it was sobering to think I had played the last two Majors of the season in a combined 22 under par for eight rounds only to be denied victory on both occasions.

The Ryder Cup at the Belfry was to provide little in the way of compensation although I was pleased to be partnered with Colin Montgomerie. Monty was asked before the contest if he was looking forward to playing with me and replied 'Oh yes. But then we're both awkward buggers, aren't we?'

On or off the course, I have seldom found Monty to be the 'awkward bugger' of his popular identikit and I was surprised by his later comment that he found 'playing with Nick hard work because he's so intense'. Perhaps it was because I was so determined to make up for my poor performance with David Gilford and give much more to my partner that I tried to be of assistance as much as possible, even to the point at one stage of stopping him just before he took a putt. 'I don't like the read,' I told Monty, who duly changed his line, and the putt went in. I received a big thumbs-up from Monty for that.

But I didn't get a thumbs up 20 minutes before teeing off on the first day. During practice I'd been fading the ball consistently but when it came to the real thing, I suddenly lost confidence in that aspect of my game. This meant that although throughout the three days of practice we'd planned on me driving off on the odd holes as they suited my game better, at the very last moment I had to ask Monty to tee off first. When I told him, Monty just shrugged in that Monty way and got on with it.

Monty and I enjoyed a fruitful partnership, beginning with a sparkling 4 and 3 victory over Fred Couples and Raymond Floyd in that first morning's foursomes. After lunch, Paul Azinger, fresh from his triumph in the US PGA Championship, teamed up with Couples in Floyd's stead for the fourballs and I doubt if Monty and I have ever played so well in the Ryder Cup without claiming a full point, both combinations' better-ball score of 63 resulting in an honourable half.

One curiosity of this match was that it had to be completed before the official start time on the Saturday morning because, after I had birdied the 17th to return to all-square on the Friday evening, it was simply too dark to continue. So, the following morning, it was pistols at dawn – all square with just the 18th to play. The 18th at The Belfry is one of the most intimidating tee-shots in golf, especially when the situation is a sudden-death shoot-out, and I was mightily relieved to sink a 12-foot putt on that final green to secure a half-point. 'Right,' I said, rubbing my hands, 'what's for breakfast?' as much through relief as satisfaction, for completing that one hole had been a mentally draining process. I had gone to bed thinking about it, woken up thinking about it, then had to put in a full practice session, working my way right through the bag from wedge to driver to make sure I was properly warmed up.

Perhaps it was the stress of our pre-breakfast game of Russian roulette, but both Monty and I found it impossible to reproduce the magic of the previous day. On guts alone, we defeated Lanny Wadkins and Corey Pavin in the foursomes, but had little left to offer against the seemingly vulnerable pairing of Chip Beck and John Cook in the afternoon, losing by one hole during a series of matches when Europe crucially surrendered the initiative. In the final day's singles, I halved with Azinger but the result had already been decided and the Americans retained the trophy by the narrow margin of 15–13, which was a bitter disappointment.

Every member of the team was clearly wearing his heart on his sleeve when HRH Prince Andrew – on his first visit to the Ryder Cup – came through the team room. I met him outside and he exclaimed, 'There are men lying back there in crumpled emotional heaps. I don't know what to do.' Feeling much the same myself, all I could reply was, 'Welcome to the Ryder Cup, sir.'

Curiously, at the start of the contest, I blithely predicted to Monty, 'I just know I'm going to hole out this week.' Walking somewhat despondently on to the 14th tee against Azinger in the singles, I told Fanny, 'Well, this is as good a time as any.' My 6-iron tee-shot took two bounces and, as predicted, disappeared into the can, which made me one of the few players to have scored an ace in the history of the Ryder Cup.

I still had the feeling that I was lacking one vital ingredient. I was willing to try anything and inspired by a picture of Sam Snead playing in his bare feet, I thought, 'Well, if I am going to give that a go, there's no better place than on a tropical island.' I was in Jamaica preparing to defend the season-ending Johnnie Walker World Championship and friend and foe alike rubbed their eyes in bewilderment when I arrived on the practice ground bare-footed. Steeling myself for the inevitable 'Twinkle-Toes Faldo' headlines, I believed it was a worthwhile exercise because it improved my balance and prevented me from using too much leg action on the downswing. If nothing else, the sight of my un-encumbered size 11s must have provided my new golf shoe sponsors, Mizuno, with food for thought.

One of those wide-eyed spectators was Seve Ballesteros. Later I came upon him trying the self-same exercise in street shoes and shorts and gave him an impromptu lesson. I have a picture of Seve with his chicken-wing legs sticking out of his shorts, which he has banned me from showing to anybody.

Far more controversial than that drill was my decision to putt using the left-hand-below-right, reverse-grip method. Since golf was invented, putting has been the bane of players' lives and when professionals suddenly lose the knack of consistently knocking in 12-footers, they will try just about anything on the greens. Although Lee Trevino ridiculed the reverse-grip action – 'If God had wanted us to putt cross-handed, he would have made our left arms longer' – I have won two million bucks using the cack-handed style, and it is not as weird and wonderful as some of the other putting styles adopted over the years.

At the Johnnie Walker, I abandoned the experiment after three holes of the opening round, eventually trailing home a distant sixth behind Larry Mize. Like the Monty Python team, I determined to look on the bright side of life and, setting myself a new goal for the coming year, resolved to become the fifth player in history – following Jack Nicklaus, Gary Player, Ben Hogan and Gene Sarazan – to complete the elusive Grand Slam of winning all four Major titles, making the US Open and US PGA Championship my two primary targets for the season. Let no one accuse me of being under-ambitious.

I arrived in the Thai resort of Phuket in February to discover my record 81-week reign as world number one had been ended by Greg Norman, depressing news that matched my depressing form on the course where I missed the cut. I was in the midst of a truly wretched run of form, four lacklustre over-par rounds at Augusta leaving me 32nd in the Masters, 17 strokes behind Jose-Maria Olazabal, Europe's seventh successive recipient of the green jacket. Occasionally, all the hard work on the practice ground and the gruelling training sessions in the gym would bear fruit and I would put together four encouraging rounds, such as in the Alfred Dunhill Open in Belgium where I beat Sweden's Joakim Haeggman in a play-off for my first tournament victory in 11 months.

Even so, I was still not entirely happy with my putting. One dilemma on my putting stroke has always been what to do with my right elbow, and the left-under-right style rids you of that problem. Technically and mechanically, putting cack-handed makes complete sense although the downside is you suddenly feel very awkward when called upon to chip. If I were to embark on my career all over again, I believe the perfect compromise would be to putt cack-handed on straightish putts of inside 20 feet, say, but to revert to the normal style when you require rather more 'feel'.

My confidence fleetingly restored after my Belgian victory, I arrived in Pennsylvania for the US Open. The Oakmont Country Club is just about the last place on God's golfing earth you want to find yourself unless every single facet of your game is operating as a precision tool. Designed by Henry Clay Fownes in 1903, one can but presume he was in Dr Frankenstein mood when he created a course described by Ben Hogan as 'a monster'. Take the bunkers – the Sahara Bunker 75 yards by 35 yards, stands guard over the 253-yard par-3 8th hole and it took 11 truckloads of sand to fill the damn thing; equally intimidating, a row of eight ball-guzzling bunkers, the Church Pews, lines the third and fourth fairways. The fiendish Fownes used heavy river sand and invented the 'Oakmont Rake' to deal with it, a vile-looking contraption armed with twin lines of teeth two inches long and two inches apart. Its use created deep furrows and, as three-times Masters Champion Jimmy Demaret bemoaned, 'If you had combed North Africa with it during World War Two, Rommel wouldn't have got past Casablanca.'

The river sand has gone now, to be replaced by fine white silicone, and the number of bunkers has been reduced from 350 to 200, but the furrows remain. Should you make it on to the green without accident, that is when your problems really begin because the putting surfaces at Oakmont are the fastest and most difficult in all America. Scottish-born Tommy Armour won the US Open here in 1927 with a 13 over par total of 301; and in the 1935 Open, Sam Parks's winning score of 299 made him the only player in the field to break 300. It has often been said that Oakmont is a course where good putters worry about their second putts before they have struck their first ones and, although Johnny Miller triumphed in the 1973 US Open after a closing round of 63 – frequently described as the greatest round of golf ever witnessed – torrential rain over the previous two days had doused the fire in the fearsome Oakmont greens.

The self-styled toughest course in the world fully lived up – or from my perspective, lived down – to its reputation in 1994 and I duly missed the cut as Ernie Els claimed his first Major with a highly creditable total of 279.

My rollercoaster form continued unabated at Turnberry, scene of the 1994 British Open, where an opening round of 75 left me with too much ground to make up despite scoring 66, 70 and 64 thereafter. In that 5 over par first round, I played a wrong ball up the 17th from the rough, costing me an eight. To Nick Price went the laurels, to me an equal eighth place as I began to give serious consideration to joining the US Tour on a full-time basis the following season.

My reasons for considering this option were many – the courses, the press, the state of my game, which I felt might improve if I was playing stateside on a regular basis, and the fact that I was about to enter my twentieth year as a professional and I really wanted to give America a proper go.

Matters came to a head on all fronts in September when my

enthusiasm for life in America was heightened by my tied fourth-place finish in the US PGA Championship at Southern Hills, Oklahoma, behind the suddenly 'hot' Nick Price; if I could come within touching distance of winning a Major on US soil as a tourist, what might I achieve as a golfing resident? After playing on the perfectly prepared fairways and greens of Southern Hills, I became extremely frustrated at the conditions on the European Tour, and I aired my thoughts that we had fallen behind the Americans in course preparation and practice facilities in a newspaper interview delivered with honesty and genuine concern. Mark James, inciting the feud between us which lingers to this day, took it upon himself to use my criticism of some of the courses in Europe to launch an attack on me, saying, 'We all thought that if Faldo had a problem he should have brought it before the Tournament Players' Committee rather than blurt it out in the press. That's typical of him in my opinion.' James went on to lambast me and label me 'a fat cat' for playing in events only when I received 'appearance money', which was arrant nonsense.

Many of the practice grounds in Europe were little better than fields at the time, with tees covered in stones from where you played over the brow of a hill so you never saw where your shots landed. I was talking in general terms about new courses built in fabulous locations with rolling hills or woodland – tracts of golfing real estate for which I would give my right arm to be employed as the architect – but where the designer had settled for the humdrum. Having become accustomed to the facilities in America, it was with a sense of frustration I surveyed the courses on which we were frequently being asked to play in Europe and found the vast majority looking distinctly threadbare. It is a great shame that our great links courses – Turnberry, Carnoustie, Royal Troon, to name but three – do not stage more European Tour events when so many poor imitations are used time and again.

Perhaps emboldened by Mark James's withering comments, even

Mark Roe was encouraged to join the 'knock Nick Faldo' club. If it had been someone of equal status – Seve or Monty, say – I would have listened to his opinions.

As a senior member of the Tour, I was trying to speak up for everybody by voicing my complaints and was deeply distressed by the reaction. As early as the 1985 Ryder Cup at The Belfry, all the team members had informed the European Tour that the three most important considerations were, in order: one, great courses, two, first-class practice facilities, three, prize money. Yes, money was a distant third on our list of suggested improvements. Sadly, our opinions were never taken up and implemented at the speed we would have liked, hence the reason I felt compelled to speak out against the Tour's reluctance to keep pace with the developments in America.

When I read Mark James's comments, I sought him out on the practice ground while at the Dunhill Masters at Woburn and asked him simply, 'What the hell was all that about?' James later described how I had approached him 'red-faced with fury and the steam coming out of his ears', which bore no resemblance to the reality. The bottom line is that Mark James and Mark Roe, and I'm sure many other players, couldn't handle the amount of appearance money being paid. But the truth is that appearance money has been the saviour of the European Tour, which at that stage had been propped up for years by half a dozen players. We were the stars the sponsors wanted and the personalities the public paid to see. If you want to stage a prestigious event, you have to have the top people and I happened to be among the players the tournament promoters wanted. I am sorry if that sounds harsh, but without appearance money, players such as Seve Ballesteros, Sandy Lyle, Bernhard Langer, Jose-Maria Olazabal, Ian Woosnam and I may have decamped full-time to the States where, at that time, the prize money was triple what was available in Europe. If you don't have the top players, you run the risk of having no television coverage. And if there's no television revenue coming in, will the sponsors find the money to fill that hole? Not if there are no top-name stars, they won't. So it is possible the event would not take place at all.

By the time the Tour had moved on to Paris for the Lancôme Trophy, speculation was rife that I would be disciplined in some way for my comments. Something had to give, and it duly did during my pre-tournament question-and-answer session in the press tent.

'Nick, can you confirm if the rumours about you going to play full-time in America next year are true?'

'Yes.'

'Was it a difficult decision to reach?'

'No.' (Should I leave it at that, or continue? I took a deep breath and continued.) 'It was the easiest decision in the world after all the shit that has been thrown at me by you guys. Last week I came into the interview room at Woburn with the intention of being constructive and you grasped the wrong end of the stick. That was the last straw. I have been misquoted for the past nineteen years and I have had enough . . .'

I had decided to get things off my chest. How did things reach such a sorry pass? Well, I had grown weary of being misrepresented at every turn: portrayed as being emotionless, ruthless, a fuss-pot, unapproachable, humourless, cold and calculating, over-ambitious and overbearing, irritable and implacable. The damning indictments leapt off every page of every anonymously penned newspaper or magazine profile. I had grown to resent being psychoanalysed in print by people I had never even met. I felt America would represent an escape route.

With so much going through my mind and so many possibilities to consider for the forthcoming year, it was perhaps surprising that I – almost – had a great close to the season. I say almost because, at the start of November, I should have won again in the Alfred Dunhill Masters on Bali. I was leading by six with seven holes to play when I was approached by an official who asked me to explain an incident that had occurred on the 2nd hole of the second round when I had removed a piece of coral in a bunker from behind my ball. As it was a European-sanctioned event, I thought I was acting within my rights but I was unaware the tournament was being played under Australasian Tour rules and thus I was immediately disqualified. I guess everything in life has to happen once, so I took it on the chin, wished the two guys with whom I was playing 'good luck and goodbye' and walked off the course.

Recalling the Sandy Lyle incident of all those years ago, my indiscretion only came to light in the last round when Australian Craig Parry also found himself behind a chunk of coral in a bunker and called over a rules official to ask, 'Can I move this?'

'No,' was the answer, whereupon Craig said, 'Oh, but Nick did the same thing earlier on.' I harbour no grudge against Craig. It was my fault and my fault alone.

Compensation was at hand when I proceeded to win the Sun City Million Dollar Challenge, putting left-under-right just to prove that sometimes a change is as good as a rest.

I had arrived at Johannesburg Airport to see a headline reading, 'Faldo: Man On A Mission' and it was true. I was on a mission after the unhappy events in Bali. I produced some marvellous golf and, partnered by Ernie Els one afternoon, I had a great opportunity of shooting a 59 – out in a 2 under par-33, during which I had eight birdie chances, I came back in 29. Throughout my career, I have been more interested in garnering titles than money, but the thought of winning one million dollars certainly concentrates the mind.

Curiously as it turned out, it was Gill who really sowed the seeds out of which grew my decision to move to America. Watching a US Tour event on television in our Windlesham home, she suddenly asked, 'Have you ever thought about going back on a full-time basis?' Gill's proposal made immediate sense and I enthusiastically embraced the suggestion, laying plans to take a nanny for the children, employ a tutor and, at a time when I was making vast sums of money each year, to fly everywhere in a private jet.

Ultimately, it was decided not to uproot the children and so Gill stayed with them in England. I, however, did go out and rejoined the US Tour; and, as things turned out, that move resulted in a life-change beyond my wildest and most fearful imaginings.

CHAPTER THIRTEEN

RYDER CUP TRIUMPH AND INNER TURMOIL

'Hi, Nick, my name's Brenna.' Enter Brenna Cepelak, a blue-eyed blonde. The third week of January 1995 found me practising in a snowy Arizona for the Northern Telecom Open. Though the weather was miserable, it did not begin to match the misery I was feeling: I was in golfing exile, on my own, many thousands of miles away from the three children I loved more than anything in the world. Perhaps that is why I proved so susceptible to Brenna's charms. I firmly believe that if you are truly happy in a relationship, you do not suddenly open yourself up to someone else; nor can someone else find their way into your heart. At the time, I was depressed and lonely, and at almost 38 years of age I suppose I was experiencing some sort of midlife crisis. Consequently when the alarm bells started ringing, I did not hear them. All I knew was that my marriage seemed to be as good as over and there I was having dinner with a girl half my age who was bubbling over with enthusiasm. There is no fool like a middle-aged fool.

I find it hugely amusing when someone is asked on a chat-show if there is anything they regret in life, and they reply, 'Oh no, I wouldn't change a thing.' Well, I would — because for the next five years I hardly made one correct decision in either my personal or business life. Never being one to do things by half, I gave my particular midlife crisis my very best shot.

Not surprisingly perhaps given my inner turmoil, I also began playing golf like an old trout, and by the middle of February I had won a mere 40,000 bucks, 10 times less than my mate Peter Jacobson who was leading the money list with 400,000 dollars. After missing the cut at the Buick Invitational in California, I returned to Lake Nona, Florida, where Gill and the children were coming out to join me during the half-term school break. It was not the happiest of fortnights because, although I had planned to spend every available moment with Natalie, Matthew and Georgia, my form was so atrocious that I was in desperate need of a period of intensive work with David Leadbetter on the practice ground.

I was once again faced with the age-old dilemma: you want to be with your family but at the same time you are aching inside over not playing well, or not doing your job properly. The only remedy I knew for the way I was performing on the golf course was to practise, to identify what was going wrong and work hard to fix it. I didn't feel I was just trying to sort out my swing — it was my entire career, and at that stage it was a huge part of my life. Things have changed now, but at the time that was how I felt.

I did set out to juggle the time between my family and my golf, with practice in the morning with Lead and family time in the afternoon. But the morning sessions ran over. We'd identify something wrong in my swing and we needed to fix it. But making the necessary correction doesn't happen to a schedule and I felt I had to stick it out until we got it right. One of the goals of my career has been to be able to say that I gave it 100 per cent, but if I could have sensed the damage that was being done over those two weeks

I would have chosen the kids every time. But that is easy to say with hindsight. At the time I was trying desperately hard, and failing, to manage the juggling trick, as, riddled with guilt, I stayed too long on the practice ground.

The crux came one morning when I rose at dawn, scoffed a quick plate of cereal, then raced off to practice. When I returned for lunch, my dirty breakfast bowl was still sitting in my place at the table. There was a message in that but I didn't see it. As a golf professional I was not doing a particularly good job, and as a dad, I was even worse.

Ironically, having waved off Gill and the children at the airport at the end of their stay, the very next week my game did come back and I edged out Greg Norman and the in-form Jacobson to win the Doral-Ryder Open in Miami, my fourth US Tour victory but my first since the 1990 Masters.

Had the whole family moved to Florida, would it have saved our marriage? In the long term, probably not, but at least our children could have grown up under the same roof as both their mum and their dad, even if we were leading increasingly independent lives. Those who regard me as being cold and calculating have no idea what a soppy dad I am: to live and work so far away from them is a heart-wrenching experience.

Professionally, I adored playing in the States, where the galleries appeared to regard me as something of a character and the press were refreshingly interested in my expertise rather than my private life. Heavens above, in this pre-Tiger Woods era, I was even described as the 'most humorous and charming of superstars'. Having won the Doral-Ryder Open, a week later I was the runner-up at the Honda Classic, so I returned to England cock-a-hoop as a golfer in mind, body and game but feeling an abysmal failure as a dad and husband. The atmosphere was decidedly frosty and every time I looked at the children I felt like bursting into tears. Could I give all this up? I had three wonderful kids and a beautiful house in

Windlesham, near Sunningdale, on which I had just spent £1 million creating the garden of our dreams. The grounds now included lakes, exotic plants, special water features, even nine holes – everything you have ever seen in the movies. It was the result of all that I had worked for over the past 20 years.

And so without considering the consequences, I allowed myself to drift into a serious relationship with another woman. My golf, not surprisingly, became as mangled as my thought-processes, the Doral-Ryder notwithstanding: Masters (tied 24th), US Open (tied 45th), British Open (tied 40th), US PGA Championship (tied 31st). I knew I would now have to depend on being granted a 'wild card' by captain Bernard Gallacher if I was to make a record-equalling 10th successive appearance in the Ryder Cup at Oak Hill in Rochester, New York. This was the first year, wrongly in my opinion, that the captain's pick had been reduced to two from three, so I had to endure an anxious few weeks' wait before Bernard, bless him, put me out of my misery by awarding me one of the two precious invitations. It was a calculated gamble on Bernard's part for, although I was not playing as well as I would have wished before our biennial showdown with the Americans, I was by now a battle-hardened veteran of the US Tour, more than familiar with Oak Hill, an attractive and challenging par-70 course of 30,000 trees (and no, I have never stopped to count them).

Gill accompanied me to Rochester as a member of the European wives' 'team', but sadly the week of the Ryder Cup marked an end to our love affair; Gill had been a wonderful companion throughout our early years together, a down-to-earth, no fuss, no frills, no drama girl who was the perfect partner and who gave me three children I idolise. It was no easy task to focus my attention on the opposition and it came as no great surprise to me, or to the rest of the European team, when Colin Montgomerie and I struggled from the very first morning. We lost our foursomes to Tom Lehman and Corey Pavin by one hole. One down after the first, it was clear I was at odds with the world, especially when Lehman putted out on the second green after I had already conceded his hole-winning putt. 'When I say it's good, it's good,' I growled. Lehman later milked the situation in the post-match interview by crowing, 'I told him to speak more clearly. Faldo claims he told me a couple of times my putt was good [which I did] but I wasn't going to put up with any crap, especially after he stretches out his arm as if to say "put the ball in your pocket, you idiot".' I certainly didn't mean to indict Tom Lehman as an 'idiot' and I have no idea how he came upon that interpretation of events; the fact remains that when an opponent concedes a putt, you should accept it.

Three down after three, Monty and I eventually clawed our way back to level on the 18th where I found the rough off the tee and a greenside bunker with my approach, which handed victory to Lehman and Pavin. This served to darken my already black mood. The only moment of relief came on the par-5 4th where my drive left Monty with 312 yards to the pin. 'Where do you want it?' asked Colin breezily. 'Well, if you can hit it two hundred yards, that will leave me a full wedge, which, with a bit of spin, I reckon I can put real close.' With that master-plan in mind, Monty proceeded to top his shot 112 yards, leaving me a 3-iron over a bunker to the flag, which was still some 200 yards away. Fortunately, I struck the shot perfectly and Monty holed a tricky putt for a birdie four. Seve Ballesteros, to whom such birdie golf is routine, would have been proud of us.

I was playing reasonably consistently from tee to green but with a putter in my hand I was a disaster and we were beaten 3 and 2 by Fred Couples and Davis Love III in the afternoon fourballs.

Monty was magnificent, a constant encouragement at my shoulder, and I think it was the camaraderie between us that persuaded Bernard Gallacher to persevere with our partnership on day two. Belatedly we put our first point on the scoreboard with a 4 and 2 victory over Curtis Strange and Jay Haas. Despite our win, the Faldo-Monty magic of The Belfry in 1993 had mysteriously evaporated – we were collectively a frustrating 4 over par through 50 holes. Bernard had finally seen enough and, after lunch, I was sent out in the company of Bernhard Langer to face Loren Roberts – acclaimed as the 'Boss of the Moss' for his putting skills – and the tigerish Corey Pavin, small in stature but blessed with the heart of a giant.

We arrived on the last tee all square. A victory for us would allow Europe to enter the final day with the overall score level at 8–8, and Bernhard and I (a pairing that had combined to win three points out of four 12 years earlier at Palm Beach Gardens) could easily have assumed we had achieved the priceless point when I was on the green in two with the opportunity of an 18-foot birdie putt, while both Pavin and Roberts were in ball-guzzling thick grass off the putting surface. Advantage Europe, or so we thought.

The closing scene of our little drama was another of those what-happened-next incidents. With Bernhard reduced to the role of spectator after missing the fairway off the tee, Roberts chipped on and putted out for his par, leaving the way clear for Pavin and me to go head-to-head on the trail of a birdie. With his partner safely down in four, Pavin could afford to be aggressive. Knowing what a master chipper he was, I had sensed something out of the ordinary might just happen, and so it came as little surprise when his chip duly rattled in the hole. So, from seemingly needing an 18-foot putt to win the hole and square the overall points score at 8–8, I now required my birdie three to prevent us entering the last day 9–7 in arrears. But my putt was a woeful one and the 18th green erupted in a blaze of red, white and blue as Pavin, America's newest hero, strode off to the clubhouse. The entire European team was despondent as we trudged, heads bowed, through a 100-yard avenue of Americans whoopin' and hollerin' as only they can. Needing 7½ points from the singles to come, was it any wonder that Ian Woosnam turned to the assembled British golf writers and groaned, 'Phone it in mates, it's time to catch Concorde home.'

At this point Bernard Gallacher proved himself to be a leader in true Churchillian mode. He did not go so far as to tell us that we would fight them on the beaches but he dispelled any notions of abject surrender by quietly explaining how, if each and every one of us played with pride, passion and a refusal to countenance defeat, we could yet pull off the most sensational and unlikely of victories before the disbelieving eyes of America. Even US captain Lanny Wadkins sounded a note of caution amid the sense of euphoria sweeping the course by admitting, 'I have twelve guys playing well but this is the Ryder Cup in which anything can happen. If we're still two points ahead tomorrow night, that will be the time to crack open the champagne.'

If I could have hand-picked my opponent from the American 12 for the closing round of singles, I would have chosen Curtis Strange, even though he had roundly cuffed me in our 18-hole play-off for the 1988 US Open at Brookline, then successfully defended the title 12 months later here at Oak Hill. Like me, Strange was also a 'wild card' entry, the choice of his old buddy, Wadkins, and his selection from outside the top 50 world rankings had led to a storm of controversy.

Our match was a war of attrition from the first tee. Strange went ahead at the 6th, I drew level at the next, fell behind at the 11th and was still one hole in arrears when we arrived on the 17th where I noticed the scoreboard was dominated by blue figures, representing either European victories or individual match leads. Doing some quick mental arithmetic, I worked out the various permutations and came to the conclusion that if Philip Walton defeated Jay Haas in the match behind me, we would have $13\frac{1}{2}$ points. If I lost to Strange, therefore, Europe would lose by a single point; if I halved my match, the Ryder Cup would be drawn 14–14 but the Americans would retain the trophy as holders; but should I win the last two holes, we would snatch victory not from the jaws but from the very bowels of defeat. All I had to do was to ensure that I won the 17th and 18th, two of the most challenging closing holes in championship golf.

The mental pressure was beyond anything I had previously endured. From tee to green 463 yards away, the 17th was a self-enclosed amphitheatre of spectators, creating an atmosphere more reminiscent of ancient Rome's Colosseum than a genteel 20th century golf course. Although heavily outnumbered, the European fans were just as vociferous in their support as their American counterparts.

Strange handed me the advantage by missing the green with his approach, whereupon I promptly returned the compliment by depositing my equally wayward second shot into a greenside bunker as the wind suddenly changed. Strange pitched on to eight feet, then I splashed out to seven feet on exactly the same line. Fanny peered over my shoulder and we studied the putt like two trans-lators puzzling over a particularly difficult word, eventually agreeing that it would break left. Having read the same line, Strange obvi-ously reached a similar conclusion and I was stunned when, instead of breaking left as we had thought it would Strange's putt veered crazily off to the right. It was a bewildering situation – is it better to go with your gut instinct or to obey the evidence of your eyes, even though you do not believe what you have just seen? Almost reluctantly, I changed my mind and aimed left edge of the hole and, lo and behold the ball broke into the hole to square the match with just the 18th to play.

If the pressure on the 17th had been almost too much to bear, it intensified even further on the 18th tee where the eyes of the golfing world were exclusively focused upon Curtis Strange and Nick Faldo. Most of the other guys had done their bit, now the destiny of the 1995 Ryder Cup lay in our hands. Surrounded by a scrum of team-mates, television cameras and radio reporters, I drove into the left rough, to the accompaniment of a European groan and an

American roar of approval, heard coast-to-coast across the United States. Strange commendably struck his tee-shot right down the middle of the fairway.

The 18th green at Oak Hill is not one you would wish to approach in a monthly medal competition, let alone at the climax of a Ryder Cup when you are carrying the expectations of your team, your friends and your family, not to mention a whole continent of sports fans. The green sits on a plateau atop a ball-devouring bank, guarded by four mammoth bunkers, so I knew there was no way I could reach the putting surface directly. I laid up short to 93 yards, leaving me, I hoped, an ideal threequarter wedge from the first cut of rough, which was my lucky break because that would naturally take the spin off the ball. Having produced such a wonderful drive, Strange then mishit his 3-iron approach, which came up short in the thick rough on the hill leading up to the green.

When I addressed the ball to make my third shot, for the very first time in my career my legs completely went. From the waist down I turned to rubber as though I had been hit by a haymaker from Mike Tyson. Mouth dry, legs shaking, heart pumping, stomach churning, I composed myself as well as I could in the claustrophobic atmosphere, reminded myself I knew exactly what to do, and proceeded to strike one of the very best soft wedge shots of my life: the ball bounced twice before stopping less than five feet from the pin. I presume that Strange was enduring precisely the same agonies as I was and you could tell by the way Strange winced that he knew his pitch to eight feet was less than ideal – he desperately wanted the ball to have rolled three or four feet closer. Averting my gaze, I could not bring myself to watch Strange's putt for a par which would guarantee the trophy remained in the possession of the Americans, but the strangled gasp that followed told me everything I needed to know. He had missed. I now faced a four-footer to keep the Ryder Cup alive. Fanny and I went through our usual procedure, lining up the left to right, fast-breaking, downhill little terror to come. I could even detect the tension in Fanny, for she knew full well that if she misaligned me she would kick herself for the rest of her life. No wonder every part of me was shaking, every part except the putter that is. Unlike the drowning man, it was a vision of my future not my past that sped through my mind on fast-forward. What if I missed? I would be handing the Ryder Cup to the Americans.

In the split-second before the 18th green erupted with European celebrations, all I could hear was the sweet, sweet sound of ball rattling into cup. The initial emotion was sheer relief as I raised my still tingling arms in ecstasy. Then all hell broke loose. Seve Ballesteros was the first to envelop me in his great arms, tears rolling unashamedly down his cheeks. Between hugs Seve whispered in my ear 'You are a great champion.' Coming from such a great champion, that accolade represented one of the highlights of my career and I later wrote to Seve thanking him for such a compliment. The Spaniard was swiftly followed by Bernard Gallacher with the words, 'You've just won us the effing Ryder Cup!' But I had done no such thing, because somewhere out in the woods of Oak Hill, Philip Walton was still doing battle against Jay Haas. Three up with three to play, then two up with two to play and visibly ageing with every passing hole, Walton now stood on the 18th tee one up with just one to play. He made a half in bogey five and the celebrations started anew. We sang, we danced, we kissed, we hugged. Somehow, against all the odds, we had won the necessary $7\frac{1}{2}$ points out of 12 and Bernard Gallacher took possession of the treasured Ryder Cup trophy. During the seemingly endless round of post-match interviews, any time anyone said something nice about my role, my eyes welled up again. 'If I had to bet my life on trusting someone to win the last hole, then Nick Faldo would be my choice,' beamed Seve. 'When Nick sank that putt on the seventeenth,' muttered Woosie through his own tears, 'I knew then we had won the Ryder

Cup.' Howard Clark sought me out to remark. 'I don't know what you've been going through this week, I don't want to know, but you have been absolutely magnificent.'

Of all my Ryder Cup triumphs, I will forever regard Oak Hill as the most precious of all but it was far from a one-man effort. Howard Clark, Colin Montgomerie, Mark James, David Gilford, Sam Torrance and Philip Walton all won their singles that never-to-be-forgotten afternoon, while Ian Woosnam secured a priceless half against Fred Couples. But never let us forget the other team members of Europe 95 – Costantino Rocca, Per-Ulrik Johansson, Bernhard Langer and Seve. All of them had more than played their parts over the preceding two days of competition as had the wives and the caddies. Finally, all credit to Bernard Gallacher and his support team, who never lost faith in us even after Pavin's outrageous chip on the Saturday evening had left the United States with a seemingly unassailable 9–7 lead.

On a personal note, our Ryder Cup victory meant as much to me as any of my five individual Majors. In terms of pressure, the threequarter wedge and putt at the 18th were as important as any two shots I had ever played before in my life. There is nothing quite like the fellowship of your team at a moment such as that to remind you of the whole spirit of the wonderful game of golf. No one player won the Ryder Cup for Europe at Oak Hill; it was a team victory from the first morning to the final, climactic evening.

So, it was off to the traditional celebration dinner, an unnecessary obligation in my opinion because if you have won the Ryder Cup, you are too physically and mentally drained to celebrate and if you have lost, you want to strike a Greta Garbo pose and be left alone to nurse your misery. Personally I would much prefer an informal barbecue where you could meet, chat, eat, then say your goodbyes and leave the enthusiasts to it.

The Ryder Cup won, Gill and I officially announced the less than earth-shattering news that we were splitting up. This process plunged me into a living hell from which I would not emerge for five horrendous years. Although we had not been living together for some months, I found the actual separation far more stressful than I would ever have imagined possible despite managing to rent a lovely old Tudor cottage in a park in Ascot about two miles away from the children in Windlesham. Gill packed up my stuff — my music, my clothes, everything — and sent it all over. It was a nasty shock to see my entire material world packed into 20 cardboard boxes. Even my trophies had to stay in the marital home for security reasons.

Of course, the well-being of Natalie, Matthew and Georgia was of paramount importance to me; how could I explain to three loving and beloved children that from now on, Dad would be living in a strange house? I sat Matthew, who was an innocent six-year-old, on my knee. The only way I could think of to explain things in a way he just might understand was to remind him of *The Lion King*, which was his favourite movie back then. 'I'm Mufasa and you're Simba, we're father and son,' I told him, 'and no matter where I am, I will always be in you, I will always be there for you.' Although Huey Lewis, who had been through the same thing, told me that as long as children from a broken home knew they were loved then they could adapt incredibly quickly, telling Matthew was a really gut-wrenching experience.

For the first few weeks, the kids were very, very quiet whenever they came over to the cottage, just wandering around and no doubt wondering in a childish way why their entire existence had been turned upside down. The fact that their lifestyle had always been built round a travelling dad probably helped them adjust more quickly than most kids in a similar situation; after all, from the day they were born, I would wave goodbye on a Tuesday and, if I had a good week, would not return until the Sunday night. If I was playing in America or Asia, of course, then I might be away for two, three or even four weeks at a time, something I am now seriously trying to change given my new order of priorities: family first and golf second.

Back then, however, I was still a full-time golfer and a part-time single father. I perfected a version of spaghetti Bolognese, throwing everything into the pot – meatballs, sausages, whatever – and seemingly the three of them absolutely loved my cooking, especially pudding, which comprised a mountain of ice cream topped off with all the little sweets they liked best such as Jelly Tots, Dolly Mixtures, Smarties and the like. 'Wow! This is great, dad,' they would say every time I placed this feast before them. I was probably rotting the poor wee souls' teeth, but they were happy. We also went out a lot, to restaurants or the cinema, but in the back of my mind during every visit I was already preparing myself for the dreaded handover, the moment I had to deliver them back to their mother.

Although Gill and I had requested privacy during this troubled period of our lives, especially for the children, newspaper reporters and photographers were often camped outside the front gates at Windlesham. I would drive the kids along a back lane, leave the car in a garden centre car park, and sneak them in through the woods, which the three of them regarded as a great adventure. But after having them to stay for a full weekend, I detested having to give them up again and for a couple of years I cried at each and every handover. One of my friends even took the kids aside and asked: 'Who puts their arm round Daddy when he cries?' 'Daddy cries?' they chorused. 'I can tell you your Daddy cries an awful lot.'

Afterwards I would return alone to my rented cottage totally crestfallen. It was a weird sensation living in someone else's house, gazing at unfamiliar prints on the wall, sleeping in a strange bed, surrounded by another family's possessions. It all just added to the depression. I can understand why, except in the most extreme cases, it makes sense for the mother to be granted custody of the children following the break-up of a marriage but I feel sure I speak for many thousands of fathers who have been through the same, agonising situation when I say that no one else can fully understand the pain, the sheer physical ache, we endure. From being able to go out to play in the garden, collect them from school, or merely cuddle them in your arms until they fall asleep on the sofa, you are instantly reduced to the role of a semi-detached parent. Living apart from those you love most, missing the day-to-day events in their young lives, is heart-rending.

The separation was no easier for Natalie, Matthew and Georgia, who found themselves under siege in their own home. Even a routine school run in the car was likely to be accompanied by paparazzi eager for a picture of their terrified young faces gazing through a window. Although I was no Michael Jackson or Madonna in the 'fame game', I had come to expect some attention, but Gill and the children should have been left alone. Some reporters even took to rifling through the rubbish bins – goodness knows what they thought they might discover – and another persistent hack left 27 messages in a single night on Gill's answering machine, promising a sympathetic ear.

Looking at our children now, Gill and I must have done something right because they have come through the various traumas unscathed, even Natalie, who, as the eldest, found the break-up the hardest to bear. For a while she was vehemently against the idea of ever getting married in the future, saying, 'I would never trust a man.' I thought 'bite your lip, Dad' and gently explained that at some future time a boyfriend might betray her or that she herself might fall in love and then out of love again, and that it was all part of growing up.

For my part, I desperately craved affection which is the only excuse I can offer for becoming embroiled in the relationship with Brenna. Constantly the media spotlight was on us, even to the extent that when we rented a house in Lytham for the 1996 Open, the *Sun* promptly leased the one next door. When I subsequently decided to book into a hotel instead, one paper carried a totally fictitious story suggesting that Brenna had demanded every curtain in the original rented house be changed because she did not like the colours.

Even when we travelled to Jamaica for the Johnnie Walker World Championship the photographers trailed us. One incident there did provide some light relief. We were returning to our villa one night dogged, as usual, by a snapper, whose camera was quite obviously under his shirt. Out stepped a Jamaican police officer to bar his way.

''Scuse me, mon, but you cannot come this way, it's a private road,' our defender informed the photographer. 'And what have you got under your shirt?'

'None of your business, mate. And I can walk where I like.'

'I ask you again, my friend, what's that under your shirt?'

'I've told you, mind your own business.'

'Well, let me tell you what I have under my shirt — a nine millimetre Smith & Wesson.'

Exit one of Fleet Street's finest.

Another story, which must have been deeply distressing to those back home, suggested that we had rented a luxury villa in Jamaica for six grand a week, where we were living it up, having apparently checked in as 'Mr and Mrs Faldo'. Arrant nonsense, we did no such thing — and for the sake of historical accuracy let me make it clear that Johnnie Walker kindly provided all the players' accommodation free of charge.

Recently I was sent a fascinating book entitled *If I'd Known Then What I Know Now* by J.R. Parrish, and if I had known then what I know now, then I would have appointed a public relations team to guide me through that particular minefield. I think part of the problem was that, although he never said it, I sensed John Simpson, my agent of the day, never really agreed with my decision to leave Gill and, in particular, the children and so left me to handle my own PR.

I can understand the need to sell newspapers via lurid headlines but, as a professional sportsman, when I leave the playing field I would prefer to be allowed my privacy. Unfortunately these days that does not happen. I trained to be a golfer, not a celebrity, whereas today you must also be an entertainer: that is one of the biggest changes in sport. The public seems to expect more of sportsmen than their skills and ability, demanding personalities too – which is why Andre Agassi, say, was always more popular than Pete Sampras. Some guys will say 'sod it' and go out to play with their heads down, but others will provide the press with what it wants. There is no right or wrong way to play professional sport, but some people have developed the happy knack of becoming bigger stars than their records merit and good luck to them.

By 1997, Gill and I had been separated for over two years and in order to move things forward and sort out her affairs, Gill issued a petition for divorce. On top of all the emotional grief, thus began my serious financial problems. I had, by then, left IMG (despite four personal phone calls from Mark McCormack on the day of my departure) to go it alone with John Simpson. Deep down, I think Mark always knew I would return one day in the future.

My decision to strike out on my own was one I quickly came to regret. My finances were in such a mess that it took over a year to sort out all the paperwork. Meanwhile Gill, no doubt thinking I was digging holes in the garden to bury a secret stash of cash, grew increasingly impatient with the painfully slow rate of progress. When you are involved in so many projects, it is difficult to pin-point exactly where all your money lies when it is scattered here, there and everywhere; seemingly straightforward issues, like working out precisely how much it cost me to operate as a professional golfer, seemed to take an eternity.

Another new day, another body blow. When I received the letter informing me that I was to be inducted into America's Hall of Fame, it should have been one of the highlights of my career but served only to cause me more heartache. In golfing terms, such an honour is the equivalent of a knighthood, and, understandably, I

wanted the children to be at my side during the induction ceremony in Florida, especially so since the organisers were planning to
re-induct all the past living champions, male and female. The Hall
of Fame is a shrine to the world of golf, like a pyramid filled with
treasures, in which you are given your own glass case containing
memorabilia and a taped message which reels off your accom-
plishments. Jack Nicklaus was due to be in attendance to witness
my joining the legends, as were Arnold Palmer, Gary Player, Gene
Sarazan, Sam Snead and Patty Berg, which was a tremendous
personal thrill because my first ever putter was a 'Patty Berg' auto-
graphed club.

At the ceremony, Johnny Miller, the only other new inductee of
my year, sat surrounded by his kids, which made my situation all
the more poignant. Gary Player introduced me, paying tribute to
my dedication and commitment and extolling my virtues as a great
human being (I blush to this day) and then I was called upon to
make my acceptance speech, which I was dreading because I had to
follow straight after Johnny who had been a television commentator for the past 10 years. I explained that I had always been good
with my hands – 'at least that's what all the girls said at my school,'
which raised a laugh – and then I was off and running. Sadly,
though, my heart was aching on what should have been one of the
most memorable days in my life. My parents and David Leadbetter
were there but my three precious children were unable to share in
my day of days.

The Americans always use the phrase 'Hall of Famer', which I
far prefer to the miserable adjective 'veteran', and I find it sad that
we do not have a sporting Hall of Fame here in Britain. When I
heard Sir Steve Redgrave was planning to chop up his boat for
charity, I commented to my friend Danny Desmond, 'Hey, we
should buy the friggin' boat and open our own Hall of Fame in
this country.' Imagine a special gallery designed to display and celebrate the feats of Redgrave, Ian Botham, Laura Davies, Jackie

Stewart, Fred Perry, Stanley Matthews, Mary Peters, Daley Thompson, Kelly Holmes, the list could go on and on; think of all the great sportsmen and women Britain has produced over the years. Perhaps if London's bid to stage the 2012 Olympics is successful, that could provide the inspiration for a Great Britain Sporting Hall of Fame.

By 1999 my business affairs were starting to unravel and as so often, when the alarm bells were ringing, I most certainly was not listening. I had enjoyed a long relationship with Mizuno, who in my opinion at the time were making the best irons in the world, and they had even given me my own personal club grinder, the 6 foot two inch 'Turbo' who was the finest master craftsman I had ever encountered. But after dealing with such blue-chip companies for 20-odd years, the decision was made to switch to Texan club-maker Adams Golf.

Barney Adams had only been in business for about three years but had hit the scene with the Tight Lies Fairway Wood, which, to be fair, was a brilliant invention, allowing you to cut through any bad lie. His was a great success story because Barney had started out with no money – paying for his hotel rooms with clubs – yet three years later his company was earning $30 million. With a projected income of $130 million, Adams Golf was suddenly listed in the Fortune 500 group of companies and Barney collected the Young Entrepreneur of the Year Award. Adams Golf offered me an incredible deal, not only promising me a 10-year contract worth twice what I was earning from Mizuno, but also giving me plenty of shares, and a place on their design team with a brief to fill the rest of the bag: everything I could have dreamed of. 'Thanks, Barney,' I thought, 'you've paid for my divorce and given me a pension fund all in one stroke.'

Gradually, however, my 'dream deal' started to disintegrate. There was a mad rush to produce a set of irons for me and although my advice had been to make 20 sets that we could refine, the word came back 'No, we're ready to push the button.' However, on the first set of irons delivered to me, the heel was way too sharp and, even before striking a ball, I knew I was going to hit it left, and left each and every ball went. But while my shots went left, the clubs went right, right back to Texas where I assumed they would be adjusted.

Ten days before the 2000 US Open I received word that I was to play with the irons. Immediately I called up and said 'Guess what? You've still got my set.' A company representative was despatched with said clubs to Orlando, where I was practising. But the problem persisted – every shot I struck flew left. I handed them back the rep and demanded 'What do you want me to do now?' 'Call Barney' was the reply, which I did, explaining that the clubs simply weren't right yet.

The irons, needless to say, did not go in my bag for the US Open and a few months later I was informed again that I had to use the irons, this time with a new shaft they had recently invented. This gave me 18 days to prepare for the next tournament so another phone call to Texas followed.

'Barney, I don't have any clubs with these new shafts and anyway, you're telling me that after playing with the same shafts for eighteen seasons I have eighteen days to switch over? That's an impossible request.'

That was the beginning of the end – things just hadn't worked out as we had all hoped and, as a result, we negotiated a severance deal and went our separate ways, with no hard feeling on my side certainly.

When I had originally signed on the dotted line with Adams Golf I believed my financial difficulties had been solved at a stroke, and I splashed out £2 million on Pentlands, a house in St George's Hill. I was then persuaded to spend a further £1 million on refurbishments, using an architect especially selected and flown in from America who had one fatal flaw – he could not work in metric. I had obviously suffered a short-circuit in the brain; at the age of 40 I was acting like a reckless teenager.

Next came the Bridgestone debacle; my advisers suggested that I should buy the rights to become the Bridgestone ball distributor in Europe. These are some of the best balls around, but my super sales force could not seem to sell them, despite John Simpson's reputation of being able to sell sand to the Arabs and ice to the Eskimos. Whatever the reason, it turned out that we could not sell golf balls to golfers, with my sales force resorting to blaming an unseasonably wet summer. Two years later I pulled the plug on the deal which cost me a million bucks. The sales director chose this moment to raise the possibility of a bonus, because we had finally managed to sell the last of our stock: I will not print my reply.

Looking back, I realise I had become something of a psychological wreck. Every part of me was affected, my emotions, my responses, my thinking, my judgement. With my private life in a mess and my business life crumbling, I lost all sense and balance. I consulted the renowned American sports psychologist Jim Lohr, who warned me: 'You're running at one hundred per cent in every area. Something's going to go bang.' I never contemplated suicide as such but I do recall one silly moment when I went off fishing in the Porsche and felt like giving the car a good, bloody whack into a wall. I just had the urge to smash the car up and leave everything to chance but luckily I arrived safely at the riverbank.

Such was the turmoil, I even considered the option of asking Gill to take me back; back to the comfort of my home and the everyday company of my children, who I hoped would be overjoyed to have Dad back with them again. But even as the notion passed through my mind, I knew it was wrong. I realised I had to take charge of my own life, which might have another 50 years to run.

Having felt I have been let down by numerous people over the years, it only highlights to me why I value my friendship with Danny Desmond so highly – he has been such a rock throughout my life. I have known Danny for more than 25 years since he lived in the manor house down the road from Tudor Cottage in Ayot St

Lawrence. He is Natalie's godfather, which is a favour I returned when his son, Charlie, was born. Although he routinely refers to me as 'Superstar', he has never been influenced by my so-called fame, and over the years has been sponsor, caddie, confidante and business adviser. Danny has always been there for me whatever my problem, without ever wanting anything from me apart from friendship.

In case you are wondering what happened to my golf career throughout these troubled years, I can safely say that the course became my refuge for a while, the one place where, despite the pressures of tournament play, I could actually take a deep breath and relax. Crazily, therefore, in the middle of this torrid period of my life, I went out and won myself a third Masters title in 1996.

CHAPTER FOURTEEN

THE NORMAN CONQUEST

After the highly charged atmosphere of Oak Hill and the 1995 Ryder Cup traumas and dramas, I naively thought it would be refreshing to return to the United States in the New Year when the press would have had their fill of my private life. Two reporters were arrested for forcing their way into Brenna's classroom at university and later brought before the courts to face charges of 'interfering with the peaceful conduct of an educational institution', a crime of which I was previously unaware.

The golf at least provided some sanctuary, a place where I could follow my daily routine without having a microphone stuck in my face. The season began in heartening style at La Costa in Carlsbad, California, where I finished joint second to Mark O'Meara in the Mercedes Championship. That was followed by equal eighth in the Buick Invitational and a tie for ninth place in the Honda Classic, an event that provided a distasteful postscript to the Ryder Cup.

The American press may not give a monkey's about their stars' behaviour in private but, in the aftermath of Oak Hill, the newspapers had lambasted captain Lanny Wadkins and a number of his players for a perceived lack of fight on that final afternoon. Even Rick Reilly, a highly respected columnist on *Sports Illustrated*, criticised the selection of Curtis Strange who, it should never be forgotten, had come within a single putt of winning the Ryder Cup. According to Reilly, 'America lost the Ryder Cup in a week when Nick Faldo made two birdies and Seve Ballesteros hit three fairways. America lost the Cup with the number one player on the PGA Tour money list, Lee Janzen, sitting on his couch at home.'

Fuelled by many such articles – and, no doubt, by several plastic cups of beer – six months after the events of Oak Hill, a buffoon in the gallery at the Honda Classic decided to make his thoughts known to Curtis Strange who, as luck would have it, was my first-round playing partner. 'Bogey! Bogey! Bogey! Ryder Cup choker,' came the cry from the other side of the ropes. I was outraged on Strange's behalf. Here was an honourable champion, a man who had won two US Opens and played in four previous Ryder Cups with distinction, being belittled by a drunk. I insisted that the marshals fling the heckler out on his ear. Better than anyone, I could fully understand the pressures Strange had been under on the 18th at Oak Hill and was not prepared to stand idly by whilst some jerk mocked his talent and reputation.

America can provide some lighter moments too, especially in the pre-tournament pro-am events where anything can, and frequently does, happen. Sometimes you find yourself sharing a round with a low-handicap player who knows his way round a course. More often, however, you are paired with a millionaire businessman who cannot tell his mashie-niblick from his elbow. On one such afternoon, Fanny and I stood on the first tee beside a young giant of the business world who had the very best clubs, a crocodile skin bag and every gimmick known to the pro shop, including fluorescent coloured golf balls. Orange ball number one was sliced into the trees. That was swiftly followed by a yellow missile, which was hooked into the lake. My companion decided enough was enough and wrote 'no return' on his scorecard. At the second hole it was orange right into trees, yellow left into water – 'no return'.

By the 13th hole he had still not set foot on a green. Belatedly, on the 14th par-3 he hit his tee-shot 100 yards or so down the middle – 'Very good,' I said encouragingly – then knocked his approach into a greenside bunker whereupon he picked up his ball and put it in his pocket.

'Aren't you going to play out?' I asked.

'No,' he said. 'Bunker play is not the strong point of my game.'

On another occasion, I was paired with a little old man in his 80s who hacked his way down the 1st eventually taking a ten.

'I think this fella needs some help,' I whispered to Fanny.

On the 2nd tee, I took him aside and mentioned, as kindly as I could, 'You've got to try and scrape the club away by taking a wider backswing.'

'No, I can't do that. I've just had both hips replaced and I'm still very stiff.'

'Well, try and get your left shoulder under your chin just a little bit.'

'I'm afraid I can't do that either. I've just had a new titanium rotator-cuff put in my shoulder as well.'

'OK, fine, then keep your eyes on the ball as you go through.'

'You're not going to believe this but this morning I picked up my wife's glasses and I'm having trouble focusing on the ball.'

'So, apart from that, everything's all right?'

'Pardon?'

Cue outbreak of hysterics from Ms Sunesson.

With my game in fine fettle, a fortnight before the '96 Masters I played the Tournament Players' Championship at Ponte Vedra Beach, Sawgrass, where, after a satisfactory opening round of 70, my second round was interrupted by heavy rain. On the Saturday morning, the course was enveloped in a shroud of bone-chilling damp mist. I was warming up on the practice ground under the eagle eye of Fanny when I heard a sickening crack in my neck, followed by shards of pain slicing through my shoulders. With the Masters two weeks away, Fanny advised me to withdraw immediately but, foolishly perhaps, I decided to continue even though I could not complete a full backswing or even follow the path of a putt because of the pain. A second round 75 was not good enough to make the cut but, happily, I had suffered nothing worse than a severe muscle spasm and by the time I descended upon Augusta, I was fighting fit physically if not mentally.

I was trying to juggle (more successfully this time, I hoped) my role as a dad to Natalie, Matthew and Georgia, who were once again visiting Florida during the Easter holidays, and my career as a professional golfer. Going into April, however, I felt something was missing, some spark, that single ingredient which can transform you from contender into champion. After the usual round of swimming outings and games of tennis it suddenly dawned on me that I had not hit a golf ball in some time and the Masters was only a week away. I decided, therefore, that I had to tell the kids a white lie about a business meeting and I nipped off to practise on Good Friday. I felt dreadful about that, but at the time my overall feeling was that the holiday had gone well. A few years later, however, I came across a photograph we had taken on Easter Sunday with the kids all dressed up. Looking at it with fresh eyes I saw the faces of three lost souls and I realised how much they were hurting.

I arrived in Augusta in reasonably good spirits. But reality dawned when, as is my custom at the Masters, I went out on the back nine to begin my first practice round and skied my tee-shot on the 10th; I trudged over to the 11th – skied it; went to the 13th and skied it twice. The Tuesday brought no marked improvement and halfway through my practice session I threw the clubs on the ground and informed Fanny, 'That's it, I'm going for lunch to try and find a new brain.' I shared a table with Bob Cotton, a police officer from Tulsa who, in the autumn of 1995, had been my minder when I dragged half of Fleet Street to Oklahoma on the announcement of my separation from Gill. He did a very good job as well. I remember one hack tried to get across a putting green to ask me some questions when Bob blocked his path with the immortal line, 'Are you tired of your teeth?' I was bemoaning my lack of form when Bob glanced up from his plate and, almost in a whisper, said, 'Just remember, you're Nick Faldo.'

Perhaps it was merely a coincidence (or synchrodestiny even, as Deepak Chopra would say), but when I reported to the registration desk to be allocated a player's badge, it was number 67. 'Sixty-seven, lovely, lovely, lovely,' I thought to myself. 'That'll do nicely this week.' Of course, that is precisely what I shot in the final round. Sportsmen are always looking for little omens like that and my mood brightened even further when I was handed my courtesy car key-ring bearing the number 111. 'One, one, one . . . three wins?'

I was on the practice ground prior to the tournament when Jerry Pate, he of the model tempo from the 1970s, wandered past and commented, 'Hey, you're just a bit quick from the top, but that doesn't matter here. You've got to be the best putter at the end of the week.' Jerry's words gave me a real boost because I was putting well, but I was determined to correct the speed of my swing. I spent hour after hour on the practice range coming through the ball as slowly as humanly possible, trying to hit it as softly as I could. It is what I called my 'powder-puff' swing after Georgia's favourite cartoon character. So after all that hard work to slow things down, who am I partnered with in the first round? John 'Wild Thing' Daly, who seems to spend his time trying to murder the ball at top speed! Quite a double act.

Experience is everything at the Augusta National – I know Tiger Woods triumphed in his first Masters but that lad is something special – and, although my best finish in a Major in 1995 had been equal

24th, I was suddenly overwhelmed by this uncanny feeling that I was destined to achieve great things. Out-driven by anything up to 60 yards by my playing partner, I nevertheless won our private first-round duel 69–71 and was somewhat surprised to find myself still six shots off the pace behind Greg Norman's course record-equalling 63. Even so, having had so little practice, that 69 gave me a great lift.

Norman had been on the verge of packing up and moving out just 24 hours previously when his final practice round was curtailed owing to back pains. He was miraculously restored to rude health by a visit to Fred Couples's personal therapist. When Fred's fiancée, Thasis, noted the Australian had outscored her intended by 15 strokes in the first round, she famously exclaimed, 'You picked one helluva time to make Greg Norman feel like a million bucks, dahlin'.' On day two a second-round 67 gave me a halfway 8 under par total of 136, still four shots adrift of the pace-setting Norman, with whom I would now be partnered in Saturday's third round.

It was nip and tuck for the first 10 holes with Norman unable to increase his advantage and me equally unable to whittle down his lead; on the 11th, the pin was way back left in a suicide spot, and I intended to play right of the pin into the fat of the green but I pulled my approach, the ball finished 12 feet from the hole just dangling above the creek. The crowd went crazy, thinking I had gone for the flag, when Fanny was heard to murmur ironically, 'Balls as big as grapefruits.' And so to the 12th, the delightfully named but devilishly difficult 'Golden Bell', described thus by Bob Ferrier in *The World Atlas of Golf Courses*:

> The 12th hole at Augusta is one of the world's great par-
> 3s; measuring 155 yards, it plays to a green which is quite
> wide but narrows from front to back. Rae's Creek crosses
> in front, pushing up towards the putting surface. A frontal
> bunker is squeezed between water and putting surface and
> there are two bunkers off the back of the green, with its

backcloth of flowering shrubs and a wall of tall pine trees. The pin is often cut on a direct line with front and back bunkers so there may only be a handful of yards between flagstick and water. And up there, above the green, tree-top high, is the wind, the great unknown factor. Players will be hitting a high pitch at this hole [I myself tend to use a seven-, eight- or nine-iron depending on the conditions] to a really minute target area. If only he could know what the wind will do to his shot, if, indeed, there is any wind, so there's little point in throwing strands of grass into the air. So this 12th hole, severe enough in its basic parts, becomes an enigma wrapped in mystery.

Still leading the Masters on 11 under par, Norman struck his worst shot in 48 holes by plonking his 8-iron straight into the murky depths of Rae's Creek, and was now faced with the distinct prospect of racking up a double-bogey five. A par-3 would bring me to within two shots of the lead, but the 12th at Augusta is, as Fanny says, 'the only hole in the world where the caddie prays' because the capricious wind can wreak havoc with the best of tee-shots. It was more than a full 8-iron, yet less than a full 7. After a lengthy debate with Fanny, I settled on a 7 and watched in abject horror as the ball sailed over the green and into the fringe rough beyond. If there is one spot on the 12th you do not wish to find yourself, it is here, confronted by a downhill chip on to the lightning-quick putting surface with Rae's Creek waiting like a shark with its jaws gaping open to swallow anything over-hit, however gently.

Norman, playing his third shot having taken a penalty drop from the water, conjured up an inspired sand-wedge from 80 yards, which pulled up 10 feet from the pin, whereas, using all my ingenuity, the very best I could do was a feathered chip to 12 feet. Still angry with myself for not depositing my tee-shot in the middle of the green, I proceeded to miss the putt for a bogey-four, a score Norman matched with a courageous 10-footer. Minutes before it had looked conceivable that I would enjoy a two-stroke swing, but I trudged off to the 13th still four strokes in arrears.

Matching each other shot for shot we both unleashed mighty drives round the corner on the par-5 13th where I missed an eight-footer for an eagle. Each registering a birdie four, the leaderboard's less than encouraging figures continued to read:

Norman 11 under, Faldo 7 under.

At the par-5 15th I was again on the green in two, but took three wretched putts from 50 feet, while Norman, in the rough from the tee and still short of the green in two, flighted home a superb pitch over the water to within six feet for an improbable birdie four and a five-shot cushion. Moving on to the 16th I hit probably my worst shot of the week when I pushed my 9-iron into the front-right bunker and made a bogey 4. By round's end, Norman's 71 for a 13 under par three-round total of 203, against my less than scintillating 73, meant I entered the final round trying to overturn a six-shot advantage held by the current number one golfer in the world. Even more dispiriting, I had had opportunities on the 12th, 13th, 14th, 15th and 16th to reduce the deficit, only to miss all five putts, the longest of which was in the eight to 10 foot range. On the positive side, however, my birdie on the 18th, inconsequential as it had seemed at the time, ensured I would be going head-to-head with Norman over the last 18 holes, which meant I would be in a position to exert a bit of pressure should he start to wobble, as many a third-round Masters leader has done.

In the press tent, I put on my usual brave face. 'Of course I can still win. I'm only six back,' I told them, and as I was talking, I actually began to believe the apparent nonsense coming out of my own mouth. 'You know what?' I muttered inwardly. 'I'm right. Six back isn't anything at Augusta. If I can get three back on the front nine, a three-shot lead on the back nine is absolutely nothing.' I woke up on the Sunday morning fully refreshed and relaxed, placed a call to my parents, which I seldom do before a final round, and became so engrossed in a Nascar motor-race on television, I did not have time for my usual hour-and-a-half warm-up.

'You've got fifty-seven minutes before you tee off,' Fanny reminded me, when I finally ambled on to the practice tee. In reality, this break in my normal routine was probably a good thing for me as it meant that I just had to get on with my practice whereas Greg had been down there early, chatting to everyone.

His name has often appeared throughout this narrative, but who exactly was Greg Norman with whom I would now do battle in the last round of the Masters? World number one for a total of 331 weeks between 1986 and 1998, Greg's abundant talent has never been reflected in Major titles, yet he can be considered one of the true greats of golf. With over 70 tournament successes world-wide, he has become one of the wealthiest sportsmen in the world through the multi-million dollar yachts, his wines, his clothing line and the grass-seed business he recently sold. But I firmly believe Greg would gladly swap his bank-book and the vast majority of those 70 plus victories for a single Masters or US Open triumph to add to his British Open successes of 1986 and 1993.

Having led going into the final round of seven previous Majors only to surrender the lead on six occasions, his critics were wont to describe him as lacking a killer streak – despite being known as 'The Great White Shark' – and being prone to nerves. Greg should have won the Masters in 1987 when Larry Mize outrageously holed out from 40 yards at the second extra hole. Greg also lost the 1984 US Open the Fuzzy Zoeller in a play-off and was denied victory in the 1986 US PGA Championship when Bob Tway holed out from a bunker to win by one shot.

According to legend, Norman's misfortunes began way back in 1982 in the European Open at Sunningdale. His name was at the top of the leaderboard on the 7th tee of the final round. One of the finest drivers in the modern game, Greg was at the very top of his backswing when a worm popped its head (or it could have been tail) through the turf a few centimetres behind his teed-up ball. Adjusting his swing to avoid sending the creepy-crawly to kingdom come, Greg, hardly surprisingly, topped his drive deep into the rough and another title was gone the way of so many before and since.

Being the type of man he is, the Australian has never allowed this litany of disappointments to sour him and he remains one of the most laid-back and chivalrous of rivals. Even with a six-shot deficit to claw back, however, I knew that, given my matchplay record – and despite the looming presence of Phil Mickelson only one further shot adrift in third place, all Augusta appreciated this was nothing less than a matchplay situation – if I could bloody Greg's nose by landing an early blow, all things were possible.

Things went to plan from Greg's opening drive at the first, which ran off the left edge of the fairway, blocking his approach to the green and resulting in a bogey five. The scoreboard now read Norman 12 under, Faldo 7 under, and I thought to myself, 'Lovely, one back after one. The perfect opening gambit. Is that the chink of light I've been hoping for?' As we stood on the second tee, I could feel the nervousness emanating from Greg. He gripped and regripped his club time and again, as though he could not steel himself to hit the ball. 'Obviously something is going on in Greg's mind,' I thought to myself. Courageously – and the White Shark has never been anything less than courageous on a golf course – he matched my birdie four on the second where he showed sublime touch by two-putting from off the back of the green, which suggested that he had pulled himself together.

On the 4th Greg mishit a 4-iron a bit high on the blade, ending up short and in a bunker, from which he made a bogey four.

Having myself bogeyed the 5th, I immediately bounced back at the next, the sweet-sounding but demonic 180-yard, par-3 Juniper.

Twice in the week — and the last day is always one of those days — the pin is placed back right on a plateau, which is raised at least four feet from the rest of the green, meaning the area you are aiming to land the ball on is about a 15-feet circle. I have always regarded this as one of the key shots of the Augusta week because you know your game is on if you can hit this spot consistently. My 6-iron landed on the plateau, the ball coming to rest about six feet behind the pin. After dropping a shot, it was important I did not surrender my early momentum and when I rolled in the putt, it sent a message to both Greg and myself that battle was truly joined. Visibly reeling from that latest blow, Greg began taking longer and longer over every shot, his seeming need to constantly regrip increasing. For my part, I made a conscious effort to stand taller, walk more purposefully, to show no reaction whatsoever to any wayward shot. That is all you can do in golf. You cannot physically beat up the other guy and I would never dream of trying to psyche someone out with a patronising remark or throwaway line. But with my stride, my bearing, my expression, I wanted to remind my opponent, 'Hey, I don't know about you, but I'm all right, mate.'

Greg, by contrast, was putting himself under increasing pressure. Augusta can play mind games with you, inducing you to question the wisdom of each and every shot, which is precisely the reason Greg pulled his approach shot into the trees on the 8th, then tried to bite off too much on the 9th where his ball spun back off the green: Norman 11 under, Faldo 9 under.

On to the notorious Amen Corner, the 10th, where Greg jammed his chip well past the hole, then missed the return putt for a par, at which point, I was later informed, his best pal on the Tour, Nick Price, walked out of the clubhouse, exclaiming, 'I can't stand to watch this happen to Greg.' When Greg three-putted the 11th from 18 feet, we were suddenly tied at the top of the scoreboard: Norman 9 under, Faldo 9 under.

Having made up six strokes in 11 holes, the contest had truly become classic matchplay, and one of the golden rules of match-play is to hit the par-3s first, especially the 12th at Augusta, the 155-yard Golden Bell. Standing on the tee, you have to make a decision on exactly where you want to land the ball; you cannot afford to pick a club then change your mind or you will have to start the thought process all over again. Given the brutish angle of the 12th green, if you intend to go for the heart of the target area then suddenly think, 'No, I'll go left,' you will have too much club, but if you decide to go right, you will come up short. It is one of the subtlest holes in world golf.

Fortunately this time there was no indecision. I selected a 7-iron and played a perfect shot to 15 feet left of the stick – precisely where I wanted the ball to be – which served to pump up the pressure even more on Greg. Whether he was indecisive about going for the pin or playing safe I cannot say, but his ball came up a couple of feet short of the putting surface and slid slowly back to disappear into Rae's Creek, where he had also found himself in the previous round. On the American sports channel ESPN, commentator Dan Patrick muttered, 'If Greg Norman blows the 1996 Masters, it will be the biggest collapse in golf history.' A double-bogey five from the shell-shocked Australian against my regulation par and the tournament had been turned on its head: Faldo 9 under, Norman 7 under.

'Bloody hell,' I whispered to Fanny as we made our way to the 13th, 'now it's mine to lose.'

I can only guess how Norman was reacting but for the first time during the round I could feel my chest constricting as the enormity of events began to sink in. The 465-yard par-5 at Augusta is not the best spot on the golfing planet to start harbouring such doubts. I found the middle of the fairway off the tee, leaving myself with around 210 yards to the front of the green and 228 yards to the pin, precisely the 5-wood distance I had been practising all week; Fanny had packed the club in my bag for four days for just such an eventuality: I was still faced with a puzzling dilemma, with the ball standing above my feet but, incongruously, on a downhill lie. When I addressed the ball, the club face would not sit still, twisting around. 'Road is left, creek is right, road is left, creek is right,' kept going through my head until I suddenly realised, 'That's enough of that'. I returned to my bag and said to Fanny, 'Let's start again. I'm OK, I want to go for it.'

On television, the commentators were dramatising events. 'Nick Faldo doesn't know what he's doing. He doesn't know whether to lay up or go for the green.' In fact we had no such doubts because I knew if I nailed a 2-iron, the ball would easily make the front edge and even if it did roll over the green I could still get up and down for my birdie four.

With the pendulum having swung in my direction, I knew one fantastic shot would send out even more forcibly, the 'I'm alright' message. The visualisation complete, I executed one of the very best shots of my life, the ball soaring as if laser-guided into the heart of the green. Narrowly up ahead, Greg had driven on to a nest of pine needles and I could tell he was considering trying to match my effort, which would have been golfing suicide from such an unpredictable lie. His caddie managed to talk him out of this adventure and after some minutes of consultation he played up short from where, and all credit to him, he matched my birdie with a fighting pitch and putt. With five holes to play, my two-stroke lead remained intact.

There was to be no let-up in the pressure. On the 490-yard, par-5 15th, I fired in a slightly fat 4-iron low-runner, which landed on the green as though it was a bed of concrete and bounced through the putting surface into the fringe at the back. Greg, meanwhile, all but holed his pitch for an eagle, only adding to the degree of difficulty of my shot to come. It was a fiendishly tricky little pitch, the classic Augusta bump-and-run — struck too timidly, the ball would not bounce up the bank to the green; too adventurously, and there was every chance it would pick up speed on its downhill route to the hole and roll into the water at the other side. With the adrenaline coursing through my veins and my throat like parchment, I made it look ridiculously easy by judging the chip to absolute perfection. The ball trickled ever so slowly towards the target, coming to rest three feet from the flag. Under the circumstances, the shot represented a miraculous recovery for a birdie four: Faldo 11 under, Norman 9 under.

It was all over on the par-3 16th. I was content to aim for the middle of the green and Greg, presumably thinking this was his last chance from two shots back, went for the flag in a last-ditch attempt to reduce the leeway. He succeeded only in pulling his 6-iron tee-shot badly left into the lake for a double-bogey five: Faldo 11 under, Norman 7 under.

Having started the final round a few hours earlier trying to claw back a six-shot deficit, I arrived on the 18th with a four-stroke advantage. It was a weird sensation for, having won my two previous Masters on the 11th green in play-offs, I had always dreamed of marching up the 18th at Augusta with my arms raised in triumph, knowing I had won the title.

With Greg being such a popular competitor, the crowd were understandably confused about how to react; on the one hand, they wanted to treat the vanquished with the respect worthy of a great champion, on the other hand, they wanted to whoop and holler at such an unlikely victor. I could sense the waves of sympathy pouring down upon Greg from the bleachers as I made my way up the fairway, so it would have been entirely inappropriate to engage in any demonstration of triumphalism. I tried to acknowledge the cheers in a dignified manner, with a smile and a nod of the head, but inside I was exultant for the 18th green at Augusta is a sight like no other – the greenest of grass, the whitest of bunkers, the bluest of skies, the clubhouse shimmering in the distance.

But I still had the final hole to negotiate and I drove into the bunker, which was fine — a far better place to be than in the trees. I plucked a 9-iron from the bag and was halfway through my backswing when the thought occurred, 'Blimey, Nick, you're playing this a bit quick.' Arriving on the green, I took a quick look at the scoreboard, and even though I knew it was a two-horse race, instinct took over and I did my maths, counted twice to double-check, and heaved a 'no-one-can-catch-me' sigh of relief. After holing out for a birdie three and my pre-ordained 67 — the number of my player's badge — my first thoughts were for Greg. I felt genuinely sorry for him. Although I had lost the 1988 US Open to Curtis Strange in a play-off at Brookline, I had not been scarred by the experience. I have no doubt whatever that Greg was scarred for life by the events which unfolded at Augusta that afternoon. To have the green jacket snatched away just as you are visualising slipping your arms into the sleeves must be soul-destroying.

The hour following the end of any Major is a blur of television and newspaper interviews and I repeatedly made a point of pleading with the press to go easy on Greg, 'because we still want him around, don't we?' That was followed by the presentation of the green jacket in Butlers Cabin and the formal Champion's Dinner. I am frequently asked why none of my three Masters blazers graces my trophy cabinet, but under Augusta National rules, the jacket must never leave the clubhouse, with the exception of during the champion's reigning year. Gary Player sneaked one out by accident, sparking an outraged phone call to his home in South Africa from the then chairman, Clifford Roberts.

'You do realise it is not allowed to remove your green jacket from Augusta, don't you, Gary?'

'Mister Roberts, the next time you're passing through Johannesburg, I'll be more than happy to hand it back.'

Like two boxers who had given their all and then some, on the 18th green Greg and I had shared a hug and a private word in front of the watching millions.

'I don't know what to say,' I told him. 'Don't let the bastards get you down over this.'

The media were eager to know what words of solace I had offered but for many years it remained a secret between the two of us, until an incident that occurred during dinner with my friend Craig Farnsworth one night in Colorado.

'Right, out with it,' cajoled Craig. 'What did you say to Greg at Augusta in 1996?'

'That's between the two of us. I'll never tell anyone the exact words.'

At that very moment, the restaurant owner came over to our table with a small coin as a memento of our visit and, inscribed on it in Latin was exactly what I had said to Greg, although the Romans did not use the expletive.

The following morning I returned to the scene of my third Masters victory to let it all sink in; I wandered around the 18th green and then sat in the empty grandstand just reliving every moment. That climactic afternoon in Georgia had been a piece of sporting theatre like no other.

Compared with the opening round of the 1990 Open at St Andrews where I had walked down the first fairway thinking to myself that I was going to win by five shots, a prediction which proved wholly accurate, I had felt anything but confident before that last round against Greg at Augusta. As it turned out, the round proved to be my finest in terms of sustaining the mental stamina you need to commit to your routine before each and every shot as the pressure and atmosphere grows. This is something I am very proud of. As I surveyed the scene of my latest triumph, the sense of relief in knowing I could still win a Major (which far outweighed any sense of triumph) was overwhelming.

The youngsters on the Faldo Series must have grown weary of hearing me go on and about it but it is a message worth repeating time and again: when you play in the four Majors, or indeed any other tournament, I believe you must treat every shot as history in that your opening drive on the first hole is as important as your final putt on the 72nd. That is the secret to tournament golf. Can you maintain the same intensity — not just for four rounds but for 24 hours a day for four days — from beginning to end? Some golfers, like Lee Trevino, manage to give the impression of being super-cool and relaxed. He is always a bubbly, talkative character on the surface, but what is going on inside his head we will never know; perhaps the more nervous he became, the more he talked and that was his own way of dealing with it. But if you are Lee Trevino on Thursday morning, then you have to be Lee Trevino on Sunday afternoon.

Before any Major, all the attention is usually focused on about 10 players, which is why you often find a relative unknown leading on 12 under par after 36 holes, only to slip back to 2 under after 72. The enormity of leading suddenly hits the less fancied contender, and what came so naturally in round one suddenly vanishes — although, of course, some recent Major winners have bucked this trend. On six occasions — three Opens and three Masters — I found the ability to live in my own little world 24 hours a day, controlling my breathing, controlling my nerves, controlling my emotions, controlling my heart and mind.

I have to laugh whenever I hear someone, usually a young, brash, American pro, wittering: 'My God, I was in the zone on the back nine.' I remember once being with Jack Nicklaus during a TV interview and when this subject came up, Jack laughed, 'Hell, I was in the zone for 20 years.' Jack shared the same ability that Muhammad Ali possessed, of being able to create — intentionally — exactly the right state of mind to produce the maximum performance, just as I did during that never-to-be-forgotten Sunday afternoon in April 1996.

CHAPTER FIFTEEN

CAPTAIN SEVE

For at least the first two years after my split from Gill, golf provided a welcome release from my emotional and financial tribulations. How else can I explain my victory in the Masters at a time when my brain was addled and my heart aching? Perhaps I was trying to prove to everyone that whereas I might be a failure in the marriage stakes, as a golfer I was still right up there with the very best. I was not to know that both my mind and body were gradually being worn down and that I would ultimately be robbed of the resilience I had shown at Augusta. I still felt physical pain every time I thought about or looked at a picture of the children: missing them so deeply was a killer. Hearing over the phone about sports day or the school play can never be the same as being there in person.

But, having won a third Masters, I was big news again in America where all the talk before the 1996 US Open at Oakland Hills, Detroit, centred on whether I could now go on to complete the elusive 'grand slam' by winning all four great championships in a single year. To add to the pressure, Lee Trevino had predicted that I would come to challenge Jack Nicklaus's record of 18 Majors, to which I laughingly replied, 'Six down, only twelve to go. It's still a long way off.' Perhaps it was due to all the build-up or merely a reaction to the physical and mental exhaustion of Augusta, but I was never remotely in the hunt, eventually finishing joint 16th behind the unexpected victor, American Steve Jones.

Next came the 125th British Open, and my 20th appearance, which was scheduled for Royal Lytham where I had won the English Amateur Championship 21 years earlier in 1975. I celebrated my 39th birthday with a 3 under par first-round 68, a score I repeated on both the Friday and Saturday only to find myself a distant second to Tom Lehman, whose third-round 64 earned him a safety-net of 6 strokes at the top of the leaderboard. How the tabloids relished this reminder of Augusta. 'I'll Spank the Yank: Faldo's Vow to Topple Lehman' screamed one Sunday morning back page, even though I had carefully avoided making any such suggestion when I had been grilled in the press tent following my third successive 68.

'Are there any similarities to the Masters?' I was asked, to which I replied honestly but deliberately deadpan, 'Yes, it's a Major, I'm lying second, and, yes, here I am with six shots to make up again.' In private, I thought Lehman might well wilt in the white heat of battle and falter he duly did with an adventuresome 73. In the end this proved sufficient and, although I managed to claw back three strokes, I trailed home a despondent fourth after being overtaken by American Mark McCumber and South African Ernie Els on the run-in.

Like so many of my fishing trips, it was another tale of the one that got away. I missed a birdie opportunity on the first, which could have set up my round, squandered two other chances on the 4th and 5th then, after a great drive on the par-5 6th, I hit an 8-iron over the green and failed to make a birdie. I was round in a one under par 70 which could have, should have, been a title-winning 66. To give credit to Lehman, he hooked numerous drives on that final afternoon but scrambled magnificently and was a worthy champion, having played from the left rough almost throughout his round.

The US PGA at Valhalla, Kentucky, three weeks later was even more depressing for me; it was played in searing heat, so suffocating that I even walked off at the 13th during my first practice round, almost an unheard of occurrence, saying, 'That'll do for me.' I became even more hot under the collar when, after a promising opening round of 69, I was never in contention, lagging home 14 strokes behind American Mark Brooks in an embarrassing tie for 65th place.

The consolation was that my tally of Majors was just one fewer than that of early heroes such as Bobby Jones, Sam Snead and Arnold Palmer: my place in golf's pantheon was secure and I could relax accordingly. At the AT&T Pro-Celebrity Tournament in January 1997, I offered to caddie for my old fishing buddy Huey Lewis, introducing myself to the crowd as 'Fanny Faldo' while wearing an Ozzie Osbourne wig, to the delight of the photographers. I forced myself to take part in such lighter situations in an attempt to find some relief from everything that was going on in my life. I suppose what I was doing was just going through the motions of having fun to try to block out other things.

Before my defence of the Masters the following year, I had agreed to compete in the Nissan Open at the exotic-sounding Riviera Country Club in Los Angeles, where the notorious O.J. Simpson used to play his golf before being declared *persona non grata* by the members. Rounds of 66, 70, 68 and 68 earned me my sixth US Tour title on a final afternoon when a young man by the name of Tiger Woods stormed up the leaderboard with a closing 69. The title was won in what I like to think is classic Faldo style, setting the pace from the first round and seeing off every challenge. Every time someone drew within two shots of me, I would immediately strike back with a couple of birdies. Craig Stadler was the first to launch a determined run at me but I shot birdie, birdie as if to say, 'send the next one right in here, please.'

I adore playing the Riviera because it is a fabulous course, brilliantly designed by George Thomas. It appears to be simplicity itself, with one dangerous bunker on each hole, greens set at an angle, cleverly-placed trees, and if you are not down the correct side of every fairway, you are in real trouble, which is why it remains one of my favourite courses in America. It is subtle and difficult, just how I like a course to be.

When I arrived in Miami for the Doral the following week, something hit me that I can't explain. I just felt different. Even though I had just come off the back of a win I suddenly thought, 'Well, that's it.' The Nissan Open of 1997 thus remains my last individual tournament victory, which I can only put down to finally snapping under the strain of my increasingly tangled life away from the golf course. I was completely drained, a state from which, seven years on, I am only now emerging.

By the time of the Tournament Players' Championship at Sawgrass towards the end of March, the American media were transfixed by the notion that a 20-year-old Augusta rookie might win the green jacket on his Masters' debut. Asked repeatedly about Tiger, I was by now too wise in the ways of the press to dismiss his chances and returned their googlies with a straight bat.

'If you go out and play Augusta totally relaxed, it's a piece of cake. If you go out and play it as the Masters, then it's pressure time and that's when you discover what a tough course Augusta really is.'

'Given the media circus, do you have any sympathy for the player who has to partner Tiger?' I was asked.

'If you want to keep on top of your own game, there's nothing worse than a lot of commotion going on,' I conceded.

In a way it was a futile question-and-answer session because one of the Masters' quaint traditions calls for the defending champion to partner the reigning US Amateur Champion, in this instance Tiger Woods. Thus we were duly paired together in the first round, and press attention switched to the resumption of my rivalry with Greg Norman.

'Last year was the worst round of my life,' Greg admitted. 'The eleventh, twelfth, thirteenth, I want to flush those holes out of my mind. But Nick put the pressure on me, he created the atmosphere. He did all the things you have to do to win a Major championship.'

This time, though, it was my turn to crack under the pressure. Once again I was juggling practice sessions with David Leadbetter with spending as much time as possible with Natalie, Matthew and Georgia, who were, as in previous years, at Lake Nona for their Easter holidays and, I was ready to snap, and snap I duly did. 'Is there any particular player whom you would like to help into the jacket?' I was quizzed by one particularly insensitive person. 'No,' I replied sharply. 'I want it to remain in my wardrobe.'

Next I had to decide what dishes to request for the Champion's Dinner on the eve of the tournament. Having chosen shepherd's pie in 1990, and steak and kidney pie the following year, this time I plumped for plain old fish and chips. Just to make sure it was the real thing, I insisted on 30 pounds of cod being flown in from Harry Ramsden's, not forgetting the individual salt cellars and vinegar jars. I am delighted to say my choice was voted one of the three best dinners ever staged at Augusta, rated right up there with Ben Crenshaw's famous Texan barbecue and Vijay Singh's Thai and sushi evening. Vijay was the first to introduce sushi to the menu, a dish Tiger now favours as a starter followed by an all-American beefburger.

And so the condemned man ate a hearty meal. Such was the outbreak of 'Tigermania' sweeping Augusta that a gallery exceeding 15,000 assembled on the first tee to witness the defending champion being out-driven by 60 yards or more. After 10 holes, I was languishing on 5 over while Woods was only one stroke better off. Designed by Dr Alister Mackenzie, a Scot who had emigrated to America where he had given up medicine to become a golf-course architect, Augusta could have been the brainchild of the devil himself that afternoon. The combination of a capricious wind and blisteringly fast greens ensured it was all but unplayable and the scores gradually rose – Corey Pavin 76, Greg Norman 77, Seve Ballesteros 81, so I was in no way disgraced by shooting a 75. Disappointed, yes, humiliated, no. All the difficulties served to make Tiger Woods's first competitive round of golf at Augusta something at which to marvel; he was out in 40 and back in 30 for a scarcely credible 70, in the worst of conditions.

A second-round 81 meant I missed the cut and I sat transfixed in front of the television in the clubhouse as Tiger proceeded to pulverise the opposition, setting the lowest ever total, 270, and the largest winning margin, 12 strokes. As dismayed as I was with my own surrender, it was nothing but a privilege to assist Tiger Woods with the donning of the 1997 Masters green jacket.

Although I had won both the previous Masters and the prestigious Nissan Open on American soil in the space of 10 months, some so-called experts across the Atlantic in England were beginning to question my right to be awarded a 'wild card' invitation by captain Seve Ballesteros to compete in the next Ryder Cup at Valderrama in Spain. 'If I was the captain,' I announced in a rare blowing of my own trumpet, 'and Seve had just won the Nissan Open, all I can say is he'd be on my team. That's my only message to Seve.'

I admit that I did not further my Ryder Cup cause when, after top-three finishes in the Volvo PGA Championship at Wentworth and the Kemper Open, my form slumped alarmingly in the US Open at Congressional, Washington DC. Down among the masses at 5 over par after three rounds, I was paired with Tiger Woods on the final afternoon. Thus I witnessed the full force of 'Tigermania':

our round was a farce, played out on a course swarming with television reporters, cameramen, photographers, journalists, security men and marshals, which caused lengthy delays on each and every hole. In the midst of this chaos, I surrendered the last vestige of my concentration when an official warned us for slow play and, suitably outraged, I informed the official that I had previously pointed out that I was ready to play but was being continually held up by the scrum of photographers. 'Please don't tell me that you're going to time us because of all this chaos. This isn't our fault, guys.' My pleas fell on deaf ears and we were timed for the next eight holes, making it all but impossible to retain our full concentration.

A triple-bogey at the 6th, where my pitch found water instead of the putting surface, summed up my day and eventually I signed for a 6 over par-76, leaving me 15 shots behind the tournament winner, Ernie Els. To be fair to Congressional, having to deal with a golfer who arrived at the first tee surrounded by eight security guards and a huge posse of photographers was an exceptional situation.

As ever, Tiger behaved like a perfect gentleman. Fanny knows him well because she is best buddies with his caddie, Steve Williams, but I cannot say I have spent much time with him. However, he has always impressed me with his dignity and decency. Like Muhammad Ali before him, he has transcended his chosen sport to become one of the most instantly recognisable athletes on the planet so that from the moment he appears in public, the world's eyes are upon him.

The nearest we have ever seen to the 'complete' golfer, Tiger has taken interest in the sport to a new level, in a way that possibly only Arnold Palmer did before him. Every professional in America, Europe, Australia and Asia should be truly grateful for that. In 2000 all the talk was that Tiger had become too dominant and that if that continued, with him having built up 10-stroke leads by the halfway stage of numerous tournaments, then the television viewers would switch off in droves. Now in 2004 we see Tiger still a phenomenal golfer but not anywhere near so dominant, particularly in the Majors. He seems to be going through – in his terms at least – a lower point in his career. As I truly believe, this is the rhythm of life, with downswings and upswings coming along at various times. It has certainly happened to me in my career and it seems to be happening to some extent to Tiger at the moment. When I finally stop competing on the regular Tour, I look forward to sitting down and sharing a beer with Tiger.

With Tiger dominating the headlines, any lingering hopes I entertained of turning around what had become a distinctly lacklustre season evaporated, when four mediocre rounds at the British Open at Royal Troon left me trailing home in joint 51st position, my worst result in the Open since Royal St George's 12 years earlier.

After missing the cut in the US PGA at Winged Foot, New York – my opening rounds of 75 and 78 tallying up to a highly embarrassing 13 over par – I faced an agonising wait while Ryder Cup captain Seve Ballesteros pondered his two wild card selections. I did not envy him the task for, although I had been hailed as the hero of the hour at Oak Hill two years earlier, both Jesper Parnevik of Sweden and Jose-Maria Olazabal of Spain were in the reckoning, having also failed to qualify via the Order of Merit. Naturally, I felt my past record in the contest should be taken into consideration but, against that, both Parnevik and Olazabal were playing well. Had not fate stepped in, I often wonder how Seve would have solved this three-into-two conundrum. Fortunately for the three of us, but unfortunately for Miguel Angel Martin, Seve's young compatriot suffered a severe wrist injury and missed the entire month leading up to Valderrama. Seve decided Martin should prove his fitness by playing in a tournament before the Ryder Cup but he refused, insisting 'it will be all right on the night', and was unceremoniously dumped. Wily old fox that Seve is, this allowed him to pick the 11th placed player on the Order of Merit, Olazabal, and nominate Parnevik and myself as his two wild card selections.

Valderrama will forever be remembered as 'Seve's Ryder Cup' for no one in the 70-year history of the contest had ever brought more passion to the role of non-playing captain. Armed only with a buggy, I think Seve must have been using an illusionist's magic mirrors, so repeatedly did he pop up from the undergrowth all over the course to hiss, 'Six-iron, Monty, three-iron, Nick.' I remember his assistant, Miguel Angel Jimenez, coming down for breakfast one morning looking for all the world as though he had been up all night fighting a deranged gorilla; his eyes were red, his hair was all over the place, he was unshaven.

'I've been up since four o'clock this morning with Seve deciding in which order to put the players out,' he explained, waving his hands in the air in affectionate exasperation. 'Olazabal wants to go out first because he's a quick player, and Langer wants to go out last because he's slow. All Seve had to do was choose matches two and three but do you think he could make up his mind? No way, Jose . . .'

At that moment we were joined by Seve's wife, Carmen. 'Another night of two hours sleep. If this goes on, I'll be seeking a divorce.'

But Seve's boyish enthusiasm spread through the team like a benign fever, even if certain sections of the media questioned his leadership abilities, dragging up his record in the Spanish Army which he had chosen to quit early. Are we really that fascinated with digging up perceived negatives all the time? Attitudes seem different in America where things are so positive. I've been in tournaments in the US where I've missed the cut and I'll be out shopping in the local supermarket and people come up to me and tell me what a great player I am. It's a different focus on life.

During practice one morning, Monty, Lee Westwood, Darren Clarke and I could not work out the best way to tackle the 17th so I said, 'Well, it's simple. Let's go back and play it again.' Borrowing Seve's buggy, we raced back to the tee to have a second attempt.

One report subsequently suggested that Seve had been incandescent with rage at our inability to master the 17th and had ordered us to try again. In fact nothing could have been further from the truth.

Many of Seve's methods were inspired. Before a ball had even been struck, he asked each of the 12 European team members to write down on a slip of paper the names of the two players he would most like to partner in the fourballs and foursomes. I opted for Monty and rookie Lee Westwood, and when Westwood nominated Darren Clarke and Nick Faldo, the identity of my latest Ryder Cup sidekick had been established. Telling Lee I would ride shotgun while he chased the birdies, we won two points out of four including a 2 and 1 victory over Mark O'Meara and Tiger Woods in the Saturday foursomes. Less pleasing was our defeat at the hands of Jeff Maggert and Scott Hoch in the afternoon's fourballs, a couple whose behaviour, I felt, was sadly unsporting. Their pacing off of distances after it had already been decided who should putt first, and the way they repeatedly questioned some of the referee's decisions certainly created an atmosphere.

The build-up to that particular Ryder Cup on the usually sunny Spanish coast was exhausting in the extreme, because it poured down continually. Talk about the rain in Spain! We endured the three worst storms on record. Day after day, we would rise from our beds at six, eat breakfast, and then set off for the practice ground whereupon the heavens would open. We would sit around waiting for the rain to ease before teeing off at around 11 a.m. completing our 'morning' rounds about four and a half hours later. We would then return to the first tee at about five o'clock and play until it was dark. After 36 holes on the sodden sponge that was Valderrama, our leg muscles were begging for mercy – so then we would repair to the physiotherapy room for treatment. That was followed by the team dinner and then bed by 10.30 p.m. Next day, we would rise at six and the whole damp rigmarole would begin all over again.

Lee Westwood and I actually completed our Saturday evening foursomes against Justin Leonard and Jeff Maggert on the Sunday morning when Lee, bless him, holed a great putt on the 16th to earn us a 3 and 2 victory, which elevated me into the position of leading points-scorer in the history of the Ryder Cup. I later sent Lee a picture of the scene on the 16th with the simple but heart-felt message, 'Thanks, mate'.

Tactical genius or lucky conquistador depending on your view (and I will forever insist it was the former), under Seve's unique style of captaincy we went into the final day's singles with the cushion of a $10\frac{1}{2}$–$5\frac{1}{2}$ lead, which may sound a certainty in our favour but with the Americans' record in the singles throughout the years we knew it was still going to be a serious battle to get the points required. Our skipper was sent into another frenzied round of soul searching when, at 10.30 on the Saturday night, I reminded him he had yet to announce his starting line-up for the final day's singles.

'I play fast, I would like to go out number one,' said Ian Woosnam.

'Right, Woosie, you go out first,' replied Seve agreeably. 'Who go twelve?'

Silence.

'I'll go twelve then,' said Monty.

'Number twelve, you got it.'

'Well, I'm playing in my eleventh Ryder Cup so I'd like number eleven,' I reasoned.

'Good, good. Nick, you go eleventh.'

I do not know if Seve realises it to this day, but, give or take the odd guy, we pretty well chose our own slots. After we had clinched the narrowest of $14\frac{1}{2}$–$13\frac{1}{2}$ victories — with me losing my singles 3 and 2 to an inspired Jim Furyk, who chipped in from all over the place — all 12 of us made a special point of complimenting Seve on his 'brilliant strategy'. But Seve's unquestionable passion for the Ryder Cup is second to none and that has got to rub off on the whole team. He had been a brilliant general and it was impossible not to share his tears of joy following our Ryder Cup triumph on his beloved Spanish soil. The two things that have never been in doubt about Seve is the size of his heart and the fact that that heart is in the right place. He has made an enoruous contribution to the incomparable contest that is the modern Ryder Cup.

My abiding memory of Valderrama is of Seve's two team talks. On the Tuesday before battle commenced, his first speech was delivered low-key.

'You dohnna have to ween . . . I dohnna wanna poot thee pressure on you . . . I juss wanna you go out there and play the best you can . . . thass alla you can do . . . you go out and enjoy, you ween, you loose . . . eet doesn't mattah . . .'

Fast-forward to the Saturday night on the eve of the singles, however, and Seve's message to his troops had undergone a perceptible change in emphasis.

'You havva to ween . . . you havva to hole e-every putt . . . I dohnna wanna you heeting eet inna bunkah . . . I dohnna wanna you heeting eet inna watah . . . and I definitely dohnna wanna you heeting eet inna trees on sixteen . . .'

It was classic Seve stuff – and somehow we did not three-putt, we did not hit it in the bunkers and we most definitely did not hit it in the trees on 16, so the man must have been dead right, about the way to win.

The Ryder Cup competition is the single most exhausting week in golf, a fact no one can fully appreciate unless they have played in it. The work-load is relentless even before a ball is struck in the competition, and that is where Seve was like an uncle to the rookies in the team, gently coaxing them through the round of photoshoots, welcome dinner, interviews and team meetings. In the midst of all that, you must find time to fit in your practice sessions, and so by the Thursday night you can find yourself drained. Perhaps it is the sheer intensity, the head-to-head matchplay format, the desire to beat the Americans, the camaraderie of being part of a team for one week every two years in what is essentially an individual game but, to me, the Ryder Cup represents the ultimate sporting contest.

Given the cachet the contest has acquired over the past two decades, by contrast the annual World Cup, a two-man team event, has surrendered a measure of its former prestige. Still, a scan down the list of former winners – Peter Thomson and Kel Nagle (Australia), Ben Hogan and Sam Snead (US), Jack Nicklaus and Arnold Palmer (US), Seve Ballesteros and Manuel Pinero (Spain) – explains why I was so proud to add the title to my collection in 1998, in tandem with David Carter. Ireland had won the World Cup back in 1958 through Harry Bradshaw and Christy O'Connor, Ian Woosnam and David Llewellyn had triumphed in 1987, and I had always been desperately keen to see England's name on the trophy, preferably before the Scots could get there.

Again, it was a crazy time in my life. I had not long ago ended my unhappy relationship but was beginning to believe there were better times ahead, so before the competition began in New Zealand, I visited a Chinese herbalist in Auckland in the hope that he could prescribe a potion which would have a calming effect. I also rented a house on the harbour beside the course rather than staying in the official tournament hotel which was a good hour's drive distant. David must have been somewhat stunned to come down for breakfast every morning to find me frying eggs and bacon for our team. Before being thrown together in England's colours, we had only been nodding acquaintances so I think he was pleasantly surprised that we gelled so easily.

In David's congenial company, I struck a rich vein of form – losing the individual title by only a single shot – and I like to think he enjoyed the whole experience as much as I did. David has always been one of the unsung heroes of the European Tour and I was delighted for him when he sank a 20-foot putt on the final hole, thereby securing an English triumph. Sadly, due to injury problems,

David has not been able to use our World Cup victory as a spring-board to further successes but I look back on our week's work together with fond memories. I still regard the World Cup as a historic and important tournament, so I was extremely pleased to be a member of the first successful English team.

CHAPTER SIXTEEN

FALLING FOR V, SPLITTING FROM LEAD

I met Valerie Bercher (whom I now call 'V') across a crowded salad bar in the sponsors' hospitality tent at the 1997 Canon European Masters in Crans-sur-Sierre in the Swiss Alps, where she was working for IMG. I would come to appreciate she was everything I had always looked for – charming, sophisticated, elegant and, as a bonus, radiantly beautiful. V was also blessed with a smile that could melt a glacier. Behaving like a smitten 16-year-old, I would trot up to her desk at every opportunity armed with a series of dumber than dumb questions such as, 'Sorry to bother you yet again, but do you have tomorrow's practice tee-off times?' (As if Fanny did not carry all such information in her computer-like brain.)

On the Saturday night, I was engaged in a session on the putting green when out of the corner of my eye I spotted Valerie standing among a group of people by the 18th where she was discussing arrangements for the closing ceremony. Do not ask me how, but I knew that if I didn't take this opportunity to arrange to see her again, I would regret it for the rest of my life. So, steeling myself against probable instant rejection, I ambled over, feigning nonchalance.

'Excuse me, could I have a chat with you?'

'Now?'

'Yes, if it's convenient.'

'Why?'

'Well, I wondered if you'd give me your telephone number.'

'Why?'

'Because I'd like to call you some time.'

'Why?'

Clearly impressed by my blundering schoolboy chat-up, Valerie, eyes twinkling with mischief, duly jotted down a series of numbers that proved to be entirely fictitious. Even more intrigued by her apparent disinterest, on my return to England I managed to track down Valerie's genuine home number in Switzerland and we chatted regularly on the phone for a month before setting a definite date to meet. I flew to Geneva where Valerie was waiting in the airport arrivals hall, arms crossed, defences up, and with a smile that registered nothing but amused suspicion.

Our first date was like one of those filmed montages so beloved of Hollywood. We strolled along the banks of Lac Leman, chatted over coffee and a pastry in a pavement café, joked with the *patron* of a flower stall. Then in the afternoon, and I do not know what possessed me, I took her to see *The Full Monty* (the movie, not my golfing buddy). That did it: I was head-over-heels in love. Here was this gorgeous French-speaking Swiss girl laughing fit to burst at British humour.

Switzerland tends to close on a Monday so that night we had dinner in a nondescript Chinese restaurant where we opened our hearts to one another. Like me, Valerie was in a relationship that had run its course, so we agreed to go off and sort out our respective lives before taking our relationship any further. I later discovered that

Ryder Cup, Oak Hill, 1995

'OK Monty, if you say you can do it, do it.'

Celebrating with Seve and Monty. As Tony Jacklin said: What is it about the Ryder Cup that makes us come over all unnecessary?

Cut the atmosphere with a knife? More like a chainsaw. This was one for the team.

PIERRE-ALAIN HUG

SYLVAN MASON

Poised to carry V over the
threshold. Check out the stance…

The most precious bump in the world: a week
to go before the arrival of Emma.

SYLVAN MASON

The Faldo family line-up: Matthew, V, me and baby Emma, Natalie, Georgia.

although she had 'vaguely heard' of Tiger Woods, Valerie had no idea who I was (so it must have been my good looks that attracted her, not my reputation as a golfer).

The financial downward spiral into which I had been plunged, protracted divorce proceedings and my alarming loss of touch with a golf club in my hands all served to unbalance my equilibrium; It would take the best part of 12 months, by which time I was just about ready for the arrival of the men in white coats, before my life was sufficiently in order to enter a new phase with Valerie at my side. And how I needed her.

On my 41st birthday, the first morning of the 1998 British Open at Royal Birkdale, I awoke in an absolute sweat. I lay in bed gazing at the ceiling and thought, 'What the hell am I doing? My marriage may have ended in divorce, I may have lost my home, but I've got this beautiful girl in Switzerland I haven't seen for months and here I am in danger of becoming an absolute wreck.' Why had I allowed myself to descend into such a pit of despair? A trail of failed relationships, laziness, confusion, there were numerous reasons but on reaching Southport I placed a call to Switzerland from the pay-phone in the locker-room. I was nervous as hell because I had not spoken to Valerie for the best part of three months and was dreading her telling me that she had patched up her own relationship. Fortunately for me, she had not, and we agreed to meet again at the Canon European Masters at Crans-sur-Sierre later that summer when we could finally discuss a future together.

Nothing went smoothly, though. Believing I was still seeing someone else (technically true although the relationship in question was in its death throes and in fact, officially ended a short while later) Valerie studiously avoided me when I pitched up in Crans-sur-Sierre. Having missed the cut (surprise, surprise), I caught the first flight home without daring to show my face. At that point the cavalry rode to the rescue in the shape of the faithful Fanny. Bumping into Valerie in the clubhouse she took her aside and said,

'I've got to talk to you, girl. I know Nick. I've been working with him for eight years and he's really in love with you. I can tell by his eyes. We have to do something to save him.'

Valerie immediately penned a letter to me which she entrusted to Fanny, who duly passed it on when she and I met up again in Paris the following week. Halfway through the first page I burst into tears, dashed to the phone, called V's cell-phone and left a cringingly embarrassing, soppy, sentimental message on her voice-mail. Luckily V was coming to Paris on business so we plotted to meet at the golf course while Fanny covered for me. We found a bench and there we planned the next stage of our relationship. V's job then took her to London where we met up again and started our life together before I headed off to the World Cup with David Carter.

When Valerie came to live with me the following February, she took one look at my American interior designer's efforts and burst out laughing. 'Hmm, I see what you mean,' I admitted, casting a now jaundiced eye over the psychedelic walls and red sofas complete with multi-coloured two-foot long trout motif. Such extravagance made Austin Powers look conservative and if it sounds hideous described in black and white, then be thankful you never saw it in glorious technicolour. No wonder I lost a fortune on this so-called masterpiece of design when Valerie and I finally managed to sell the house and move into our present one in Old Windsor in the spring of 2001.

One of our first trips together was to the 1999 Honda tournament in Florida where I finished high on the leaderboard on the Sunday afternoon, necessitating a mad rush to the airport check-in. 'ID, sir,' requested the polite young man behind the desk, at which point I remembered our passports were still locked away in the safe back at the hotel. Guess whose fault that was? By the time we had collected the documents and made the return journey to the airport, the final flight had departed. Even worse, there was no car for rent; the only vehicle available was a white van. But we had such a laugh, that was the day I realised I was not only in love with V, but that I loved her deeply.

As V was walking through the front door into my life, David Leadbetter was making a much-publicised departure. The flash point had come when I was busily preparing for the 1998 US PGA Championship at Salahee, Washington, and, as was my custom, I rang Lead to discover his travel plans for the tournament.

'Oh, eh, ah, I'll let you know my schedule when it's finalised . . .' he mumbled. I thought his response was odd and then I learned that he had fallen behind the agreed deadline for a coaching manual he was writing and had decided to send an assistant to watch over me in his stead, but neglected to tell me directly. Let us not forget that this was a man with whom I had won six Majors, a man who had turned me into a serial champion, and a man, some would say, whose reputation had to a certain extent been forged on the back of those triumphs. At this delicate time in my life, such action felt like a vote of no confidence to me. I tied for 54th place at Salahee, after which there followed six weeks of deafening silence from Lead. Finally I decided to make contact, penning a brief but to the point letter terminating our working arrangement. Perhaps it would have been better if I had told David of my decision face to face but I felt badly let down: he knew that I was in the middle of a dispiriting slump in form but still skipped the US PGA at a time when I really needed him.

I regarded Lead's decision as a lack of commitment to me, even though I appreciate he had his reasons; what I did not appreciate was the subsequent mud-slinging. Having belatedly talked on the phone and agreed to maintain a mutual and dignified silence, it later transpired that he had already given a magazine interview in which he proceeded to tear strips off me for, among other things, my lack of commitment (ha!) and the manner of our 'divorce'.

We never became close but I am disappointed in the nature of our parting. Nevertheless it was still an incredible 13-year partnership. We both honed our skills. And boy did we graft to get it done. As our careers have developed over the years I would genuinely regard David's techniques as groundbreaking. He would analyse my swing down to the smallest detail and whenever I came back from a tournament he would have new things for me to try.

Lead's 'dynamics of golf', which he was introducing in the month preceding our split, came as a shock to me, however. In layman's terms he videoed my swing next to a curious contraption that provided a visual print-out showing how to achieve 100 per cent impact and illustrating where I was losing power. We then embarked on a series of weird exercises, whacking balls with baseball bats while performing extra-fast movements with the stomach. David even dreamed up a putting technique in which I moved the club's head back only an inch but propelled the ball 20 feet and more. Lead's ideas seemed to be applying martial arts power to golf. I threw myself into his routines because this was the great Lead talking.

After a while I realised it was affecting my tempo and rhythm and from my experience now I know that is something you are given. To mess with that – my hallmark if you like – was a very dangerous thing. And with the form of practice we were undertaking my arm felt as though it was dropping off, to such an extent that I had to pull out of the Scottish Open at Loch Lomond with acute tendonitis and all but missed the Royal Birkdale Open the following week. Perhaps this was all just an experiment too far.

My various rebuilds, painful as they may have been, were not without their lighter moments, however, and several amusing incidents occurred during the countless practice sessions at Wentworth.

'Do you mind if I watch?' came a voice once from over my shoulder as I tipped out the balls. I far prefer working in private but, having been brought up to be polite, I replied, 'Yeah, that's fine,' whereupon I proceeded to hit four 5-irons slap-bang down the middle. No exaggeration, the four balls finished up on all four corners of a square yard. Flexing my muscles, I thought 'Well, that's all right'. I took a practice swing at which point I heard 'Excuse me, but did you know your practice swing is nothing like your real swing?' The next six balls flew left, right, left, right, left, right, all over the place, at which point I packed up and went home.

On my next visit, I was blithely chipping to all the various markers before chipping them back to my bag when another gentleman hove into view.

'I'll help you,' he said.

'No, I'm fine, thanks.'

'No, I insist,' he pressed, grabbing a club and shanking the ball straight into the door of my Mercedes with an ugly 'dong!'. Most people would have been so embarrassed that they would have made their excuses and exited stage left, but not this fella.

'That won't happen again,' he promised, whacking a second ball into the car, this time into the wing.

'Hello, is there anybody home?' I spluttered, ending the session before my Merc was wrecked.

Preparing for a trip to Switzerland, I needed to test a few 3-woods and so I grabbed six clubs and whizzed off to Wentworth late one evening to decide which one suited me best. I painstakingly marked all the balls (about a dozen for each club) and put a corresponding mark on the six 3-woods so that I could monitor distance and accuracy. I had whacked all 72 balls when I saw a little head pop up through the bushes about 150 yards away. I packed my clubs away in the car and set off down the fairway to see which club had performed the best but, as a big favour to me, my watcher had scooped all 72 balls into a neat pyramid.

'I thought I'd help,' he beamed.

'That was very kind of you,' I managed through gritted teeth.

Call me a loner? Now you know why.

Far more distressing than David Leadbetter's departure was my subsequent brief estrangement from Fanny in the winter of 1999. Ironically, it coincided with the approach of the 10th anniversary of our partnership. Fanny had become much more than a mere caddie over the decade. She was my first lieutenant on the course and a trusted confidante in my turbulent private life. Blessed with a wicked sense of humour and a thousand megawatt smile, she was surprisingly practical when the situation demanded and I had developed complete trust in her instincts.

To celebrate our 10 years together, I bought Fanny a Jeep Wrangler in Swedish blue, which I knew she had been eyeing for some time. Valerie and I had been invited round to Fanny's for a celebratory lunch and we decided that was the moment for the ceremonial handing over of the keys. We parked the car out of sight, planning on springing our surprise once we had finished eating, but throughout the meal, Fanny became increasingly uncomfortable.

'I've got something to tell you,' she suddenly blurted out. 'I think we need a break from each other.'

Unwilling to interrupt her in mid-flow, I looked at her across the table in silence.

'I feel unappreciated. I find it difficult to cope with everything that's been going on away from the golf course. I want to feel like a major helper. I don't want to be simply a bag-carrier, I want to be a contributor to our team. I need to be more involved . . .'

I let Fanny finish her big speech before inviting her outside to show her the sparkling new Jeep.

'There, that's how much you're not appreciated,' I told her.

The poor girl just stood there.

'I feel such a dick,' she finally managed.

'Well, it's your decision, Fanny, but do me one favour. Let's get through this season, the last two tournaments, then you've got six weeks off to think about it. If you don't want to come out with me again, then don't come out. I can't force you. But whatever you decide, the car is yours.'

So we went off to Taiwan together but Fanny came down to breakfast on the first morning visibly agitated, her words tumbling forth in a rush.

'I've been thinking about nothing else and I still reckon we should split up for a while.'

'Oh, Fanny, that wasn't the deal,' I replied.

For the first time in 10 years, I was annoyed with her, because I had to go out and play a tournament in which I now knew she had no wish to take part. We endured a miserable week in each other's company at the end of which I grudgingly agreed, 'OK, let's call it a day.'

Fortunately, it was the most amicable of separations with Fanny issuing a statement saying: 'Our success is well documented and I know it will be difficult to attain anything like it elsewhere. Nick has been fully understanding of my decision, which has been extremely tough to make. However, I do feel the time is right for me to move on.'

For my part, I knew I would miss Fanny dreadfully but I was determined not to make her feel any sense of guilt or regret. 'It'll be hard getting used to not hearing Fanny say something like "Do you know there are seventeen different types of humming-bird in this town?"' I told the press on my arrival in Melbourne for the Australian Open, 'but, seriously, I'm going to miss her.'

Fanny went off to work with Sergio Garcia for a spell, among others, but throughout this time we stayed in constant touch and remained close friends. Finally, after the 2001 Masters, we were reunited amid emotional scenes, agreeing to work together until my retirement whenever that might be. Thirteen years in the company of Nick Faldo – Fanny Sunesson, you are a star.

Valerie also entered my life in a more permanent capacity when we became engaged on a four-day holiday in Paris with my children. It was a laughter-filled break during which we took a boat trip along the Seine, climbed the Arc de Triomphe, went to the top of the Eiffel Tower and scaled the steps into the tower of Notre Dame at the precise moment the bells rang out at 12 o'clock. The night before I proposed, I gathered the three kids around me at a table in a pavement café and explained. 'I would like to marry Valerie. What do you think?' 'No,' was their combined response. 'OK, but what would change? She already lives with me and I think it would create more stability in your lives knowing she'll never leave us.' I could see they were comfortable with this when Natalie asked, 'Can we see the ring?'

The said ring was a work of art, a square diamond and blue topaz setting I had designed myself and had crafted by a jeweller friend. He had had a selection of stones sent from Amsterdam which I would secretly study in the Wentworth car park, offering helpful Del Boy observations like, 'Nice diamond, Racquel' at appropriate intervals. The children were suitably impressed.

Needless to say, every time Valerie and I drifted off to look in a shop window, you could hear three voices in the background whispering, 'He's going to do it now, he's going to do it now . . .' Early the following morning, while the kids were still fast asleep, I invited Valerie for a walk in the Tuileries Gardens and there, on a pathway, I went down on one knee and asked, 'Will you marry me?' Cue tears all round. As we were leaving the gardens hand in hand, a passing Frenchman told us, 'You look like a very happy couple, you should get married.' Cue more tears.

On 28 July, 2001, therefore, I awoke in my Thames-side hotel room (our house in Old Windsor having been taken over by Valerie, her maid-of-honour, Virginia, and assembled girlfriends) to the hottest day of the summer. By 11 a.m. it was 84 degrees and I was mightily glad I had chosen a James Bond-style BMW Z8 soft-top to collect my bride-to-be for the journey to London, where we had planned a very private registry office wedding followed by a reception for around 25 close friends and family. Being the logical person I am, I sensibly put my good jacket and dress shirt on the car's back seat to avoid them being crushed and donned an old T-shirt for the journey. I arrived at the house with the roof down and the five-litre engine roaring away. Standing there on the doorstep with my hair resembling a burst sofa, I made a bad thing worse by neglecting to comment on how beautiful Valerie looked within the first millisecond of laying eyes on her. V did look absolutely gorgeous in dress number one, the first of three different outfits she wore during the day, all designed by Nicole Godat, a Swiss designer friend of V's. Casting a jaundiced eye over me, V's first words were, 'What *do* you look like?' before proceeding to give me an almighty rollicking.

'How come you're not dressed? You're even wearing the wrong shoes.'

'It's over eighty bloody degrees out there,' I tried to explain to her retreating back, as the sweat ran down my arms and legs. It was only then that I fully appreciated how stunningly gorgeous she looked in her lacy, crocheted, halter-neck cream gown.

I combed my hair, changed my shirt, pulled on my jacket, and off we set in stony silence. After 20 minutes of this less than heavenly atmosphere, over the radio came Mica Paris singing 'My One Temptation' which, by a stroke of good fortune, just happened to be our song, and very seldom played. With romance back in the air, we duly presented ourselves before the registrar where Valerie surprised and delighted me by repeating a set of vows she had composed herself.

'Do you, Nicholas Alexander Faldo . . . ?' began the registrar. As my body temperature soared from 98.4 to about 298.4, I was struck dumb, unable to repeat even my own name. Panic-stricken, I looked round frantically for support only to catch sight of a sea of faces all looking as apprehensive as I was. Not a word could I speak; and then the tears started. Of course, when I began crying, that set Valerie off, which set her mum and dad off, then my mum, and then even Dad lost it, followed by everyone else assembled, and so, by the time it came to kiss the bride, the atmosphere was so emotion-charged I think even the registrar was weeping.

Having informed the press of our wedding plans, we posed for a series of previously agreed pictures outside the registrar's office which were sent out on the wires because we did not want to do a deal with one of the glossy magazines for exclusive photographs. We drove back to Windsor with the roof down, music playing, followed by our families and closest friends in a dozen silver BMW 7-Series, after which I presided over afternoon tea on a hotel terrace overlooking the Thames, while Valerie returned home to supervise arrangements for the ceremony of blessing and the party to come, which was stage-managed by the remarkable Steve Foxcroft, head of entertainment at all the Johnnie Walker golf events.

When the 120 guests arrived, they were offered platters of wonderful canapés, including duck pancakes prepared by Anton Mosimann, who was in attendance, and signature cocktails on the lawn to the music of a jazz quartet. We had spent six months working on the garden to ensure it looked like the Garden of Eden, with pink floodlighting, flaming torches lining the drive, and even importing banks of lilac and white flowers from Holland and South Africa to match the colour scheme of the evening. Then, from behind the hedge, came the sounds of the London Gospel Choir singing 'Love Train', and the guests were led in a column to the formal pond, where we had built what the newspapers described as a 'love temple' for the service of blessing, which was more spiritual than religious. Valerie was now resplendent in dress number two, a clinging white silk number studded with diamonds and feathers. To the strains of 'My Heart Can't Lie', we were 'married' a second time, exchanging rings and releasing a flock of doves into the sky.

Our guests, including New Zealander Michael Campbell and his wife, Julie, representing the world of golf, were invited to launch a fleet of little candlelit boats on the pond, just as they do in Thailand to rid themselves of worries and cares, before crossing the decking and assembling in a marquee for the formal dinner, speeches and party. As the dancing got underway, and totally unbeknown to V, out stepped Mica Paris herself on to the stage.

'I believe this is someone's favourite song,' she announced, launching into a live rendition of 'My One Temptation', at which point the tears started flowing all over again.

Mica performed four or five numbers before making way for a cover band called Zigzag. Remembering my musical efforts at Muirfield in 1992 when I strangled Frank Sinatra's 'My Way', the highlight of the evening – well, in my opinion at least – came when I took the stage accompanied by my best man, Dale Richardson, plus Steve Foxcroft, Kjell Enhager, Chris Perfect and one of my golf course architects, Brian Curley. I also persuaded Mica to join us and we regaled Valerie with the Andy Williams classic, 'You're just too good to be true.'

About one o'clock in the morning, Valerie disappeared to re-appear in dress number three, a startling see-through, silver, Cinderella creation, in which she danced the night away until the final guests left at about 4 a.m., allowing us to fall into a bed strewn with pink rose petals. With the pink lighting and torches, the house looked like a fairytale castle and the fairytale would have been complete had Natalie, Matthew and Georgia been with us. As with my induction to the Hall of Fame, their absence introduced the only note of sadness to the proceedings. They have since watched the video and little Georgia, bless her, has asked Valerie if she can borrow her dress (she has selected number two) when it is her turn to walk down the aisle.

We began our married life by spending three relaxed days in a house on the coast outside Newquay, walking the beach and gener-ally chilling out before flying off to Bermuda for our official honey-moon. There, for 13 idyllic days, we had our own private beach and, just to prove how romantic I can be, each and every morning for 13 days Valerie woke up to a little gift on her pillow – designer sandals, handbag, perfume, lingerie. Three years on, every day is a honeymoon in Valerie's company.

CHAPTER SEVENTEEN

PUTTING THE RECORD STRAIGHT

Although we were still in the early days of our life together, how I came to appreciate V's calming presence at my side during the grim summer of 1999. Exactly how Mark James ever came to be appointed Ryder Cup captain I will never comprehend because, to put it politely, he has always been a funny old chap. Our lingering public feud dated all the way back to the 1994 British Masters at Woburn when I had criticised the standard of many of the courses and practice facilities of the European Tour. James had responded by branding me a fat cat who only played in tournaments offering substantial appearance money. As I have previously explained, I was speaking up for the long-term benefit of the Tour.

I did not play particularly impressively in the 1999 Masters, the Open at Carnoustie or the US Open at Pinehurst, missing all three cuts, but I was a seasoned Ryder Cup campaigner with 11 successive appearances to my name; and I was not the only one who believed I was worth consideration as one of the captain's two wild card selections. 'An eighty per cent Nick Faldo would always be on my team,' insisted Colin Montgomerie in a fraternal show of solidarity, while Lee Westwood commented: 'A Ryder Cup without Nick Faldo would be a weaker European team.' But Mark James did not agree, dismissing my past record with the pronouncement, 'We have too much strength in depth for me to hand a wild card to someone playing on a wing and a prayer. Nick knows that to be considered for selection you have to show some form. I would love to have an on-form Faldo, an on-form Seve and an on-form Woosie on the scene, but there comes a time when everyone has to move over and if it's this year, then so be it.'

Determined to 'show some form' to my harshest critic before the announcement of the team, at the 11th hour I rearranged my schedule to fly to Germany from America to compete in the BMW International in Munich, the last tournament before James would reveal his two captain's picks. Spotting him in the hotel lobby, I approached and asked, 'What's the position here, Mark? If I win this week, will that be enough to get me in?' To which he replied dismissively, 'Even if you win, it's unlikely I'll pick you.' I was devastated by such a negative reaction; I cannot believe Tony Jacklin would have acted in such a manner. I returned to a friend who I had been sitting with and recounted James's words. He was equally amazed and insisted I must have got it wrong, so I went back up to the Ryder Cup captain and said, 'Sorry, Mark, could you just run that by me again?' I hadn't misheard him.

In my view James's words and tone were not a justifiable reaction to a player who holds the record for not only the most appearances in the contest but also the most matches won (23), ahead of Arnold Palmer (22), Bernhard Langer (21), Billy Casper (20), Lanny Wadkins (20) and Seve Ballesteros (20). James should at least have given me some encouragement as Tony would have done – 'Go out there and prove me wrong, Nick. You're not in the team at the moment, so win this week and make me pick you.'

Having been a permanent fixture in the team since my debut in 1977, I was both crestfallen and angry. The Ryder Cup had come to mean everything to me and I had achieved sufficient top 20 finishes in the US that season to suggest I could put some European points on the board in Brookline. I made my thoughts public and went on to say that when it came to the Ryder Cup contest itself, I trusted James would have learned the meaning of the word 'motivation'. James promptly turned my words round. 'He's been complaining that I haven't talked to him all year and now he suddenly doesn't want to hear what I do have to say,' he responded. 'If I say nothing, he's not happy. If I say something, he's not happy.'

I was seething. Having worn myself out in both America and Europe in the hope of persuading James that I still had something to offer – after all, I had not been in vintage form when I beat Curtis Strange to turn around the 1995 Ryder Cup at Oak Hill – I pointed out, quite reasonably in my opinion, that if his mind had already been made up before Munich, he should have had the decency to tell me so and save me another transatlantic flight. 'He's nothing but a big crybaby,' came James's stinging response. James had certainly had the opportunity to discuss with me his views on my selection. Earlier in the summer, I played a practice round with him before the Open at Carnoustie but he didn't say a single word about my game or the Ryder Cup.

Another mystery then arose in Munich. It was widely believed (on what basis I don't know) in the locker-room that Bernhard Langer had been told he would be awarded the final wild card selection, Sweden's Jesper Parnevik having already been promised the first slot. But when it came to the formal announcement following the final round, and with an ashen-faced Langer sitting a few feet away from him, James read out the 12th name as Andrew Coltart.

With seven rookies due to make the journey to Brookline, here was a youth versus experience argument that was set to run and run. Coltart, not surprisingly, defended his inclusion like a voracious dog guarding a bone. 'I think Nick was a great benefit to the team two years ago but he hasn't really done anything in the last couple of years. He's been beaten and bettered by younger players. Maybe the others aren't in awe of him as they used to be and he's no longer one hole up standing on the first tee.' In the event, Coltart would make only one appearance in the contest in the final afternoon's singles when, unsurprisingly, he was beaten by Tiger Woods.

Even before the action started in Brookline, I unwittingly plunged myself into a further round of Ryder Cup controversy during the Canadian Open at Glen Abbey, where I finished a heartening eighth. Asked to give my opinion on Colin Montgomerie's refusal to leave the European Tour to sample the more competitive atmosphere of America, ever the diplomat, I said that Monty was happy to live in England surrounded by his friends and family but that if he wanted to win Majors, I was surprised he had not sought a fresh challenge. But this was his choice, which I felt was important, and I added that I could fully understand Monty's reluctance to uproot his wife and children because he was such a great player, he was the king in his own backyard.

Surprise, surprise, when I was quoted what appeared was nothing like what I had actually said. It seemed the US writer was trying to create negative media before the Ryder Cup, which resulted in Mark James being angry at what he regarded as an attempt to undermine morale in the European Ryder Cup team. Nothing, and I stress nothing, could have been further from the truth. I telephoned Monty to explain the truth behind my words and within a millisecond he interrupted me to say he fully understood I had meant no harm whatsoever and was, in fact, merely offering my advice. I closed our conversation with the following battle cry for Brookline: 'Monty, you've got to be the man on the golf course and off the golf course. You're our number one, remember that, and the very best of luck to you all.'

Before setting off to play in San Antonio, I also penned a letter:

16 September 1999

To the Ryder Cup captain, Mark James, and the European team, the Country Club, Brookline, Massachusetts

As Tony Jacklin said to me: 'Good luck and play well goes out the window. Just win.' I believe you can bring back the Ryder Cup to Europe again where it belongs. I am right behind you and will be supporting the team throughout the event, even though it is from 2,000 miles away.

My very best wishes to each of you. Above all, enjoy it.

Nick Faldo

Given the circumstances surrounding my exclusion from what would have been my 12th successive Ryder Cup appearance, did I truly mean those sentiments? Yes I did, 100 per cent. Even though I was not actually competing on this occasion, once a member of the European team, always a member is my belief. I was bitterly disappointed, too, at the outcome and disgusted by the behaviour of certain Americans during what will go down in sporting history as the infamous Battle of Brookline.

My feelings of disappointment and disgust, however, were nothing compared with what I felt when Mark James subsequently published his Ryder Cup diary, *Into the Bear Pit: A Captain's Log . . .*, from which I offer the following extract:

The [Colin Montgomerie] outburst came at such a crucial time that I can only think it was deliberately designed to undermine the team's challenge. In the eyes of the team it was unpardonable . . . Faldo has said in the past that he would like to be Ryder Cup captain but I think that will depend a lot on his relationship with the players. A lot of them do not like him because he has been critical of the European Tour, tends to keep himself to himself, and tends not to acknowledge people. Somebody the players do not particularly get on with will probably not make a good captain. Just because he has achieved what he has does not automatically qualify him for the captaincy . . .

I would have ignored all that both at the time and in these pages had James not gone on to reveal something which made my blood boil.

Nick Faldo sent a good luck note. Similar missives from the likes of Seve and Ian Woosnam had been pinned on our notice-board and were much appreciated. This one was not pinned up because I took one look at it and could not believe that Faldo had sent it. Not only had he had a serious barney with me relatively recently, but he had also slagged off Monty just before we came to Boston.

When all hell broke loose in the newspapers over this revelation that Mark James had destroyed my letter without showing it to the team, he explained his actions thus: 'My first inclination was to throw it away, but first I decided to seek the views of a few other people, including some of the players, and everyone's reaction was the same: bin it. I had no hesitation in accepting their advice. There was no room on our notice-board for someone who was not one hundred per cent behind us.'

I don't know to this day whether Monty spoke to Mark about our conversation. Perhaps not because Monty has a reputation for sitting on the fence. I just don't know whether he did fully explain my side of the story, but of course if you are not there in person to represent yourself then there is little you can do. And what's the life lesson here? I should have called Mark James first and explained things myself and that would have been it. But I didn't and as things turned out I was grievously hurt that my heartfelt letter of support had been blithely ripped up and tossed away.

Backed into a corner, James later said the 'pin it or bin it' decision had been based on an almost unanimous vote of the team; again, as I understand it from the feedback I was given, he showed my letter to at most half a dozen players only. But it certainly was not a unanimous vote.

My sense of grievance deepened when, before the 2000 Scottish Open at Loch Lomond, the *Daily Mail* published a photograph of me under the headline: Is This The Most Hated Man In British Sport? I am delighted to say that, judging by the reaction of the great British sporting public and my fellow professionals, I was anything but; however, it is decidedly unpleasant to be so branded.

Since James had also taken it upon himself to question my credentials as a future Ryder Cup captain, let us look at what he brought to the role. Having chosen Andrew Coltart in preference to Bernhard Langer or me, James proceeded to cast him in the role of cheerleader throughout the first two days, which he spent on the sidelines beside two fellow rookies, Frenchman Jean Van de Velde (who had come so agonisingly close to winning the Open at Carnoustie earlier that summer only to lose to Paul Lawrie in a play-off) and Finland's Jarmo Sandelin. If Coltart was deemed a more worthy team member than Langer or me, why was he shunted into exile in Brookline? I was also surprised to hear suggestions that there may have been some premature celebrations on the Saturday night with the job not yet done. I certainly hope that these rumours aren't correct and Captain James didn't think that Sunday's victory was a done deal given Europe's 10–6 lead, especially with the Americans' dominance in the singles.

In view of the contents of his book I questioned Mark James's right to serve as chairman of the European Tournament Players' Committee and as 2001 Ryder Cup vice-captain to Sam Torrance, a role to which he had already been appointed. The 2001 contest at The Belfry was, of course, later postponed for 12 months in the aftermath of the 11 September atrocities. I sought a meeting with Tour chief executive Ken Schofield to air my grievances. Schofield intimated that James's literary efforts would be referred to both the Ryder Cup Committee and the Tournament Players' Committee for discussion. So convinced was I that James had contravened Tour regulations, which state that a player 'is obliged not to attack, disparage or criticise a fellow competitor', that I grew increasingly determined there should be no whitewash. I arranged a further meeting with Schofield to press my argument that, having broken the code of conduct, James should be charged with 'bringing the game into disrepute'.

I did not want blood, merely justice, and derived no pleasure from the fact that James was duly 'invited' to resign his 2001 Ryder Cup vice-captaincy amid mounting criticism. The European Tournament Players' Committee was strangely reluctant to take any disciplinary action against its chairman and my outrage deepened when, on my return to America, I received a call from Neil Coles, chairman of the PGA European Tour, informing me that some of my previous comments could also be construed as 'having brought the game into disrepute' and perhaps I should 'back off', especially if I still harboured ambitions of captaining our Ryder Cup team in the future.

I totally accepted the decision not to undertake any disciplinary action against James, and have done so ever since, but I still don't fully understand it. What I do recall is that James later said, having since talked to others and having heard my side of the story, he would think about a correction in the paperback version of the book. My biggest issue was that he had reacted to what he had read in the papers rather than discuss what actually happened with me. However, to the best of my knowledge, no such corrections or retractions have ever appeared.

As a postscript to this unpleasant affair, at a book signing in St

Andrews prior to the British Open, Mark James looked up to see Melissa Lehman, wife of Tom, about whom he had been particularly savage in print, standing before him. Whereas James – and you could imagine the sweat running off his forehead – might have been expecting a handbag around the ears, Mrs L had a far more mischievous retribution in mind. I guess she said something like, 'Could you inscribe it "To my dear friend, Tom. The best of luck, play well and may God speed you".' An embarrassed Mark James did as asked.

This was not to be the last time I was to have a difference of opinion with the Tour authorities that year. At the beginning of November various players, unsolicited, were coming up to myself, Seve, Bernhard Langer and Jose-Maria Olazabal voicing concerns about the presentation of the Tour's accounts. As a result, the so-called Gang of Four decided to represent the players by raising the issue at a forthcoming AGM, which required, under the terms of the Tour's rulebook, a signed petition. We therefore spoke to the players at the Volvo Masters at Montecastillo in Spain and 60 of the 61 signed, only Monty failed to join us. What we were requesting was an independent audit of the Tour's accounts and the Tour counteracted by asking whether we should be allowed to see this, given the fact that Seve and Bernhard were tournament promoters in their own right and therefore, according to the Tour, there might have been a clash of interests. As it turned out, the Tour had already canvassed the votes ahead of the AGM, which we were unable to do as we didn't have all the players' telephone numbers in order to contact them. At the meeting we voiced our concerns but the vote was already against us. Although we lost, however, the good news is that the Tour has taken on board our comments and the players are now much more involved in the financial aspects of the Tour.

Our sole reason for taking the action we did was for the benefit of the future of the Tour but we were never really able to get that across and so, when the meeting finished, I decided that that was that and I would just move on and no longer be involved. But it is interesting to hear Seve return to the theme in May 2004 claiming he had been victimised for his membership of the Gang of Four when he was disqualified from the Italian Open after being penalised for slow play. As Seve explained: 'Most of the players are against the regime, a big number. But the problem is this big number have no guts. When they are called to say whatever they have to say, they are afraid because there is no freedom to speak up. When somebody is against the system, they become the number one public enemy.'

And what of my own ambitions to serve as European Ryder Cup captain in 2006? I had already withdrawn my 'unofficial application' to skipper the team in 2004 long before Bernhard Langer's appointment, in order to try to qualify as a player, but I prize the honour highly and I would love to experience what Sam Torrance experienced at The Belfry in September 2002. I relish being part of a 12-man team – a dozen different personalities, a dozen different foibles, a dozen different likes and dislikes – bonded together by a single goal.

Ah, but Nick Faldo is an entirely different species from Slammin' Sam, you might think. Sam shed a waterfall of tears for all of Europe at the moment of victory. Could I bring the same passion to the job? Are you kidding?

I was on the periphery of the action at The Belfry two autumns ago in a television commentary box, and although I thoroughly enjoyed my stint at the microphone, it hurt like hell not being down there on the 18th green amid those scenes of jubilation. I want to be part of all that again as either a player or skipper, because, through the remarkable transformation of European golf over the past two decades, the Ryder Cup has become one of the most fascinating and talked about events in world sport.

It would be wonderful to have a crack at the captaincy in 2006. There are so many great young players coming through. Everyone is talking about Paul Casey, Justin Rose, Luke Donald and Ian

Poulter but there is a whole pack of youthful talent emerging across Europe, and it is my burning desire to lead them into battle. So what are my credentials? Apart from my record as a player, I sincerely believe I could bring something new to the captaincy, harnessing all the skills I have learned from the numerous victorious skippers under whom I have served – the psychology and man-management of Tony Jacklin, the attention to detail and tactical awareness of Bernard Gallacher, the passion and inventiveness of Seve Ballesteros, together with a few new ideas I have up my sleeve.

One skipper I would not try to emulate is 1991 American captain Dave Stockton. Stockton, as you may recall, was thrown into the sea by his jubilant team at the finish of a traumatic event, to say the least: four months later a Christmas card dropped through my letterbox with a picture of his sodden figure emerging from the waves on the front. Inside this festive greeting card just one word was printed: 'Rejoice!' Charming.

I imagine the seemingly simple task of juggling the possible four-ball and foursome permutations is enough to keep you awake for weeks. I can see that some partnerships come together like ham and eggs – Ballesteros and Olazabal immediately spring to mind – whereas with others there may be a multitude of permutations that might or might not work (as Carmen Ballesteros would testify!). What flash of divine inspiration persuaded Tony Jacklin to pair Ian Woosnam, the dedicated party animal, with me at Muirfield Village in 1987, where we contributed $3\frac{1}{2}$ points out of four to Europe's stunning 15–13 triumph? Chalk and cheese Woosie and I might have been off the course, but for two days we operated like a mind-reading double act, the notorious free spirit Welshman in tandem with the meticulous Englishman, who would not even trim his fingernails during a tournament lest it interfere with his touch.

CHAPTER EIGHTEEN

WHAT IT TAKES
TO WIN

If I can be greedy and ask for a second Ryder Cup wish, it would be that at some point in the future, one or more graduates of my Faldo Series qualify to represent Europe against the Americans. The Series is designed to help produce the next generation of champions. The idea first came to me when I was playing a practice round with Robert Floyd (son of Raymond) in Florida and asked the lad about his forthcoming plans. His diary was packed with 72-hole events, which set me wondering why there were so few similar opportunities for juniors in Europe. The Swedes cottoned on to the importance of helping youngsters years ago. Way back in 1982, the Swedish association sent three of their junior players to study me at close range. They shadowed me throughout practice for the Open at Royal Troon, watching how I prepared for a Major. With such foresight, is it any wonder that Sweden's golfers have such global presence?

I could have simply pumped in the money to set a Junior Series in motion and employed a team of teaching professionals and advisors to look after the fledgling players but that is not how I wanted to do things. For a start, I enjoy my time with the youngsters and I think it is important to them that I am actively involved. I dedicate the best part of three weeks a year to working closely with them, which may not sound a lot of time to set aside for such an important venture, but considering my other commitments, it represents a significant chunk of my working calendar. I believe I am now in possession of the formula to create a champion, the 'next Nick Faldo', if you like, offering an understanding of the transition from amateur to professional in all aspects of the game – technical, physical and mental – and I am more than happy for the youngsters in the Series to pick my brains to their hearts' content. Everything I have learned, I am happy to pass on to those who will follow after.

Nick Price apparently reckoned I had the natural ability to win a dozen Majors, which does leave me with a slight sense of under-achievement. Maybe I could have proved Nick right but, given the knowledge I had at the time, I probably achieved as much as I could. That said, winning one Major could be construed as a fluke, two is 'Thank God, I can play this game', three is 'Hang on a minute, that's a bit special', so six has to be no mean feat. Dare I hope that one of the members of the Faldo Series will equal, or even surpass, my tally?

Instead of whacking thousand upon thousand of balls all day as I did as a kid, I like to teach the importance of 'feel'; I like to see the youngsters developing their shots, hitting fades and draws, finding a way to shape their shots to the target. Yes, you have to understand the techniques of playing golf, but 'feel' is every bit as vital – maybe trying to hit a 6-iron the way you would use a wedge, for example, creating your own shots. Such adaptability is perhaps more important now than ever before. Ever since Tiger appeared on the scene kids love smashing drives 300 yards down the fairway, which is obviously a great advantage, but they have to be encouraged not to neglect their short game or putting. As the old cliché has it, 'You drive for show and putt for dough'.

Greg Norman was the best player I've ever known with a persimmon driver in his hands – 260-odd yards. Today, there are probably a dozen guys who can do that with their 3-wood, and often to narrower fairways. The sweet spots today seem larger than the heads we used to use. The game has changed that much. So how can you gain an edge today, when the second shot more often than not is played with an 8-iron, requiring much less finesse than the second iron shots of my era? What it means is that it is that much harder in today's game to differentiate yourself from other players. This is where touch and feel come in. If you have that it will give you a greater self-awareness and will certainly give you the edge on the tougher courses on the Tour and without doubt in the Majors. I firmly believe that over the course of a four-day tournament, one-dimensional power players will get caught out at some point. Shot-making ability through touch and feel will make all the difference.

It was Craig Farnsworth, an American 'sporting eye' specialist, who had worked with the US Olympic shooting team, baseball players and even fighter pilots, who helped me truly appreciate the visual understanding of putting. Craig can examine your eyes and tell you whether you miss your putts short left or whatever, because – and this was something I did not know – your eyes pull in different directions. Fortunately, there are exercises you can do to train your eyes to focus on the same spot, but some golfers go through their entire careers unaware that they are actually looking way off line. They do not realise they have a problem because they have unwittingly developed the knack compensating for it. Before the 1996 Masters, Craig gave my eyes electrical stimulation massage and, guess what, I was the number one putter throughout the week. We have always known that the putting stroke, its pace, and your ability to read greens were important, but for decades professional golfers have been ignorant of the fact that their eyes can be the most vital tool of all.

The brain can also represent an extra 'club' in your bag; one of my most trusted lieutenants within the Faldo Series set-up and also tournament play is Swedish sports psychologist Kjell Enhager, to whom I was introduced by Fanny. Kjell has been one of the main forces behind Sweden's emergence as a major force in women's golf through his work with Annika Sorenstam, Helen Alfredsson and Sophie Gustafson among others. When Kjell first gathered the Swedish women around him, he asked them what constituted a satisfactory round.

'Seventy-two,' they chirruped as one.

'Why not fifty-four?' he asked. Cue unbounded mirth and merriment all round.

'*Fifty-four?*' Ho-di-ho-di-ho . . .

'Well let me ask you this,' continued Kjell undaunted. 'Who in this room has birdied the first at your home course?' All the hands were raised. 'And the second?' Again, all the hands, and so on until Kjell arrived at the 18th, each and every hole having been birdied or better.

'So there you have it. Who said you had to reach every green in regulation figures followed by two putts? Have you actually met the person who told you that? We make too many assumptions.'

Such a score remains a pipe dream needless to say, but it is worth recording that the Swedish ladies' scores have dramatically lowered in recent years, with Annika Sorenstam shooting an amazing 59.

What leading sports psychologists like Kjell provide is a road map pointing you in the right direction. I believe you can build a better golfer if you utilise the right psychological tools. When the young Ivan Lendl set out to become the world champion in tennis, he found that only one serve out of every 10 was in, while his training partner's strike-rate was nine out of 10. The difference between them was that the other guy was tormented by the notion that he was missing that one — why could he not achieve a maximum 10? — whereas Lendl was concentrating his thoughts on the one good serve, ignoring the missed nine. Gradually he improved his ratio to two, then three, four, until he could make 10 out of 10 almost with his eyes closed. Lendl went on to win eight Grand Slam titles, but we do not even know the name of the other lad.

Bjorn Borg possessed amazing mental powers which he actually developed — even in practice he played every point as though it was match point at Wimbledon. Naturally, when he did find himself at match point against John McEnroe on the Centre Court, he had rehearsed that feeling thousands of times. He was the proverbial ice man. If Borg lost a point to a bad call or unlucky bounce, instead of railing against the injustice of it all, he would simply spin his racket to reset his mind. Tiger Woods gives himself a few seconds after a poor shot and as he walks forward he sees an imaginary line and he knows, once he crosses it, he will have forgotten about the shot.

Even popular child psychology can be transferred into the sporting arena. Parents tend to talk in negatives. When they see their beloved offspring carrying a plate to the sink, for instance, what do mum and dad say but 'don't drop it', thereby painting a picture of a dropped plate in the child's mind. It is no surprise when the kid promptly trips over some invisible object and duly drops the plate. I read a recent report about a school where there was one poor mite who never received a single mark in his spelling tests; every week, every word was spelt wrongly. Then the teacher, God bless her, decided that she would mark a few words with a tick for correct, even if the answers were wrong. With the teacher slowly building up the number of ticks, the lad underwent a complete transformation and, having rid himself of the fear of failure, within weeks his spelling really was 10 out of 10. It was as simple as that.

What all great champions possess, and none more so than Jack Nicklaus, is the ability to switch to automatic pilot when needing to play your best on the Sunday of a Major. That is when you have to know how to control all senses and emotions, how to conquer the nerves we would all feel in that kind of pressurised situation. The difference between Nicklaus and a talented amateur, though, is that the amateur will start jabbering to himself, 'This is when I usually tighten up and, yes, here it comes, I'm tightening up. My backswing always gets shorter when I tighten up . . . and, yes, my backswing's getting shorter.' The trick is to say, 'Yes, I'm nervous, it's natural, but I know exactly what to do to deal with this.' If your shoulders are tightening up, take a moment to relax them. If you are nervous your breathing will be high in your chest, so you need to concentrate on lowering your breathing to your stomach. Some people even advise imagining you are breathing from your heart.

Jack Nicklaus used to say to his caddie at times of stress, 'Tell me two things – the yardage and that I'm the best in the world.' Amateurs do not usually have the luxury of a caddie, which is why your own 'mind caddie' can be so important. If you listen to a high handicapper, you will hear him muttering, 'I'm useless at bunker shots. Every time I go in a bunker, I thin it across the green.' Twang! He duly thins it over the green. But if he had a professional caddie standing at his shoulder, he would be told, 'Take your time. Have a practice swing . . . take a good look . . . hit two inches behind the ball . . . follow through . . . you can do it.' It is amazing how golfers torture themselves. They would not dream of getting into their cars saying, 'Every time I go round a roundabout I go the wrong way and crash.' Yet they will stand with a driver in their hands and think, 'Every time I stand on this tee I hit it into the trees.' Surprise, surprise, into the trees they go.

I believe the application of modern techniques will enable golfers to improve at a faster rate than athletes in almost any other sport. I was part of an era which saw so many changes, not only in the swing but in attitudes. 'Oh, don't touch weights,' people used to tell me. 'You'll become too muscular and you won't be able to putt.' Well, young guys like Tiger have found ways to develop serious muscles and achieve a fabulous touch on the greens too. No one ever told me to do stretching exercises to aid flexibility and there were no special sports drinks, although Fanny knew of some from Sweden which she introduced into my regime long before anyone else was drinking them that I know of. Modern players should enjoy far greater longevity because in the era when I was at the top of the game we had no idea what a punishing effect jumping on a plane, flying for 12 hours, playing a tournament, then racing to catch the next plane would have on our bodies.

From a personal point of view, one of the things I have finally done right is to assemble a team of specialists consisting of specific technical coaches, a physiotherapist and a chiropractor to support me in my efforts to reinvent myself as a serious contender before I reach 50 and have to think about joining the US Champions Tour, as their Seniors Tour is now known. I have come to terms with the fact that my best years as a player are now behind me. I am not being negative in saying that, I am simply acknowledging the truth: my golden years are gone and there is nothing to be gained from railing against the passage of time.

However I would like to repay my team by winning at least one more tournament in Europe – my victory speech would sound like an Oscar winner's, so many people would I have to thank. I have not won an individual title since the 1997 Nissan Open in America, seven long years ago. I remain convinced I will triumph again in Europe, even if I have to be brutally honest with myself and acknowledge that a seventh Major is probably beyond my powers with so many great young players in the ascendancy. Why have I not won an event in such a long time? The reasons are myriad but mostly personal, directly associated with the long-running saga of my divorce, the fluctuating fortunes of various business schemes and management dramas. For many years I was carrying very heavy baggage. I still love tournament golf with an abiding passion. It fascinates me. I have never found it a chore or hard work – although I do work hard at my craft – but I suppose a certain fear of failure has crept into my mind. I gave 100 per cent of myself to golf because I wanted to be the very best in the world; I did not want to reach the age I am now and regret not giving it more. I met one of my old school mates recently and he said to me, 'Look at you. You're a lucky bugger. I was lazy and never did anything with my life.' I would hate to feel like that.

I always dreamed of winning Majors, I dreamed of being world number one: those were my goals and I am proud to have fulfilled them. I am fitter, wiser, technically more proficient and much more of an athlete now than I was when I was winning everything, which is maybe why the older I get, the more I appreciate what I achieved. When I scan the record books it gives me a golden glow inside, especially winning the Majors and periods like that in 1992 when I won six tournaments in a six-month period.

It is truly uplifting to be a part of the history of this wonderful game. A recent magazine article listed the various eras of golf beginning with that of Harry Vardon, followed by those of Gene Sarazen, Ben Hogan, Sam Snead, Arnold Palmer, Jack Nicklaus, Tom Watson, Nick Faldo and Tiger Woods. On paper, therefore, I seem to be among the legends, which I am growing to accept, although I used to feel uneasy with that tag.

My particular era fell between 1987 and 1996 but if I did not think – no, make that believe – that I am capable of winning at least one more important tournament, then I would strap on the saddle-bags and ride off into the sunset with V. I do not relish the prospect of being out there simply to make up the numbers, even if that might allow me to pin a little sign on my back announcing, 'Hey, I'm out here for fun.' I certainly do not require a sympathetic round of applause every time I walk up the 18th. When you are in the doldrums, there is a very grave danger of becoming the forgotten hero, the lost star if you like. In golf you probably have five to seven great years (only the very best can stay at the top for two decades as Nicklaus did) and I have had mine. But I trust I have made my parents and children proud of me, and that my grandchildren will be equally proud some day in the far-off future when they will no doubt be able to watch grandad's Open victories on a tiny television screen set into the face of their wristwatches.

At times I can still compete with the very best as I proved during the 2003 Open Championship at Royal St George's where, for 44 holes, I played better golf than anyone, clawing my way up the leaderboard from 10 over after six holes of the second round to level par with four to play on the final afternoon. This performance followed a very distressing evening spent with my mum in hospital after she was suddenly taken ill.

Having reassured myself that Mum was comfortable and stable, I set myself a target for that final round. I aimed to shoot a 65, which would have put me on 2 under. In the event that would have been good enough, and I would have won my seventh Major. But having finally got back to even par with a birdie at the 14th, I made a crucial error. Throughout the last round I had stubbornly refused to look at the leaderboard, instead concentrating entirely on making my 2 under target. Then I aimed to sit back and watch to see what would happen as the other scores came in. But on my way to the 15th, for some reason I can't explain, I lost my focus and glanced up at the scoreboard to see Ben Curtis on 5 under. 'Bloody hell', I thought. 'I'm still five back. Ben Curtis is going to win the Open. Who is this guy?'

And that was it. I dropped shots at the 15th, 16th and 17th to end in a tie for eighth place on 3 over. It was just bad timing I guess, glancing up at the scoreboard when I did. If it had been, say, just 30 minutes later, Curtis was beginning to drop shots and noticing that might have had just the opposite effect. As I drove home that day I couldn't help but think 'What if, what if . . .'

CHAPTER NINETEEN

FALDO ENTERPRISES

The professional golfer of today, such as Tiger Woods, fully under-stands the commercial and business aspects of life as a top sportsman, receiving valuable advice and coaching in the skills required right from the outset. Support like that simply wasn't avail-able when I first turned pro and in business I was still operating as a naïve 'rookie' even during my reign as world number one. I was involved in numerous commercial activities – some of which were extremely lucrative – but by no means all of them proved as successful in reality as they had promised to be on the spreadsheet. Now, as various business ventures assume increasing significance and demand more and more of my time, I can reflect on the mistakes I made in the past and, equally importantly, on those committed by others on my behalf. I am determined not to repeat any of them.

Looking back, I can identify three key lessons that I have learned. The first of these is that there is no point in blaming others when something goes wrong. Even if you were not directly involved in whatever error was made, when it is your name on the contract then you are the one who has ultimate responsibility and you should be in control. If you are not, then the fault rests entirely with you and there is little to be gained from laying into the people who work for you.

There have been times when I have become extremely irate when deals in which I was involved have gone pear-shaped or been mis-handled, but I now realise that such anger originated from the desire to blame someone – anyone – else. When you acknowledge your own role in making, or not making, a success of things, then you eliminate the need for blame and, guess what, the anger vanishes. You learn from your mistakes and move on. Being in control of my own destiny has therefore become my business philosophy: the buck stops with me and that's exactly the way it should be. After all, when I am out on the course I'll happily listen to Fanny's advice, but ultimately it is my responsibility whether I hit a 5-iron or a 6-iron. Why should that situation change when it comes to my business affairs? It is my duty to read the contract, understand the bottom line and then ensure that I do everything in my power to fulfil my end of the bargain.

Clearly, it is impossible to perform as a one-man band, especially when you are playing in tournaments virtually all the year round: hence the need for an agent. Throughout most of my playing career I was associated with one of the very best – IMG, created by Mark McCormack who saw the commercial opportunities of Arnold Palmer and in effect defined sports marketing and management as it is today – who were excellent in the art of representation, securing me some highly profitable deals and sponsorships. Of course, that is precisely what I paid them to do but through their great expertise they earned me a fistful of money. In my opinion what even the major sports agencies lack is the time and the resources to 'manage' their clients, in the sense of managing all aspects of your career, not just brokering deals but planning for the future. That requires a lieutenant at your side looking out for you at every turn. If no such aide is there 24/7 while your own focus is understandably concentrated on your sport, then that is when your business dealings can go horribly awry. Just look at what happened to me if you want an example.

What I would have liked to have done was to forge a lifelong relationship with my sponsors and the companies with which I was linked, but for reasons I have never fully been able to analyse, I was never able to develop ties as close as that. There always seemed to be a distance between 'them' and 'me'. Not that I recognised this as a problem at the time because when you are playing and winning, and the money just keeps rolling in, then you tend to think 'thank you very much' and go with the flow. But that is not a satisfactory long-term strategy; it is not the brand building which I regard as critical. Such relationships are not impossible to achieve. Just look at Sir Jackie Stewart and his 40 years' association with Ford. The name Faldo may not carry the clout of Rolls-Royce or Coca-Cola, but I hope that people know that I would not put my name to any product which could harm my reputation. There have been some attempts over the years to try to develop the Faldo brand but, unfortunately, not over an extended period. The Faldo range of Pringle sweaters, for instance, was very successful in the UK and continental Europe but never really cracked the US market and was discontinued when the company's emphasis switched from golf gear towards the high street.

Not being 'managed' in the sense I am discussing had other implications for me, implications of which I should have been more aware and sought means to rectify. Having read these pages you will have gathered by now that I have a reputation for being aloof, distant and uncommunicative. That is the popular perception in some circles but, at the risk of repeating myself, those charges are just not true. Sure, on the golf course I can be like that when I am focusing on my game, wrapped up in a private cocoon, and I have no objection to being characterised like that in those circumstances. But as a husband, father, son, friend, coach and businessman such an image could not be further from the truth.

I can appreciate why this misconception has arisen. I once appointed a personal assistant who did a fantastic job and in fact was so thorough in protecting me from all and sundry it made it look like she was the 'keeper of the gates'. With others around me adopting a similar approach, sponsors, companies with whom I was associated, even close mates had trouble actually making contact with me. It is not difficult, therefore, to understand why I came to be regarded as stand-offish. As a professional golfer concentrating on winning tournaments, I was totally unaware of the gate-keeper's role and blissfully ignorant of my consequent image problem.

On reflection, I suppose it was as though I was standing on the bow of a ship cutting through the water, playing tournaments, winning, losing, and becoming world number one, without any conception of the havoc I was wreaking. As I powered forever onwards, I was completely unaware of the mountainous waves being created behind me. Now, sometimes those waves represented exciting opportunities but equally they might also carry potential dangers because of something I might have said or done, however unwittingly. With hindsight, what I needed was someone always present just one step behind me, someone with only my best interests at heart, who could scoop up and pursue the positives while alerting me to any possibly harmful negatives.

Preoccupied as I was, I didn't bother to look back at the flotsam and jetsam left trailing in my wake, while those who were paid to do so might at times have been concentrating their efforts on other priorities. Important phone calls weren't always made or returned, faxes were not sent and arrangements not confirmed. When things like that happen, it is my name to which the mud sticks and people who don't know me jump to the conclusion that I do not care enough. Thus a series of deals which with proper attention to detail could have lasted many, many years fell apart – Jaguar is one example. I was blissfully unaware of the misrepresentations that were happening around me and it is only now that I see this and I blame myself for not taking control.

The modern young player – and those who take a substantial percentage of their earnings to advise them – will, I hope, heed this valuable lesson. As I have said, when I was making my way as an innocent teenager, sportsmen were merely sportsmen. I was never advised to act or behave in a certain manner to give the public and my fellow professionals an accurate portrait. A quiet word whispered in my ear to suggest that I should make an immediate apology for having screwed up, or offer an honest explanation for a certain incident that may have cast me in an unfortunate light, would have worked wonders in my professional relationships – and probably in my private life as well. Even when everything was sweetness and light, a manager with foresight would have advised me to spend a bit more of my off-duty time with my sponsors – not for another cheque, but as a goodwill gesture designed to cultivate long-term relationships.

I am not alone amongst golfers who have needed good advice. At one time poor Colin Montgomerie, for example, was on the receiving end of some bad press in the US, often being ridiculed as Mrs Doubtfire; I wonder what would have happened if someone had suggested in good humour that Monty dress up as the redoubtable nanny? Monty might well have regarded wearing a wig and a print frock as being a bit embarrassing, but in one instant by being prepared to poke fun at yourself, it is possible to gain great respect.

The good news from my point of view is that it is entirely possible to transform your image. For all his sporting genius with a tennis racket, John McEnroe was routinely booed on sight by the Wimbledon crowds and yet he is now adored throughout Britain for the wit and expertise he brings to the commentary box. McEnroe is the first to acknowledge the faults of his past; he does not offer trite excuses but discusses his indiscretions with such great humour and honesty that we have taken him to our hearts.

Although it is vital to take control of your own destiny, you also need the very best people around you, people in whom you can place complete trust. Trust has always been very important to me; just as I place absolute faith in Fanny on the first tee where we are a team, it is no less important that I can have the same faith in the team at Faldo Enterprises. I have to be certain that we are all working towards the same goal, which is the promotion of the Faldo brand. I launched my own management company primarily to manage my own interests but also to use the experience I have gained over the years to help manage other young golfers as they take their first steps. I intend no criticism of my previous agents; I simply wanted more of an input from them. In 1997, I split from IMG for the first time to combine forces with John Simpson. John and I worked together for around four years but even though I was the reigning Masters Champion when we began our association (and just think what that profile and position represented in marketing terms) our partnership was less than successful – a significant factor being, I confess, the downhill slide my life was on.

One commercial activity I was particularly keen to develop was golf course design, but we never quite managed to get the strategy right. A year later, we brought Nick Edmund on board. Now Nick is a self-confessed golf nut and his enthusiasm for Faldo Design should have acted as a fantastic springboard for a stream of new commissions. But for some reason Nick became bogged down in the office and was unable to channel his abundant enthusiasm into securing all the golden opportunities that were out there interna-tionally. It is a sobering fact that up to the end of 1999, with hundreds of courses in construction all over the world, we had designed but two of them. In January 2000, therefore, I decided on a change of strategy, giving Nick his own office with our first architect Guy Hockley, under my direct leadership. In the four years since then we have completed four courses, have six under construction and have more than 20 signed contracts globally, for example in Mexico, Portugal, Canada, Melbourne in Australia, Ireland, Olympia in Greece, a site in Moscow just 10 minutes from Red Square, a plot of land in Beijing 20 minutes from Tiananmen Square, and the resort of Macao Beach in the Dominican Republic, a turquoise, ocean-side position complete with jungle, mangroves and spectacular natural rock formations.

On my last visit to this site I met the legendary Pete Dye, at 78 still creating courses which never fail to attract some sort of controversy. Although riddled with cancer, Dye puts in 14 hours a day, seven days a week, and so when he invited me to view his latest site down the coast – an 8,000-yard monster – I jumped at the opportunity to watch the master at work and listen to his wondrous tales. As we travelled up a picturesque par-3 in our buggy I happened to notice a line of three bunkers 50 yards right of the green.

'Pete, what's the strategy behind this?'

'Damned if I know,' he drawled.

That was the tone of our conversation throughout our afternoon together. Why did you do this, Pete, why did you do that, I quizzed him constantly.

'Damned if I know why I did that either. I guess my wife wanted it that way and since she's won 43 amateur titles, when she tells me to put a bunker there, I put a bunker there.'

It has become a real joy to stand in the middle of a plot, be it field, desert or cliff-top, envisaging the scene as it will look some day. I like to think a Faldo design is completely different from, say, a Jack Nicklaus or Tom Weiskopf one. I am not a fan of so-called signature designs because I prefer to be in synch with nature, not to fight the contours of the land but to accept them for what they are and build on what God has already created, as did the great architects like Alister Mackenzie, Harry Colt and A.W. Tillinghast during the golden era. When I walk out on to a site and gaze upon

Being a shot maker in my style of play, I understand strategy golf and I know what players like and dislike on a course. It is important to create a few holes that the players are wary of in order to stretch them. I believe that the fear factor is an important element in course design. If players are worrying about what they will have to contend with on the 14th when they are on the 7th that creates a challenging and interesting golfing experience. When I am looking at the design plans in front of me, I envisage the shots players will have to make to score well and I change bunker shapes and green positions accordingly. But no matter how precise and detailed your plans are nature will still always dictate exactly how the end result will turn out. The paper designs can be close, but they are never spot on.

For all that I love course design, there are some distinct downsides to the job, mainly to the liver and waistband. Whenever we go on site visits, everyone, so it seems, is intent on inflicting 'death by hospitality' upon us by way of gargantuan breakfasts, lunches and dinners. In Moscow, for instance, I was treated to a 10-course meal that was accompanied by the traditional toasting of all present before each and every dish with 100 per cent proof vodka.

Eating and drinking also featured prominently in one of my forays to China, although those gastronomic delights turned out to be the very least of my problems. On the first trip, we were heading out to Wu Han for my first site visit. Our destination was 1200 miles from Hong Kong and as I had been forewarned against taking a Chinese airline if I could possibly avoid it, we chartered our own flight. Our take-off from Hong Kong was reassuringly smooth but in mid-flight we were informed that we had to land to pick up a 'navigator' and pay an unspecified levy. Our papers were painstakingly scrutinised and although ours passed muster, as did the plane's, the pilot was taken away for an hour for questioning. Finally came the news that there was a problem with his paperwork and that we would not be allowed to continue our flight. We had no choice, of course, and had to wait a couple of hours on the tarmac before we could take off back to Hong Kong. What we did not know, however, was that a massive reception had been arranged for our arrival at Wu Han and when we didn't show up, it is fair to say that Nick Faldo wasn't the most popular golfer in China. Another blow to my reputation.

All was forgiven a year later when we finally succeeded in reaching our intended destination. An even bigger reception was arranged to greet our belated arrival and we were honoured with the presence of a Chinese army general who hosted yet another Desperate Dan-sized dinner, including numerous toasts with first red wine (which I tried to mix with coke as the festivities threatened to get out of control), followed by what I can only describe as firewater, a lethal concoction which etiquette demanded be downed in one to toast each and every individual around the table. The alcohol was clearly taking its effect when, to my alarm, the general challenged me to a thumb war. As the contest wore on, my opponent decided he needed more leverage and rose out of his chair to apply real pressure – to the point where I really thought he was going to break my thumb. Putting discretion before valour, I made my excuses and headed back to my room. Only then did I realise that I might have offended protocol in some way. There I was somewhere 1200 miles inside China, at the mercy of a possibly insulted general. In fact, the opposite was true; my new buddy, as it turned out, was in tears downstairs at the thought of having offended me. I rejoined the party, apologies were offered all round, another series of toasts was launched, and we made it back to Hong Kong in one piece.

Despite these little local difficulties, China is a country that interests me greatly in terms of design. In addition to Wu Han, I have designed and opened one of the courses at the Mission Hills complex, one in Beijing, and have two more under construction. The Chinese have a fervent interest in golf and in creating quality courses. As yet, there are only about 100 in the whole country, but I expect that figure to rise above 500 in the next 10 years or so.

To return to my management theme: in May 2001 John Simpson and I mutually agreed to part company. After we split, I had a discussion with Mark McCormack and I agreed to rejoin IMG. I also employed Simon Crane, whose responsibility was to build the Faldo brand, but the blurred lines between Simon's responsibilities and the role of IMG made things difficult for all concerned. Also, at that time my company appeared to be under-achieving. Deals that I had been led to understand were worth $300,000 turned out to be valued at less than ten percent of that and a proposed restaurant chain of 33 suddenly turned into three. When Simon and I sat down to discuss exactly where and why we were going wrong both in financial projections and my brand's direction, he offered his resignation and I agreed with him that the best solution would be for us to separate in the autumn of 2002.

Even though things hadn't really worked out as well as I'd hoped in terms of representatives over those years, I was still very much of the opinion that I needed to find a true manager if my business life was to move forward. But it wasn't until January 2003 that I met Iain Forsyth, whom I thought might possess all the attributes for which I had been searching in vain for so long. Iain, who had been at Nike for 12 years, shared my belief in a 100 per cent management style and so we agreed to give ourselves a trial period to discover if I could work with him, and, more importantly, he with me. Nike were very supportive and things have worked out fantastically well for us. I can now say that Iain is the first 'real' manager whom I have ever employed. He nurtures no hidden agenda to further his own interests but is completely focused on Nick Faldo business for the benefit of all those who work at Faldo Enterprises. Iain supervises every aspect of my career and business and we communicate very closely and very, very honestly. It occurs to me that he is the very first associate whom I have personally chosen: another instance of finally taking control of my own destiny, I guess.

Although I joined forces with Iain, I was still on the IMG client list and I could foresee some areas of potential conflict of interest on the horizon in relation to my ambitions and those of the other leading golfers they represented and after the tragic and untimely death of Mark McCormack in May 2003, I felt that my personal contact with the company was gone. Events came to a head in September 2003, when I felt that the only way to build the Faldo brand was to go it alone, and accordingly it was mutually agreed that we would end my personal management agreement.

The task of the team who work for me now is to build business success through the Faldo name. In many respects, I now find myself in a very fortunate position. Greg Norman proved that it is entirely possible to build a brand while still at the top of your sport but for reasons I have tried to explain that was a chance denied to me. I also chose to continue longer with my full-time playing career while Greg has had serious business interests for at least ten years, but despite those lost years of opportunity, I firmly believe it is not too late. I am still playing well and, although perhaps not featuring at the top of the leaderboard at every tournament these days, I am regularly in the frame going into the last afternoon. The game in which the Faldo label has currency is golf – and, as everyone knows, golf is a very powerful sport in that it opens so many doors. It is hugely popular in business circles and by its very nature it allows people to meet, chat, and get to know one another on common ground. I don't claim to be close pals with Donald Trump, but when the chance arose for us to play a round together, we both jumped at it.

One area in which the Faldo brand has worked well is the Faldo Golf Institute by Marriott. First established in 1997, we now have four locations in the US designed to help golfers of all ages and ability improve their skills in wonderful surroundings. The idea for the institute came when I was introduced to Steve Bradley and Pete Watzka in Orlando, both of whom were senior executives in Marriott Golf. Steve was an 18 handicapper but with real potential and I assured him that I could get him down to single figures – all he had to do was create a $14 million practice facility. They went ahead and set up the first one in Orlando and, sure enough, Steve's handicap plummeted. A pretty expensive reduction mind you.

I remain convinced, too, that my experiences, both good and bad, can be of real value to youngsters just starting out on their golf careers. I have experienced just about everything golf and life has to throw at you and have learned a great deal as a consequence. I know what a golfer wants and needs, and how things can suddenly change. All too often, when a young pro suddenly hits the big time with a tournament win, those around him aren't prepared for the incredible changes that will follow overnight. Plans need to be in place so that if and when success comes along, the transition from relative unknown to star status is as seamless as possible.

I have been lucky to enjoy my fair share of successes and feel I can offer practical advice on how to cope with the frenzy that will surely follow an important tournament victory and how to use that victory to the player's best advantage. I have also endured failures and few sportsmen know better than me that it is often the failures that attract most attention from the press. You need to put yourself on the line to win but, by doing so, failure becomes an ever-present companion. I read an interview with the Oscar-winning actress Susan Sarandon recently in which she said something along the lines of 'I'd rather work with a director who has had good failures than mediocre successes'. I agree with that sentiment wholeheartedly. I believe that in order to be a successful golfer, then you have to allow yourself good failures in order to learn how to win.

So this is where I am today. I have taken control of my commercial activities, and I have the very best people in their various fields around me, people I can trust. I also retain a will-to-win attitude.

I am not a businessman by training but I am determined to become as successful in the boardroom as I was on the golf course by applying the same dedication and focus. Whenever and wherever I identify a fault or a weakness, I will henceforth put it right. I – and I alone – will bear the responsibility for my own actions, my successes and my failures. In recent months, we have been engaged in a cleaning up exercise – putting right deals that weren't working and accepting that some others had run their course and should be ended in an amicable manner. I have a burning desire to keep the Faldo name alive after I have stopped playing; being successful is a buzz and, to be brutally honest, I want to make some serious money too.

What are my hopes and plans now? Well, I will certainly be sticking to golf-related businesses because that is where I have the experience, the passion and where my name means something. Just attaching the label 'Faldo' to any old product in order to make a fast buck holds no appeal. Did I say 'golf-related'? I have to confess to one interest which has become a business – wine. Last year I launched the Faldo Selection label, a range of Australian whites and reds which in my opinion represent the best quality for the price on the market. I have come to enjoy my wine-tasting trips Down Under greatly, even if I have never quite mastered the knack of spitting the wine out. These wine tastings last all day so it is mighty hard work: but someone has to do it . . .

In this transition phase I am in, between player and businessman, there is a whole range of new opportunities opening up to me. Television commentary is one area I am particularly interested in and at this year's British Open, although I would far rather have made the cut at Royal Troon, I did enjoy my stint behind the microphone for both the BBC and the American broadcaster ABC. I hope I can bring a new approach to the craft as I have experienced every emotion on the golf course and believe I can spot telltale signs that others might miss, indications that might reveal, for instance, when nerves and pressure are getting to a player even at the start of a round. On the technical level, because of the style of golf I play, I would hope to be able to both see and explain the type of shot required, and the strategies that lie behind decisions the players make. My predictions aren't too bad either. On the Saturday morning of the Open I named Todd Hamilton as my dark horse for the championship because as a Texan, I reckoned he would be able to cope very well with the wind. And cope he did – beating Ernie Els in the play-off.

Finally, the aspect of my non-playing activities that probably takes up more of my time than any other is the Faldo Series, which I touched on in the previous chapter. We are now in our eighth season and I am delighted to say that we have recently been awarded charitable trust status. The Series has always been run as a completely non-profit-making endeavour although there is obviously a commercial side to the venture for the simple reason we must generate money through sponsorship to be able to operate. Becoming a charitable trust is an important step forward, because in the past we may have been deemed to be elitist. This couldn't be further from the truth, unless you regard taking only handicap golfers as elitist. That has to be the case as the aim is to help bring on potential professionals but it is in no way elitist in terms of where our players come from.

Tom Philips, who runs the Series, receives 2000 applications, some from such unlikely golfing nations as Russia, for 500 places, which are selected on a simple balloting procedure. There are 18 regional events with three tournaments in each region. The age group was originally from 13 to 17 but as the popularity of the Series has increased, we have extended the upper limit to age 20. The winner from each age group after all three events then goes through to a grand final for which all expenses are paid. The brightest prospects (in my opinion) then join me on an all-expenses-paid trip to the US for a week's intensive instruction from a team of experts on all aspects of becoming a successful golfer. One of our key aims as we develop the Series is to move into more inner cities to attract young players who perhaps don't have such easy access to courses but who nonetheless are talented and enthusiastic. Asia is also another area being earmarked for expansion and there has been considerable interest from Hong Kong about taking the Faldo Series east.

Hopefully, the Series will ultimately attract a sponsored scholarship programme which will allow the youngsters to graduate into the professional ranks with a financial safety net for their first two years. My role as 'professor' is to impart as many of golf's secrets as I can. If they are smart enough, they will realise that the real secret is not so much to learn from the things I have done right, as from the things I have done wrong.

As part of the Series we also run 'Team Faldo' in which in 2004 there are 11 members, all blessed with exceptional talent, whom we hope can be developed into successful professional golfers. They are given access to my team of specialists – diet advice, physio and coaches – and I spend as much time as possible with them, not only talking about improving the technical aspects of their game but also on the mental side of things, the realities of the tour, and on the basic details that you have to get right to be successful. For example, the importance of wearing comfortable old shoes for important games rather than rushing out to buy a smart new pair that haven't been broken in. It may sound obvious, but such apparently trivial details can make the difference between winning and losing.

The members of Team Faldo are not selected merely because they may have won one of the events in the Series. That obviously helps, but what we are looking for are players who have that extra something. When assessing possible entrants I need to see that they have real drive, passion and commitment to be the best there is. Having the talent is one thing, but there has to be something deeper. Now who does that remind you of?

CHAPTER TWENTY

FINDING LIFE'S
DELICATE BALANCE

One of Kjell Enhager's favourite philosophical yarns concerns an old monk and a young monk making a pilgrimage together on foot when they come across an aged woman standing on a riverbank, watching the treacherous currents swirling by and wondering how to reach the other side. Without pausing, the old monk hoists up his cassock, lifts the old woman on to his shoulders and carries her across the torrent with her legs wrapped round him. On reaching the other side, the two monks walk on for several miles before the young one, forsaking his vow of silence, can hold his peace no longer.

'How could you do that? You know we're not even allowed to look at a woman, let alone touch one.'

'My young friend, I left that old woman on the riverbank,' replies the older monk. 'You are still carrying her weight on your shoulders.'

It has been a long and winding road to personal happiness and

I have been accused frequently of jettisoning people on the other bank but you cannot go through life continually carrying the burden of regret. You are bound to make some mistakes along the way; the trick is to learn from them and thus discover how not to repeat them. One of the things I learned on my visit to the outward bound school in the Lake District all those years ago is that there is no straight route up a mountain and there is no straight route through life.

Writing this book has been an incredibly traumatic experience for me. As I have read through the text before tournaments, and thought back over my life, all sorts of old memories and emotions have been rekindled. These were often recollections I thought had been put away in my mental box, with the lid tightly shut. Lifting that lid has proved very hard indeed. Cruel memories have come back to haunt me, such as an incident that occurred before my defence of the Masters in 1990. Natalie, at the time a little curly-haired bundle, twirled in front of me saying 'look at me in my pretty, pretty dress' and then, with Michael Bolton's song in her head, trilled 'How Am I Supposed To Live Without You?'. Only too aware how frequently I was absent from her life, pursuing my desire for greatness, Natalie's voice was like a knife through my heart.

One of the reasons the publication of *Life Swings* has been delayed so long has been the pain of reliving such incidents. I have found the whole process far more emotional than I ever imagined and in the end I had to take a six-month sabbatical from the project to concentrate on my golf. I never dream of people from my past, so to be confronted by all the old demons has been a tough exercise. I thought producing my autobiography would be a gentle stroll down memory lane charting my greatest triumphs with a few humorous anecdotes for light relief; instead of which, it has been a surprisingly difficult process.

Thankfully, I have been blessed with two wonderful parents who have been in my corner for every single moment of the last 47 years. I was raised in a home suffused with love, where laughter was the most often heard sound of my childhood. That laughter continues to this day, especially at Christmas when Mum displays a curiously idiosyncratic choice in presents. A few years ago, I opened a gift-wrapped parcel to reveal an old metal box about one foot long and four inches wide. Gently prising open the lid, I discovered a series of intriguing shapes rolled up in tissue paper. Out came a little Corgi toy car, followed by a Rolls-Royce Silver Ghost. 'Very interesting' thinks I, dipping into the box again to reveal a tiny yellow Bugatti, followed by a gold Aston Martin James Bond model. Suddenly I twigged – these had been my toy cars when I was a kid and Mum and Dad had wrapped them up and given them back to me. 'We thought you'd like that,' glowed Mum, immediately wrapping up the prized possessions of my childhood ready to take them home again!

Thus began a new Faldo family tradition – strange Christmas presents. A couple of years later I was given a spirit level that they had found in an antique shop. Unable to think of anything else to say, I mumbled, 'What a lovely piece of wood.'

'I told you, George,' cooed Mum, rubbing her hands together in satisfaction. 'I told you our Nick would think it was a lovely piece of wood . . .' Being Mr Perfectionist, I have to admit my spirit level is in constant use and I would hazard a guess that the pictures on our walls are amongst the straightest in the land.

Another Christmas morning, another surprise. I walked into our lounge one year to find two large black plastic bags joined together with sticky tape under the tree, Mum having evidently decided she was not going to splash out on several rolls of Woolworth's finest gift-wrap. Breaking through the plastic. I found a golf bag, but not just any golf bag: this was my 1983 Ryder Cup bag which had been lying forgotten in my parents' loft and which I thought had been lost forever, although I was still in possession of the other 10. I thought that was really touching.

I have also been very lucky with the friends I have made. It is impossible to name and thank each and every one – they know who they are and thank you all. But I will be forgiven for mentioning two couples in particular. During my many turbulent times off the golf course Chris and Rowena Perfect have been amazing supports, spending many an evening with me offering great advice, keeping me sane and letting me get things off my chest. And there were more than a few times when I needed all the help they could give. More recently, in Orlando Sue and Mike Dunnington have been incredible in helping us organise our lives stateside. Sue, in fact, is my PA in America and has become a very close friend to V and Emma.

One of Kjell's most frequent questions is, 'What have you done that makes you walk with a straight back?' In other words, of what are you most proud in life, even if others might disapprove of your motives or methods? Well, I am proud of my career and the fact that I committed myself to it 100 per cent. I am also extremely proud of my children, and as they grow up I, like any parent, want to help them. And I am certainly proud of the Faldo Series.

I am fortunate that my career success has allowed me to help others in a variety of ways. When I celebrated my 20th British Open appearance at Royal Lytham in 1996, I thought it would be nice to mark the occasion in some way so I donated 20 wheelchairs. It has long been a tradition that if you win the Open Championship, you provide three wheelchairs, if you are runner-up, you buy two, and if you finish third, one. I decided to take the 20 recipients to the Open and present them in person. One 16-year-old lad, whom I will never forget, looked the picture of health but was in fact terminally ill. That is when it really hits home that you must do everything you can to help, even if there are those who will dismiss your efforts as nothing but a public relations exercise.

I realise my public image has been in urgent need of a polish every now and then. For many years during the peak of my powers, I wanted to invite a television crew to film 'a week with Nick Faldo' to offer the public a rare insight into the real me, but there were those in my immediate circle who liked my image as a man of mystery and decreed it would be foolish to open up in front of the cameras. Now possessing a certain mystique when you are world number one is all very well, but when the tournament victories dry up and your ranking starts slipping, no one wants to know you. From mystery man you quickly become forgotten man. A moment which seemed to underline this was when I was invited to appear on the BBC's 'Century of Sport' awards programme and I was afforded a whole three seconds of screen time. Compensation of sorts occurred during the 2003 BBC 'Sports Personality of the Year' awards ceremony when Martina Navratilova leaned over to shake hands and said, 'I like the way you play golf, we need more people like you out there.' Such a remark from the greatest woman athlete of all time I took as a compliment indeed.

Public relations is one of the many areas of my life to have changed significantly since V's arrival. She is very open to new ideas to improve my image, which has had a positive effect, although I must say that many of the papers have also changed their style of reporting and have become more interested in me as a person, rather then settling on constantly knocking the old perceived image. V's attitude has been a big part of this shift and it is amazing how the public responds. Following our trip to Egypt for *Hello!* magazine, people would come up to me in all sorts of places and ask 'How's Val?' which I have found a wonderful and very interesting way for the public to react.

There are a couple of books that have made a big impression on me and which I have mentioned previously. The first is *Being Happy!* by Australian artist and cartoonist Andrew Matthews, which David Leadbetter gave to me. The second is *If I'd Known Then What I Know Now* by J.R. Parrish. Yes, I often wish I had mapped out a different course as a young man but there is some upside to having gone down the road that I did. Recently I was thinking about my children, who like everyone, will face big decisions and challenges in their lives. Some opportunities they will carve out for themselves, some will just be presented to them, whilst they will undoubtedly face some problems of their own making. What I say to them all is that as their lives progress, both the good and the bad, I will always be there for them. I will always offer advice if they seek it – not to preach in any way and I certainly won't tell them what to do. But after all the ups and downs of my own life I'd just like to be able to talk things through with them, perhaps to offer them the benefit of the lessons I have learned.

I have a deep well of experience to call on. I have met an incredible range of people over the years. Some of them have deliberately misled me, lied to me and betrayed me. Some have fraudulently tried to take money from me and others have fabricated stories about me and even about themselves and their life history in order to try to gain my trust. I've even had my beloved Porsche attacked by someone wielding a 9-iron. On the positive side, I have also met people who have been very generous and very supportive and others who have offered unconditional love. I have been lucky enough to meet kings and queens, truly inspirational sportsmen and women, and even some amazing thinkers such as Deepak Chopra. So I do hope that my children feel that with this broad spectrum of life to draw on, it would be worth giving their old dad a buzz if they are ever worried about anything.

Of course everyone – no matter what advice they may or may not receive or how successful they may or may not have been – experiences some failures in life. I have said before that I believe life has a natural rhythm, it swings, and sometimes you are following the upward path and at other times you are on the downward one. The important thing is how you react to the setbacks. Two famous Americans always spring to mind when I think about this. Abraham Lincoln failed at so much and then became President of the United

States, while Thomas Edison, on finally working out how to make the light bulb, said of his years of frustrating failure, something like, 'Now I know 5999 ways not to make a light bulb and one way to do so successfully.'

Everyone blithely talks about the balance of life but to me the word 'balance' is of massive importance. My golf swing is now balanced and, more importantly, my mind is now balanced. Did you know that an opera singer cannot hit all the right notes unless he or she is completely balanced? It is the same in martial arts where a little fella weighing only 90 pounds dripping wet can bring down a giant if he is perfectly balanced when he lands the decisive blow. I guess David was perfectly balanced when he raised his sling and slew the mighty Goliath.

Being a car buff, I visited the McLaren Formula One headquarters in 1992. Team chief Ron Dennis took me on a guided tour of the factory where all the latest NASA technology was being applied to the development of their newest car. Over lunch, I posed the question, 'What's the most important thing in building a car?' 'Balance,' replied Ron unhesitatingly. Not horse power, not the gearbox, not the chassis, but balance.

I only wish some journalists had been a bit more balanced in their view of me during our long and troubled relationship, which was founded on mutual suspicion. I appreciate that there are two pavements on Fleet Street, with the quality broadsheets on one side and the red-top tabloids on the other, and that they have altogether different agendas. I know golf is seldom big news except during the British Open, so my exploits off the course have always been of more interest than my achievements with a club in my hand. Reporters have mortgages to pay, children to feed, and therefore it is understandable that in order to keep their jobs, for entirely their own reasons they may be required to find a story to fit a headline such as 'Faldo Is A Selfish Swine!'.

It is far too late in the day, but I know now that I should have had media training right at the start of my career. I have never quite understood how someone can totally fabricate an article one week and then stand in front of you with notebook in hand the next saying: 'Tell me about your round, Nick.' Once I told a particular journalist who had penned some unfavourable articles about me that if I saw his face in the press tent again, I would stand up and walk out. Guess what? The very next day there he was.

'Either you go or I go,' I told him. He stood there smiling defiantly, so I stood up saying 'Fine, OK lads, thanks,' and departed. Was I right or was my reaction pathetic? Somewhere between the two, to be honest.

But there has been many a major brouhaha in which I was the entirely innocent victim, such as an incident following England's victory in the Dunhill Cup with a team which did not include me, captained by Jamie Spence. The following week we were in Valderrama for the end-of-season tournament during which Argentine Eduardo Romero traditionally throws a splendid party for the troops. Sitting opposite Jamie and the recently vanquished Colin Montgomerie, I leaned across the table and said with a grin, 'Well done Jamie, good to see you stuffed the Scots.' A newspaper published this 'story', and all hell broke loose north of the border. I was inundated with mail from irate Scots men who had taken umbrage at my light-hearted remark. As I have said many times, I love Scotland and its people. We have shared three Major triumphs (when I won my third Open I arranged for a bottle of whisky to be delivered to every clubhouse in Scotland) and I could not understand how one jocular throwaway line could land me in such bother. Have you never gone in to your workplace on a Monday morning and ribbed your mates because their football team has lost 4–0 to Partick Thistle? Perhaps the Scots have never fully forgiven me for mangling 'My Way' on the 18th green at Muirfield. What I found most disappointing about the whole affair – although perhaps I shouldn't have been surprised — was that the press knew the context of my comment, that it was a good-humoured dig at Monty, but yet they chose to ignore that and put a completely erroneous spin on the events.

One of my biggest regrets is that I did not have the foresight to keep a diary. Oh, how I wish I had done so. Psychologists have proved that if you write something down in vivid detail the night before, the words seep deeper into your mind as you sleep, creating stronger neurological pathways. Keeping a diary is a discipline I intend to encourage my children to follow. I am going to buy them nice leather-bound, five-year diaries and ask them to write down every night just the most important thing they have learned that day and the most enjoyable thing they did. What a great record to look back on 50 years later.

Communication, or the lack of it, has also been something about which I have some regrets. There have been a number of occasions on which, if I had just taken the time to stop and think things through, I could have identified exactly whom I needed to talk to in order to sort out a problem right at the outset. But I didn't always make such connections and situations spiralled out of control. The dispute with Mark James is a classic example of this, after my supposed negative comments about Monty before the 1999 Ryder Cup. The same lack of lateral thinking applied all too often to my home and my business life.

This reflective chapter would not be complete without trying to find the words to explain what V means to me; impossible, really, because she is such a very, very special person. She is my wife, my truest friend, and the young woman who finally gave me the chance to become 'me'. One of my favourite movie lines is uttered by Jack Nicholson in *As Good As It Gets* when he explains, 'I take these pills because they make me a better person.' In that sense Valerie is my daily pill. Having been fortunate enough to earn a vast fortune compared with most people, over the years I have grown accustomed to paying for everything and everybody, so I was deeply touched when I opened my card on our very first Christmas together in 1998 to find tickets for a summer holiday in Provence.

V truly is a marvel, making me realise that golf is my business, not my life – changed days, indeed. She has also taught me the meaning of the word empathy. In the past, I guess I was completely wrapped up in my own world but now I have become far more sociable and genuinely interested in other people. Before V, stuck for conversation at a dinner party, my opening gambit was invariably, 'Do you have a dog?' Now I am happy to natter away about any subject under the sun. Somewhat belatedly, with V at my side I have acquired social skills I never knew I could possess. We have probably had to cope with 20 years' worth of dramas of one sort or another during our six years together and I shudder to think what would have become of me had we not met.

Valerie has also taught me how to become a tourist, introducing me to the enjoyment of different places, after 25 years of a routine comprising only airport–hotel–golf-course–hotel–airport. Among other places, we have been to Egypt, sailing up the Nile to visit all the pyramids in Luxor, and also made a whistle-stop tour of Beijing. It is our intention now to see all the wonders of the world, starting with the Taj Mahal. We have plans to visit Cambodia too because we both want to see Angkor Wat, then our list includes whales and the Grand Canyon.

We are soulmates to a spooky degree. On our first date in Geneva, on an impulse I bought V an M People CD to which she responded, 'That's weird. I tried to buy this only yesterday but couldn't find it.' On another occasion before the 2000 US Open at Pebble Beach, we were staying in the Post Ranch Inn above the rugged coastline on Big Sur. During a walk through the redwood forest populated by condors and albatrosses, V suddenly demanded out of the blue, 'Have you ever made an albatross?' Stunned that she even knew what an albatross was in golf, I replied, 'No, not a single one in my whole career.' The very next morning in practice, I holed out with a 2-iron on the par-5 16th – as I had told her, something I had never achieved in the previous 30 years. Our thoughts on almost every subject are so in tune it is uncanny. I certainly always know that I'll never be allowed to pinch a bit of her chocolate cake, that's for sure!

So V, an exceptional young woman, has bestowed upon me the gift of contentment, something I had not enjoyed for the previous decade or more, the gift of laughter and the gift of love. On the day of our marriage, she also presented me with another precious gift, a simple card she called her 'baby voucher'. It bore a handwritten message offering the prayer that one day I would become a father for the fourth time. Fifteen months later, I was lying in a hotel bed in Hong Kong shortly before Christmas, rubbing the sleep from my eyes, when I noticed a blurred V smiling at me from across the room.

'What are your plans for August?' she asked softly.

'Well, I'll be in America, I suppose, for the PGA. Why?'

'Because I'm pregnant; you're going to be a dad again.'

Although, as I have explained, Natalie, Matthew and Georgia had each been induced to allow me to attend their births whilst also fulfilling my golfing obligations, V and I agreed there and then that we would let nature run its course this time round. Although that meant missing the 2003 US PGA at Oak Hill – thereby bringing to an end my proud run of 66 consecutive Major appearances – it was among the easiest decisions of my sporting career to make.

Like a large number of parents-to-be, we suffered an agonising scare three months into V's pregnancy when, during a routine examination at the hospital in London, a blood test suggested there was a slight risk that our baby might be born with Down's Syndrome. A lot of tears were shed following this revelation but, having been through the same trauma before Matthew's birth, I repeatedly strove to soothe V's fears by reassuring her, 'If it's a one in three hundred and eighty chance and we turn out to be that one, we'll come through it together.' Blessedly, a subsequent test showed our baby to be completely healthy.

To the unheralded Shaun Micheel went the US PGA title but to me came an even more precious prize when on 28 July (our second wedding anniversary) I was able to cuddle the newly born Emma Scarlett. Bearing in mind the series of coincidences that have characterised our lives together, guess what was the first song to be played on the car radio as V and I were driving Emma home from hospital? 'My One Temptation,' our song as sung by Mica Paris.

I feel that I am a very lucky man indeed. Not only have I been given the chance of building another relationship but I am now experiencing the joys of being a seriously soppy dad for the fourth time. Equally importantly, Natalie, Matthew and Georgia are absolutely besotted with their new half-sister. When Natalie asked to be Emma's godmother, both V and I were deeply touched. I am so proud of this, and of them. Emma is such a lucky girl to have three such wonderful siblings to watch out for her. The children are the reason that I have decided to curtail my golf schedule from 2005. Henceforth, the family will be my number one priority, with golf a distant second. My three older children love Emma and I want them all to grow up together, so I have vowed to cut down to playing maybe 15 or 16 events a year which will allow me to spend two more months at home.

A defining moment occurred when Emma was three months old and I was due to embark on three weeks away on the circuit. I went upstairs to change her nappy, whereupon Emma granted me a gorgeous gooey smile. I returned to V in tears. I sobbed for hours and the thought struck me that if my kids had cried even half that much every time I used to walk out of the door, I could not bear – or inflict – that kind of hurt any longer.

Natalie, Matthew and Georgia are great individual characters, very well-mannered and with amazingly different personalities.

Natalie has a passion for the film world, Matthew is a natural sportsman with a strong business head and Georgia is a natural entertainer with a fabulous voice. Having spent so much time apart from them during their early years, my selfish ambition would be to have them join me in business in one way or another. They are very fortunate because they will always have a choice in life, a luxury that very few youngsters enjoy. If they decide on one career and do not like it, they will have the freedom to go off at a tangent and try something else. Matthew has already intimated that during his gap year when he is 18 he wants to caddie for me on what will be my rookie season on the US Champions' Tour. Matthew, my son, I would be privileged to have you carrying my bag.

So what of the future? Well, as I have already said, with my playing schedule reduced I will be able to create more breathing space for my family. That is the number one priority. Golf will continue to be hugely important to me – if not quite the obsession of my younger days – because I still believe I can be competitive in even the biggest tournaments; that said, this summer has been a very interesting experience.

After a disappointing Masters where I failed to make the cut, I decided, back in June to attempt to qualify for the US Open, the first time I have been required to qualify for a Major since the 1976 Open championship, so it was a nerve-wracking decision to choose to go down that road again 28 years on. But I am determined to continue to challenge the best and was very focused on competing in the US Open at Shinnecock Hills. There was only one problem – I committed a serious rookie error, exactly the type of mistake I encourage the members of Team Faldo not to make. On discovering that Lake Nona in Orlando, Florida, my home course when I am in the US, was one of the qualifying courses, I immediately signed up to play there. Did I shoot myself in the foot, or what? It was only when I arrived at Lake Nona that I realised that of the 61 competitors, only the top three would qualify. A one-in-twenty chance does not represent great odds, especially when you consider that the qualifying event in Hawaii guaranteed qualification to one in 11. I knew, therefore, that I had my work cut out for me.

Prior to the 36-hole qualifier, I was out on the practice range when my predicament really hit me. There I was, almost 47 years of age, hitting balls in the company of a bunch of college kids, many of whom had employed their girlfriends to act as caddies; boy, did I feel old? But with age comes experience, so I kept my head down and focused on the job in hand. My morning round of 70 left me a handily placed fourth just two shots off the pace, and I knew I was in with a chance. I set a target of shooting 68 in the second round but on my 18th (the par-5 9th at Lake Nona) I was in the left green-side bunker in two, leaving me to get up and down for a potentially vital birdie and a total of 69. But would 139 be enough? At that stage there was no way of telling due to the absence of scoreboards on the course. As I remembered from my youth, playing in qualifying events is the slow lane of golf.

I escaped from the bunker to six feet, holed the putt and as I walked off the course, I heard a female voice say: 'There's a rumour that might be enough.' That's how low-key the whole tournament was. As it turned out, the lady's forecast was spot on. It was enough; I had made it, which, in golfing terms, turned out to be just about the only real high of my summer.

I arrived at Shinnecock Hills for the US Open under-prepared both physically and mentally, hence my opening round of 81 which left me sorely disheartened. I am not out there just to make up the numbers and after a round like that – with no chance of winning or even making the cut unless I shot a miraculous 64 on day two – I seriously contemplated packing it all in and going home. But that is not like me. I have never been a quitter and so I came to my senses and realised that, if nothing else, another round of championship golf would be great practice for The Open at Royal Troon a few weeks later. I played well and had a putt on the 17th to go three under (which would have been my third birdie in a row); alas, I missed and went on to double-bogey the last, for a respectable round of 70, but ultimately it was a frustrating week.

For whatever reason, things are just not right with my swing at the moment and I have toyed with the idea of making a few tweaks here and there to try and improve things. But I haven't had the time to concentrate fully on the practice required. I also decided to give the belly putter a try but I gave up on it after only a couple of days' practice. One terrible putt was all it took.

The British Open at Troon brought no better joy I am afraid. I gave myself plenty of time to practice before the tournament but I was out of sorts all week and missed the cut at 11 over, but at least I was still able to be part of the tremendous atmosphere of the Open over the weekend because of my spell of commentary with the BBC and ABC.

The final Major of the season, the US PGA, proved to be my most successful of the year – if you can count coming in tied at 49 as a success. It was the only Major cut I made all year and I played some great golf at times during the week, which has given me back some belief in my game.

The Whistling Straits course, designed by Peter Dye on the shores of Lake Michigan, is breathtaking. The scale is enormous and it successfully combines American target golf with the look and feel of an Irish links course. I am more than happy to admit that I have taken away a few pointers from Whistling Straits as to how to design a truly wonderful course.

As for my golf, I shot a satisfactory level par on the Thursday, a round that was good from tee to green but which let me down on the greens where I missed a couple of short putts which could have improved my position no end. On the first nine on my second round (in fact the second nine of the course) I played as well as I have in a long time, shooting four birdies, and by the time I reached and birdied my 14th, I was within three strokes of the lead. And then it all went horribly wrong. Don't ask me why – oh how I wish I knew – but my self-confidence deserted me. I'd moved into contention and suddenly I became scared of playing aggressively, and paid the price with bogeys on the last three holes.

I was very happy to be there on Saturday and Sunday but my golf never matched Friday's heights (forgetting those final three holes). Saturday was a very mixed bag with five bogeys, but at least I fought back with three birdies. Sunday was a much more difficult course, which I parred all the way round except for a bogey at the 3rd and the 15th.

And so the Majors are over for another year and I find myself in a period of transition in my professional life. I will finish off this season and then have the luxury of a relaxing break to recharge my batteries and get myself ready mentally and physically for the challenge of the new season ahead. I've already worked out my game plan for next spring and I'm looking forward to it. But I will be weighing the golf alongside my business life. From now on I want to have my life firmly stowed away in boxes – family, golf, business – so that I won't get things all mixed up as I have before. I am determined to differentiate between these activities and prioritise accordingly. I am enjoying the business side of things, being entrepreneurial, and I intend to develop that further. At the moment I particularly love course designing. On the days that I can currently devote to it I am having such fun, and I have found a genuine desire to create some great golf courses around the world. And of course there is the Faldo Series. That is, and will continue to be, a big part of my life.

But most of all my future will be my family. Just as I did as a child in Welwyn Garden City all those years ago, I still gaze up the stars in the night sky from our garden in Old Windsor, painting pictures of my four children's futures in my mind's eye. Do I hope to bequeath them my 'desire for greatness'? No, merely the happiness and love I have found with V.

CAREER RECORD

(To 1 September 2004)

THE MAJORS

THE OPEN

Year	Venue/Winner	Score	Position
1976	Royal Birkdale (par-72)	78-71-76-69=294	28th=
	Johnny Miller (US) 279		
1977	Turnberry (par-70)	71-76-74-78=299	62nd=
	Tom Watson (US) 268		
1978	St Andrews (par-72)	71-72-70-72=285	7th=
	Jack Nicklaus (US) 281		
1979	Royal Lytham (par-71)	74-74-78-69=295	19th=
	Seve Ballesteros (Spain) 283		
1980	Muirfield (par-71)	69-74-71-70=284	12th=
	Tom Watson (US) 271		
1981	Royal St George's (par-70)	77-68-69-73=287	11th=
	Bill Rogers (US) 276		
1982	Royal Troon (par-72)	73-73-71-69=286	4th=
	Tom Watson (US) 284		
1983	Royal Birkdale (par-71)	68-68-71-73=280	8th=
	Tom Watson (US) 275		
1984	St Andrews (par-72)	69-68-76-69=282	6th=
	Seve Ballesteros (Spain) 276		
1985	Royal St George's (par 70)	73-73-75-74=295	53rd=
	Sandy Lyle (UK) 282		
1986	Turnberry (par-70)	71-70-76-70=287	5th
	Greg Norman (Australia) 287		
1987	**Muirfield (par-71)**	**68-69-71-71=279**	**WON**
1988	Royal Lytham (par-71)	71-69-68-71=279	3rd
	Seve Ballesteros (Spain) 273		

Year	Venue/Winner	Score	Position
1989	Royal Troon (par-72)	71-71-70-69=281	11th=
	Mark Calcavecchia (US) 275		
1990	**St Andrews (par-72)**	**67-65-67-71=270**	**WON**
1991	Royal Birkdale (par-70)	68-75-70-68=281	17th=
	Ian Baker-Finch (Australia) 272		
1992	**Muirfield (par-71)**	**66-64-69-73=272**	**WON**
1993	Royal St George's (par-70)	69-63-70-67=269	2nd
	Greg Norman (Australia) 267		
1994	Turnberry (par-70)	75-66-70-64=275	8th=
	Nick Price (Zimbabwe) 268		
1995	St Andrews (par-72)	74-67-75-75-291	40th=
	John Daly (US) 282		
1996	Royal Lytham (par-71)	68-68-68-70=274	4th
	Tom Lehman (US) 271		
1997	Royal Troon (par-72)	71-73-75-72=291	51st=
	Justin Leonard (US) 272		
1998	Royal Birkdale (par-70)	72-73-75-75=295	42nd=
	Mark O'Meara (US) 280		
1999	Carnoustie (par-71)	78-79	(missed cut)
	Paul Lawrie (UK) 290		
2000	St Andrews (par-72)	70-71-75-71=287	41st=
	Tiger Woods (US) 269		
2001	Royal Lytham (par-71)	75-71	(missed cut)
	David Duval (US) 274		
2002	Muirfield (par-71)	73-69-76-71=289	59th=
	Ernie Els (South Africa) 278		
2003	Royal St George's (par-71)	76-74-67-70=287	8th=
	Ben Curtis (US) 283		
2004	Royal Troon (par-71)	76-77	(missed cut)
	Todd Hamilton (US) 274		

THE MASTERS – Augusta National (par-72)

1979	Fuzzy Zoeller (US) 280	73-71-79-73=296	40th
1983	Seve Ballesteros (Spain) 280	70-70-76-76=292	20th=
1984	Ben Crenshaw (US) 277	70-69-70-76=285	15th=
1985	Bernhard Langer (Germany) 282	73-73-75-71=292	25th=
1988	Sandy Lyle (UK) 281	75-74-75-72=296	30th=
1989		**68-73-77-65=283**	**WON**

Beat Scott Hoch (US) at 2nd hole of sudden-death play-off

Year	Venue/Winner	Score	Position
1990		71-72-66-69=278	WON
	Beat Ray Floyd (US) at 2nd hole of sudden-death play-off		
1991	Ian Woosnam (UK) 277	72=73-67-70=282	12th=
1992	Fred Couples (US) 275	71-72-68-71=282	13th=
1993	Bernhard Langer (Germany) 277	71-76-79-67=293	39th=
1994	Jose-Maria Olazabal (Spain) 279	76-73-73-74=296	32nd
1995	Ben Crenshaw (US) 274	70-70-71-75=286	24th=
1996		69-67-73-67=276	WON
1997	Tiger Woods (US) 270	75-81	(missed cut)
1998	Mark O'Meara (US) 279	72-79	(missed cut)
1999	Jose-Maria Olazabal (Spain) 280	80-73	(missed cut)
2000	Vijay Singh (Fiji) 278	72-72-74-75=293	28th=
2001	Tiger Woods (US) 272	75-76	(missed cut)
2002	Tiger Woods (US) 276	75-67-73-72=287	14th=
2003	Mike Weir (Canada) 281	74-73-75-73=295	33rd=
2004	Phil Mickelson (US) 275	76-75	(missed cut)

US OPEN

Year	Venue (par) / Winner	Score	Position
1984	Winged Foot (par-70)	71-76-77-72=296	55th=
	Fuzzy Zoeller (US) 276		
1988	Brookline (par-71)	72-67-68-71=278	2nd
	Lost 18-hole play-off to Curtis Strange (US) 71-75		
1989	Oak Hill (par-70)	68-72-73-72=285	18th=
	Curtis Strange (US) 278		
1990	Medinah (par-72)	72-72-68-69=281	3rd=
	Hale Irwin (US) 280		
1991	Hazeltine (par-72)	72-74-73-72=291	16th=
	Payne Stewart (US) 282		
1992	Pebble Beach (par-72)	70-76-68-77=291	4th=
	Tom Kite (US) 285		
1993	Baltusrol (par-70)	70-74-73-72=289	72nd=
	Lee Janzen (US) 272		
1994	Oakmont (par-71)	73-75	(missed cut)
	Ernie Els (South Africa) 279		
1995	Shinnecock Hills (par-70)	72-68-79-72=291	45th=
	Corey Pavin (US) 280		
1996	Oakland Hills (par-70)	72-71-72-70=285	16th=
	Steve Jones (US) 278		

Year	Venue/Winner	Score	Position
1997	Congressional (par-70) Ernie Els (South Africa) 276	72-74-69-76=291	48th=
1998	Olympic (par-70) Lee Janzen (US) 280	77-72	(missed cut)
1999	Pinehurst (par-70) Payne Stewart (US) 279	74-74	(missed cut)
2000	Pebble Beach (par-71) Tiger Woods (US) 272	69-74-76-71=290	7th=
2001	Southern Hills (par-70) Retief Goosen (South Africa) 276	76-70-74-75=295	72nd=
2002	Bethpage (par-70) Tiger Woods (US) 277	70-76-66-73=285	5th=
2003	Olympia Fields (par-70) Jim Furyk (US) 272	75-75	(missed cut)
2004	Shinnecock Hills (par-70) Retief Goosen (South Africa) 276	81-70	(missed cut)

US PGA CHAMPIONSHIP

Year	Venue/Winner	Score	Position
1982	Southern Hills (par-70) Ray Floyd (US) 272	67-70-73-72=282	14th=
1983	Riviera (par-71) Hal Sutton (US) 274	74-77	(missed cut)
1984	Shoal Creek (par-72) Lee Trevino (US) 273	69-73-74-70=286	20th=
1985	Cherry Hills (par-71) Hubert Green (US) 278	70-77-73-74=294	54th=
1986	Inverness (par-71) Bob Tway (US) 276	76-71	(missed cut)
1987	Palm Beach (par-72) Larry Nelson (US) 287	73-73-77-74=297	28th=
1988	Oak Tree (par-71) Jeff Sluman (US) 272	67-71-70-71=279	4th=
1989	Kemper Lakes (par-72) Payne Stewart (US) 276	70-73-69-69=281	9th=
1990	Shoal Creek (par-72) Wayne Grady (Australia) 282	71-75-80-69=295	19th=
1991	Crooked Stick (par-72) John Daly (US) 276	70-69-71-76=286	16th=

CAREER RECORD

Year	Venue/Winner	Score	Position
1992	Bellerive (par-71) Nick Price (Zimbabwe) 278	68-70-76-67=281	2nd=
1993	Inverness (par-71) Paul Azinger (US) 272	68-68-69-68=273	3rd
1994	Southern Hills (par-70) Nick Price (Zimbabwe) 269	73-67-71-66=277	4th=
1995	Riviera (par-71) Steve Elkington (Australia) 267	69-73-70-67=279	31st=
1996	Valhalla (par-72) Mark Brooks (US) 277	69-75-74-73=291	65th=
1997	Winged Foot (par-70) Davis Love III (US) 269	75-78	(missed cut)
1998	Sahalee (par-70) Vijay Singh (Fiji) 271	73-72-71-73=289	54th=
1999	Medinha (par-72) Tiger Woods (U.S.) 277	71-71-75-75=292	41st=
2000	Valhalla (par-72) Tiger Woods (US) 270	79-68-69-73=289	51st=
2001	Atlanta (par-72) David Toms (US) 265	67-74-71-70=282	51st=
2002	Hazeltine (par-72) Rich Beem (US) 278	71-76-74-78=299	60th=
2003	Oak Hill (par-70) Shaun Micheel (US) 276		did not enter
2004	Whistling Straits (par-72) Vijay Singh (Fiji) 280	72-70-74-75=290	49th=

THE RYDER CUP

1977 ROYAL LYTHAM

Foursomes
Faldo & Peter Oosterhuis beat Ray Floyd & Lou Graham   2 & 1

Fourballs
Faldo & Oosterhuis beat Jack Nicklaus & Floyd   3 & 1

Singles
Faldo beat Tom Watson   1 hole

Match Result: Great Britain & Ireland 7½, United States 12½

1979 GREENBRIER, WEST VIRGINIA

Foursomes
Faldo & Peter Oosterhuis lost to Andy Bean & Lee Elder   2 & 1
Faldo & Oosterhuis beat Bean & Tom Kite   6 & 5

Fourballs
Faldo & Oosterhuis beat Elder & Mark Hayes   1 hole

Singles
Faldo beat Elder   3 & 2

Match Result: United States 17, Europe 11

1981 WALTON HEATH

Foursomes
Faldo & Peter Oosterhuis lost to Tom Watson & Jack Nicklaus
   4 & 3

Fourballs
Faldo & Sam Torrance lost to Lee Trevino & Jerry Pate   7 & 5

Singles
Faldo beat Johnny Miller   2 & 1

Match Result: Europe 9½, United States 18½

1983 PGA NATIONAL, FLORIDA

Foursomes
Faldo & Bernhard Langer beat Lanny Wadkins & Craig Stadler 4 & 2
Faldo & Langer beat Tom Kite & Ray Floyd   3 & 2

Fourballs
Faldo & Langer lost to Tom Watson & Jay Haas   2 & 1
Faldo & Langer beat Ben Crenshaw & Calvin Peete   4 & 2

Singles
Faldo beat Haas   2 & 1

Match Result: United States 14½, Europe 13½

1985 THE BELFRY

Foursomes
Faldo & Bernhard Langer lost to Calvin Peete & Tom Kite   3 & 2

Singles
Faldo lost to Hubert Green   3 & 1

Match Result: Europe 16½, United States 11½

1987 MUIRFIELD VILLAGE, OHIO

Foursomes
Faldo & Ian Woosnam beat Lanny Wadkins & Larry Mize   2 holes
Faldo & Woosnam halved with Hal Sutton & Mize

Fourballs
Faldo & Woosnam beat Sutton & Dan Pohl   2 & 1
Faldo & Woosnam beat Curtis Strange & Tom Kite   5 & 4

Singles
Faldo lost to Mark Calcavecchia   1 hole

Match Result: United States 13, Europe 15

1989 THE BELFRY

Foursomes
Faldo & Ian Woosnam halved with Tom Kite & Curtis Strange
Faldo & Woosnam beat Lanny Wadkins & Payne Stewart   3 & 2

Fourballs

Faldo & Woosnam beat Mark Calcavecchia & Mark McCumber
2 holes

Faldo & Woosnam lost to Chip Beck & Paul Azinger   2 & 1

Singles

Faldo lost to Wadkins   1 hole

Match Result: Europe 14, United States 14

1991 KIAWAH ISLAND, SOUTH CAROLINA

Foursomes

Faldo & Ian Woosnam lost to Payne Stewart & Mark Calcavecchia
1 hole

Faldo & David Gilford lost to Paul Azinger & Mark O'Meara
7 & 6

Fourballs

Faldo & Woosnam lost to Ray Floyd & Fred Couples   5 & 3

Singles

Faldo beat Floyd   2 holes

Match Result: United States 14½, Eruope 13½

1993 THE BELFRY

Foursomes

Faldo & Colin Montgomerie beat Ray Floyd & Fred Couples
   4 & 3

Faldo & Montgomerie beat Lanny Wadkins & Corey Pavin
   3 & 2

Fourballs

Faldo & Montgomerie halved with Paul Azinger & Couples

Faldo & Montgomerie lost to John Cook and Chip Beck   1 hole .

Singles

Faldo halved with Azinger

Match Result: Europe 13, United States 15

1995 OAK HILL, ROCHESTER, NY

Foursomes

Faldo & Colin Montgomerie lost to Tom Lehman and Corey Pavin
   1 hole

Faldo & Montgomerie beat Curtis Strange and Jay Haas   4 & 2

Fourballs

Faldo & Montgomerie lost to Fred Couples & Davis Love III
   3 & 2

Faldo and Bernhard Langer lost to Loren Roberts and Pavin
   1 hole

Singles
Faldo beat Strange   1 hole

Match Result: United States 13½, Europe 14½

1997 VALDERRAMA, SPAIN

Foursomes
Faldo & Lee Westwood lost to Fred Couples & Brad Faxon
    1 hole
Faldo & Westwood beat Justin Leonard & Jeff Maggert   3 & 2

Fourballs
Faldo & Westwood lost to Scott Hoch & Maggert   2 & 1
Faldo & Westwood beat Mark O'Meara & Tiger Woods   2 & 1

Singles
Faldo lost to Jim Furyk   3 & 2

Match Result: Europe 14½, United States 13½

Totals	Played	Won	Lost	Halved
Singles	11	6	4	1
Foursomes	18	10	6	2
Fourballs	17	7	9	1

RYDER CUP RECORDS

Most Appearances	Nick Faldo	11
	Bernhard Langer	10
	Christy O'Connor Snr.	10
	Dai Rees	9
	Billy Casper	8
	Raymond Floyd	8
	Lanny Wadkins	8
Most Matches Played	Nick Faldo	46
	Bernhard Langer	42
	Neil Coles	40
	Seve Ballesteros	37
	Billy Casper	37
Most Matches Won	Nick Faldo	23
	Arnold Palmer	22
	Bernhard Langer	21
	Seve Ballesteros	20
	Billy Casper	20
	Lanny Wadkins	20
Most Points Won	Nick Faldo	25
	Bernhard Langer	24
	Billy Casper	23½
	Arnold Palmer	23
	Seve Ballesteros	22½

CAREER RECORD

AMATEUR TOURNAMENT VICTORIES

1975
English Amateur Championship
The Berkshire Trophy
British Youths' Open Amateur Championship
South African Amateur Strokeplay Championship

PROFESSIONAL TOURNAMENT VICTORIES

1977
Skol Lager

1978
Colgate PGA Championship

1979
ICL International (South Africa)

1980
Sun Alliance PGA Championship

1981
Sun Alliance PGA Championship

1982
Haig Whisky Tournament

1983
Paco Rabanne French Open
Martini International
Car Care Plan International
Lawrence Batley International
Ebel Swiss Open

1984
Sea Pines Heritage Classic (US)
Car Care Plan International

1987
Peugeot Spanish Open
The 116th Open Championship

1988
Peugeot French Open
Volvo Masters

1989
The Masters (US)
Volvo PGA Championship
Dunhill British Masters
Peugeot French Open
Suntory World Matchplay Championship

1990
The Masters (US)
The 119th Open Championship
Johnnie Walker Classic (Hong Kong)

1991
Carroll's Irish Open

1992
Carroll's Irish Open
The 121st Open Championship
Scandinavian Masters
European Open
Toyota World Matchplay Championship

Johnnie Walker World Championship (Jamaica)

1993
Johnnie Walker Classic (Singapore)
Carroll's Irish Open

1994
Alfred Dunhill Open
Million Dollar Challenge (South Africa)

1995
Doral-Ryder Open (US)

1996
The Masters (US)

1997
Nissan Open (US)

AWARDS

Rookie of the Year (1977)
European Order of Merit winner (1983, 1992)
MBE (1988)
BBC Sports Personality of the Year (1989)
United States PGA Player of the Year (1990)

WORLD NUMBER 1 FROM

2 September 1990 – 14 October 1990 (six weeks)
3 February 1991 – 31 March 1991 (eight weeks)
19 July 1992 – 30 January 1994 (81 weeks)

INDEX

INDEX